THE
REGICIDE'S
WIDOW

For Hugo, Jason, Christian, Sam and Kirsten

THE REGICIDE'S WIDOW

Lady Alice Lisle and the Bloody Assize

ANTONY WHITAKER

SUTTON PUBLISHING

First published in the United Kingdom in 2006 by
Sutton Publishing Limited · Phoenix Mill
Thrupp · Stroud · Gloucestershire · GL5 2BU

British Library Cataloguing in Publication Data
A catalogue record for this book is available from the British Library.

ISBN 0-7509-4434-X

Typeset in 11/14.5pt Sabon.
Typesetting and origination by
Sutton Publishing Limited.
Printed and bound in England by
J.H. Haynes & Co. Ltd, Sparkford.

Contents

Foreword

For the first forty years of her life, fortune smiled on Alice Lisle. She was herself an heiress, and in 1636 she married John Lisle, a wealthy and well-born widower and a rising man. Rise indeed he did, becoming a staunch Parliament supporter, a party to the trial and execution of King Charles I and an apparatchik of the Cromwellian regime that followed. During these years John enjoyed, and Alice no doubt shared, the rewards and celebrity that rub off on those close to the seat of power.

But with the Restoration in 1660 all changed. John, as a regicide, was an obvious target for royalist vengeance. He escaped to the Continent just in time to avoid seizure here. But he was hunted down by royalist assassins and murdered in Lausanne in 1664. Alice, for her part, lived a retired life at Moyles Court, a house near Ringwood in Hampshire that she had inherited from her father. Until 1685. In that year, elderly, infirm and nearly deaf, she was charged with treason, tried before the Lord Chief Justice and a jury, convicted, and beheaded in what is now The Square in Winchester. Her crime? Harbouring a Presbyterian minister who had, to her knowledge it was said, supported the rebellion led by the hapless Duke of Monmouth.

Miscarriages of justice come in two shapes. They may involve the conviction and punishment of the innocent. Or they may involve the conviction and punishment of those who may or may not have been guilty but who should not have been convicted at the trial that led to their condemnation. The history of this country and others, from early times until the present, reveals unhappy and sometimes shameful examples of both kinds of miscarriage. No one, I think, would now consider, even allowing for the standards and temper of the time, that Alice Lisle was justly convicted after a proper trial. But which kind of miscarriage was it?

For many years she was believed to have been an innocent victim, and her daughters procured the reversal of her conviction by Act of Parliament, very promptly after the Glorious Revolution, in 1689. But Antony Whitaker persuasively argues, in this very carefully researched book, that she is unlikely to have been innocent. A modern jury would be sceptical that she knew quite as little as she claimed about a man hidden in her house. So she may very well have been guilty. But that cannot excuse the cruel unfairness of her trial.

It was what we would now call a show trial: not, as trials should be, a fair and even-handed procedure to determine whether, in the judgment of an independent and impartial tribunal, the crime charged and denied has been committed, but an event mounted by the executive authorities of the state to establish the guilt of the accused in a public forum for political purposes. To this end those accused of treason, although facing the most barbaric of all punishments, were subjected to special procedural disadvantages, and prosecutors abandoned any restraint, as the Attorney-General had done when prosecuting Sir Walter Ralegh nearly a century earlier.

There is some doubt about the reliability of the trial record on which Whitaker has relied. But he argues that it is essentially accurate, and there is no good reason to disagree. From this record it appears that the prosecutor acted properly, so far as he was allowed to act at all, and the jury, to its great credit, resisted the pressure powerfully exerted on it by the most notorious of all English and Welsh criminal judges: George Jeffreys.

Alice Lisle's trial was the prelude to what became known as the 'Bloody Assize', and Lord Jeffreys, the Lord Chief Justice, still only about 40 and still aiming higher, was determined to strike terror into the hearts of those awaiting trial for their part in the rebellion, throughout the West Country. He saw himself as the agent of royal retribution. Whitaker says what can be said to redeem the character of Jeffreys, as does Paul D. Halliday, who records, in his article on Jeffreys in the *Oxford Dictionary of National Biography*, that 'virtually no complaints survive of his conduct as a judge in civil proceedings'. The same cannot be said of him as a criminal judge, where his reputation (amply confirmed by the record relied on here) is of a cruel and ruthless bully, using his undoubtedly brilliant talents as an advocate to insult, humiliate, intimidate and entrap. That he chose to overlay his invective with an unconvincing veneer of religiosity does nothing to commend it to the modern reader.

The records of largely forgotten trials long ago can make for dull reading. But as Whitaker tells the story, the tableau comes alive. We can see Jeffreys in all his pride and power on the bench. We can see the elderly widow shrinking in the dock. And the sound of frightened witnesses running for cover is audible across the centuries. A good story well told.

Lord Bingham of Cornhill KG

Acknowledgements

Many have helped with pictures, suggestions and information over a long period. Foremost was my father, the late Austin Whitaker, who in his retirement became Winchester City Archivist. He was an inexhaustible fund of local knowledge and of where to find it. Second, my wife Pat, whose kind (and justifiably chivvying) encouragement and sympathetic editing left the text appreciably sharper. Richard Dean, headmaster of Moyles Court School, supplied pictures of the house's underground tunnels; John Hardacre, of Winchester Cathedral, identified the position of John Lisle's house in the Cathedral Close; the library staff at Longleat deciphered some of Muddiman's more enigmatic diary entries; the descendants allowed the use of the portraits of John and Thomas Penruddock; the 17th Duke of Valderano elaborated his memories of Moyles Court in the thirties; the graphics department of the *Sunday Times* compiled the map of Salisbury Plain; The Witt Library of the Courtauld Institute of Art, London, sanctioned the use of *The Arrest of Alice Lisle*. Constable Publishers gave permission to include extracts from Sir John Oglander's *A Royalist Notebook* translated by Francis Bamford. Mary Ferrant in her own time and in the early stages helped with many routine chores, and the kind people at Sutton Publishing – Christopher Feeney, Hilary Walford and Elizabeth Stone – produced it in its final form. Finally, the interest shown by my family, friends and colleagues kept the spark of creativity alive, seeing the book through to completion.

Author's Note

But for two historical accidents it would have been impossible to write this book.

First, the report of Alice Lisle's trial has survived only by chance: one of the prosecuting counsel took a full note. Thirty-four years later, when in his seventies and probably the only lawyer involved who was still alive, he bumped into the publisher Salmon, who had the first edition of his *State Trials* already in the press. Luckily, the barrister had kept his original note and was able to transcribe it; and, despite a publication deadline that had passed, Salmon held the presses for him and, by deftly renumbering the later pages of volume III, was able to slip Alice Lisle into the chronological sequence where she belonged.

Second, Moyles Court, Alice Lisle's home for most of her life, also survived against the odds. Rebuilt probably around the middle of the seventeenth century as a comfortable country home, it was looked after by the Lisle family for most of the next two centuries. It was then bought by a nineteenth-century playboy banker for whom its charm all too swiftly evaporated – he got rid of it in 1829. By the 1860s it was in ruins; but a Victorian squire took it on, and, despite strong advice that demolition was the only answer, he had the determination, and the means, to carry out a sensitive restoration. It twice fell into serious disrepair during the twentieth century, but sympathetic hands again came to the rescue, and it now remains one of the more attractive country houses of southern England.

Antony Whitaker
March 2006

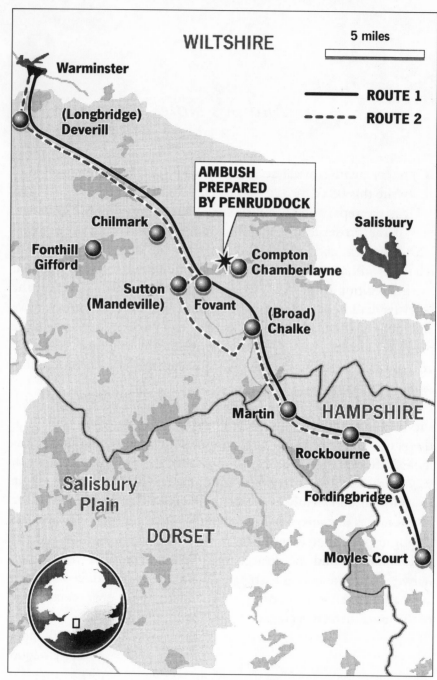

WILTSHIRE

5 miles

ROUTE 1
ROUTE 2

Warminster

(Longbridge)
Deverill

AMBUSH
PREPARED
BY PENRUDDOCK

Salisbury

Chilmark

Fonthill
Gifford

Compton
Chamberlayne

Sutton
(Mandeville)

Fovant

(Broad)
Chalke

Martin

HAMPSHIRE

Rockbourne

Salisbury
Plain

Fordingbridge

DORSET

Moyles Court

Dunne's routes across Salisbury Plain – first on his own, and then with Hicks, Nelthorp and Barter, from Warminster to Moyles Court.

Introduction

Campaigners against injustice usually plough an uphill forensic furrow. Of the suspect convictions of the past forty years, perhaps the most notorious are those involving the groups known as the Guildford Four, the Birmingham Six and the Maguire Seven. They represent the unacceptable face of injustice, when the system buckled under public outrage at terrorist bombings and the need to assuage it with putting culprits, actual or supposed, speedily behind bars. It was a legal descent to Avernus, where the poisoned pasture returned a corrupt harvest. Innocence, and the chance of proving it, were buried. In 1980, Lord Denning, then Master of the Rolls, refused to allow the Six to bring civil actions, on the ground that the risk of the police being found guilty of perjury and assault was 'too appalling a vista' to contemplate.

By contrast, the long road back to sanity demonstrated that rehabilitation can never be had just for the asking. Only a single-minded determination to expose the disease, condemn the crop and uproot the tree, in the face of equally implacable opposition from the authorities, is likely to succeed. Fortunately, all those involved in the above cases were cleared and released, albeit some fifteen years after the event, and some steps taken to ensure that others did not follow the same route to jail. Whether this restored public confidence in the British legal system is not for debate here.

This book concerns a widow whose execution for treason took place more than three centuries ago, on Wednesday, 2 September 1685. Since then, the execution has generally been regarded as disgraceful and unjust: disgraceful, because the penalty seems disproportionate to the nature of her offence; unjust, principally because a doubting jury was bullied into finding her guilty. Four years after she died, her conviction was officially reversed by Act of Parliament, which many regard as confirmation of her innocence.

Judge Jeffreys, who conducted her trial, has gone down as the villain of the piece, having been more concerned to proclaim her guilt than to test it.

This assumption of Alice Lisle's innocence has been powerfully reinforced by a number of factors. By today's standards at least, her jury's doubts should have entitled her to an acquittal; but in the highly charged aftermath of the Duke of Monmouth's defeat at Sedgemoor, the government's priority was to secure convictions in order to ensure that the rebellious West was taught the error of its ways.

The rebellion apart, Alice Lisle was a political pariah, and from the moment of Charles II's Restoration in 1660 she was consistently described as 'the Regicide's wife'. This derived from John Lisle's part in Charles I's trial and execution in January 1649. Resentment against her was kept alive by her continuing and overt support for Nonconformity, which she and her husband had espoused under the Commonwealth, but which the Clarendon Code legislation of the Restoration severely repressed. An acquittal was not the publicity the authorities wanted.

This book started out as an attempt to discover why, despite the political pressures of the day, Alice Lisle's seemingly valid defences should have been so brusquely disregarded. At first, the answer appeared to be simply that she was the political victim of a cruel king and an ambitious judge. While undoubtedly one reason for her conviction, and highly discreditable, this turned out to be only part of the story. Further investigation revealed that Alice Lisle's main line of defence was self-defeating; and that, with more homework, the Crown could have demonstrated this without difficulty. It could have been done without bending the rules or bucking the system in the way that Jeffreys himself, to his eternal disgrace, actually did – or Lord Denning, three centuries on, implicitly endorsed.

The image of Alice Lisle as a martyred innocent is appealing, but false. A victim of injustice she certainly was, but not for the reason most people believe. The unique tragedy of her case is that she was wrongly convicted in spite of her guilt – a double failure of the system – but not because she was innocent. Her conviction was a far greater disgrace for the law and those who administered it than it was for Alice herself.

PART ONE

ONE

Alice and John Lisle

The pressure was intense, the jury's dilemma as acute as it could be. A half-hour retirement had left them wondering whether they could sidestep the question of guilt on a point of law. On balance, they were inclined to acquit the accused. But their requests for guidance brought no comfort: the judge, hostile and patronising, dismissed their doubts, virtually telling them it was their duty to get on and convict. Yet they knew precisely what would happen if they did: the accused, a widow whom some of them knew personally, would be burned at the stake, which was the normal penalty for women traitors. An acquittal, on the other hand, would invite not merely explosive judicial wrath, but the censure of their royalist friends, many of whom could scarcely utter the accused's name without some expression of loathing or disgust.

In the candlelit hall of Winchester Castle it was eleven o'clock at night on Thursday, 27 August 1685. Replete with political overtones, Alice Lisle's trial for treason had lasted barely six hours. She was charged with sheltering a member of the Duke of Monmouth's defeated rebel army at her home a month before. On the face of it, the issue was straightforward: did she know, as the prosecution claimed, that he was a fugitive rebel? Or did she honestly believe, as she asserted, that he was no more than a religious refugee, a Nonconformist priest and friend who had been her guest many times in the past? As she had said during her defence: 'I did not in the least suspect him to have been in the army, being a Presbyterian minister, that used to preach and not to fight.'[1] Though sheltering persecuted priests was a crime, it was hardly a serious offence, the penalty usually being a nominal fine.

The judge was also under pressure. He faced a tight schedule, which depended on the speed of the jury's deliberations. The first of those connected with the rebellion, Alice Lisle's case was, as the court reporter noted, 'a cause of great expectation and moment', involving a well-known Hampshire figure whom the authorities wished to see convicted. It was late at night; it was far from certain the jury would convict; if they did, Alice Lisle had still to be sentenced, along with a number of other criminals; the next assize, 20 miles away at Salisbury, was due to open the following morning. Unless he was staying in Winchester, the judge had at least an hour by coach back to his lodgings before he could get any sleep. During the jury's second retirement, he became visibly more fretful and impatient.

It was a long quarter of an hour before they finally made up their minds.

* * *

Alice Lisle was born in the New Forest village of Ellingham around the end of the third week of September 1617. Although the entry is faint, the parish register records her baptism on Sunday, 24 September, so it is reasonable to assume she was born a day or two before that.[2] The elder daughter of Sir White and Lady Edith Beconsaw, she grew up at Moyles Court, the house 3 miles north of Ringwood that she inherited jointly with her sister Elizabeth, and that would remain her home for most of her life. On 23 October 1636, a month after her nineteenth birthday, she was married in Ellingham parish church to John Lisle, a widower aged 27 from the Isle of Wight.[3] He was the eldest son[4] of a family who lived at Wootton and owned extensive estates there. His father was Sir William Lisle, a dissolute but engaging individual whose main recreations were the bottle and the brothels of Newport. White Beconsaw died in 1638, and, by arrangement with her sister, Alice alone inherited Moyles Court, where she became mother to eleven children.

For an ambitious lawyer, John Lisle's first marriage, on 15 February 1632, to Mary Elizabeth Hobart, may not have been wholly uncalculating. The daughter of Sir Henry Hobart, Attorney-General and later Chief Justice of the Common Pleas under James I, she brought a substantial dowry. John's godfather, Sir John Oglander, considered these advantages far outweighed her beauty: 'Mr Lisle had with her £4,000, the greatest portion that ever Isle of

Wight man had, and he showed his masterpiece both in getting her, and in his will for marrying her, for she was none of the handsomest – as you may perceive by these lines made at her wedding:

> Neither well-proportioned, fair nor wise:
> All these defects four thousand pounds supplies.'

Sir John noted that Sir William Lisle brought the money down from London 'improvidently, with two men and himself, on tired horses in ready gold'. But on 15 March 1633, eight months before John Lisle's call to the Bar, Mary Elizabeth Lisle fell victim to one of the most fearsome hazards of the time: childbirth. She died four days after the birth of their son William, who subsequently died in infancy.

John Lisle's main aspirations, however, were political. As recorder of Winchester, he was chief adviser to the Corporation, and was deeply dissatisfied with Charles I's indecision over the renewal of the city's charter in 1637. Elected one of Winchester's two representatives in both the Short and Long Parliaments of 1640, he developed progressively anti-establishment views, in contrast to his royalist fellow-member for the city, William Ogle. He sided against the monarchy on the outbreak of the Civil War; and three months before Ogle surrendered Winchester Castle to Cromwell in October 1645, he made a widely publicised speech in London against the king. Two years later he was one of the Parliamentarian representatives who tried to reach a settlement with Charles I – who was then a prisoner in Carisbrooke Castle on the Isle of Wight – and he took a leading part in the momentous proceedings in Westminster Hall during January 1649.

As frequently happens when self-appointed tribunals of victors charge their enemies with treason, the purpose is less to establish guilt, which is foregone, than to consolidate the victors' mastery and moral authority over those they have conquered. But the right to accuse a king demands recognition for its effective enforcement. Charles saw that this was the Parliamentarians' weakest point, and confined his defence to a challenge to the court's jurisdiction, which he symbolised by wearing his hat throughout the trial. John Lisle was present at most sessions, acting as deputy to Bradshaw, the president, but he did not sign the royal death warrant. This may well have been due to pressure from Alice, who told the court in 1685 that she wholeheartedly deplored the execution that took place on 30 January 1649.

Whatever her feelings, that event was the turning point of her husband's career. He was already influential and prosperous in Hampshire. Apart from his position in Winchester, he had been elected a burgess of Christchurch in 1641, where he bought the Abbey lands and subsequently secured the appointment of his Nonconformist friend, John Warner, as vicar. Large portions of the family estates had come to him in 1642 in return for paying off his father's debts, and in 1644, on the eviction of the Laudian cleric, Dr Lewis, he became master of St Cross, the almshouse hospital south of Winchester, with its valuable income. His father's death on 21 October 1648 brought him most of the remaining family property. He was at the peak of his fortunes and accumulated wealth, and it was probably around this time that he reconstructed Moyles Court as a smaller and more comfortable country house,[5] the main outlines of which survive today. Of particular interest is the network of brick-built underground tunnels, also probably built during the 1650s. Some of these have only recently been explored and appear to have connected the house not merely with outbuildings but also with Ellingham Church, about a mile away, and possibly with Ringwood itself, 3 miles to the south. One can only surmise that their main purpose was to improve the smuggling facilities afforded by a house close to the Avon estuary.

Within a week of the monarch's execution, John Lisle was promoted to central government, as a joint Commissioner of the Great Seal (the Commonwealth equivalent of Lord Chancellor) and a bencher of the Middle Temple. With Bulstrode Whitlock, his fellow Commissioner, he rented Buckingham House in Chelsea,[6] then a village 2 miles west of the city and separated from it by marshland. The house cost £40 a year, having been 'much defaced by the soldiery quartered in it'.

While he relinquished his position at St Cross, probably because of the demands of office on his time, the suppression of the Anglican Church gave him a house in Winchester Cathedral Close, just north of where the Pilgrim's School grounds now lie, and enabled him to buy the ecclesiastical manor of Chilbolton, north-west of the city. His eldest son, Beconsaw, was entered as a Middle Temple student on 1 May 1650. In December 1653, John Lisle swore Cromwell in as Lord Protector, and the following summer he received further promotion, adding the offices of President of the High Court of Justice, Member of Parliament for Southampton and Commissioner of the Exchequer to the one he already held.

John Lisle accepted his appointment as President in the middle of June 1654 with some reluctance: he felt he lacked experience, and he had only just recovered from illness. Modelled on the tribunals that had tried the king and some of his more notable supporters, the High Court's function was to enforce various statutory extensions of the offence of treason for the purpose of making Parliament the supreme authority. The law now proscribed proclaiming or promoting Charles Stuart as successor to the abolished throne, declaring government by Parliament without a king to be 'tyrannical, usurped or unlawful', plotting against the government or the Council of State and counterfeiting the great seal, which had been re-designed as a cross and a harp. Trials for these crimes were to be by government-nominated High Court Commissioners instead of judges and juries. The draconian impact of this departure was recognised by the sunset clause on the tribunal's existence: the inaugurating statute, passed the previous November, was due to expire on 1 August 1654.

The court convened in June following the arrest of John Gerrard, Peter Vowell and Somerset Fox for planning to assassinate Cromwell, and a large crowd greeted their appearance in Westminster Hall on the 19th before John Lisle and some twenty commissioners. Fox and Gerrard pleaded not guilty at the outset, but Vowell took a number of preliminary points. John Lisle rejected his pleas for more time to prepare his case, for representation by counsel and for trial by jury, but Vowell then challenged the validity of the legislation under which he was charged. He maintained that 'compassing death to the Protector' was too recent an extension of the law for him to have notice of it. The court replied that it had always been treason, both at common law and under the 1351 Statute of Treasons, to kill the 'supreme magistrate', regardless of title or status. Vowell argued that the new Act's denial of jury trial, as guaranteed by Magna Carta, was incompatible with Cromwell's oath to observe the laws of England. The Solicitor-General countered that Cromwell had power to alter the law as the nation's welfare required. Vowell finally urged that it was unfair to put him on trial for his life under a law that was subject to alteration and therefore only temporary, to which the Solicitor-General answered that all laws were temporary in that sense, but remained in full force until repealed. These arguments, or variations of them, were to be heard on many subsequent occasions during the Protectorate.

Vowell eventually agreed to accept the court's jurisdiction, and pleaded not guilty. But the evidence, mainly that of accomplices, was all too plain. According to John Lisle's summary, 'there was a design to assassinate and murder the Lord Protector with some of his Council, to seize upon the guards and, in this confusion, to proclaim Charles Stuart king'. It had been 'a-hatching [since] the beginning of Lent last', having been devised with the cooperation of Prince Rupert and Charles Stuart in France. The conspirators planned to raise around 5,000 men to assassinate Cromwell on his way to Hampton Court, overwhelm the guards at St James's, occupy Whitehall and force the Lord Mayor to proclaim Charles Stuart king.

The commission had no difficulty in finding the accused guilty, and on 24 June they were sentenced to hang, though without the indignities of drawing and quartering. John Lisle's judgment is full of the well-rehearsed rhetoric seventeenth-century judges habitually heaped on traitors, condemning the enterprise and outlining its potentially calamitous consequences. Such addresses were aimed more at the public at large than the prisoners.

But the example of these three was scarcely a deterrent. A more serious, if short-lived, challenge to Cromwell's authority erupted nine months later, in March 1655, when another group of royalists tried to rally the West to Charles's cause. On the eve of the spring assize, on Monday, 12 March, 200 men occupied Salisbury shortly before dawn, turned the judges out of their lodgings and threatened to hang them and the sheriff – symbols of Commonwealth power – in the market-place. They freed the prisoners from the gaol, proclaimed Charles Stuart king and then rode westwards in search of reinforcements and popular support. But Dorset, Somerset and Devon were unresponsive, and by the time they reached Cullompton on Wednesday morning they were deeply dispirited, their ranks having shrunk to barely a hundred. While settling down for the night at South Molton, they were surprised by Cromwell's troops under Unton Croke,[7] and four hours later the enterprise was over. Croke captured sixty, and imprisoned all of them in Exeter Castle.

A year later Cromwell dubbed them 'a company of mean fellows, alas, not a lord, nor a gentleman, nor a man of fortune, nor this, nor that, amongst them'. But that was the hindsight of the arrogant victor, and hardly accurate. Their leader was Colonel John Penruddock of Compton Chamberlayne in Wiltshire, and for him the defeat could not have been more disastrous. He was 40, handsome, wealthy and well educated. His affectionate and intelligent wife, Arundel, had borne him eight children, and he had risked everything in a three-day burst of loyalty to Charles Stuart. That he had few illusions about the outcome is clear from his note in the family accounts the previous November, where he wrote: 'I hope God will so bless me that I shall be able to go through this great trouble.'

In his letter to Arundel two days after the battle, and aware of Cromwell's fondness for children, he pressed her to take some of their own offspring with her when she went to plead for his life. He told her to get a cousin to intercede with Rolle and Nicholas, the judges he had saved from the gallows in Salisbury. He outlined the details of his will, and asked her to bring their three eldest, Jane, George and Tom, to see him. Between 14 April and his trial at Exeter on the 19th, Arundel did everything she could, including sending petitions to Cromwell and his son Richard, as well as going to see them. But John's position was perilous in the extreme. Despite sparing two judges, he had proclaimed Charles king at Salisbury and Blandford. He had also been extremely active in the planning stage of the rebellion. An attempt to topple the government was a classic case of 'levying war' under the 1351 Statute of Treasons, and plainly he had to be dealt with for the ringleader he was.

John Lisle was one of the six commissioners who travelled into the West to try the rebels. They were not High Court Commissioners empowered to hear treason cases on their own – that method of trial had come to an end the previous August with the expiry of the provision permitting it[8] – they were simply assize judges sitting with juries, and the county sheriffs tried to secure that only jurors loyal to Cromwell were available. John Lisle's companions included Rolle and Nicholas, who played a minor role, given their involvement at Salisbury. Seven rebels convicted there on 12 April were later executed and another thirteen still at large had their estates confiscated in their absence. A week later, Penruddock appeared as the principal defendant of the twenty-six charged in Exeter Castle who pleaded, or were found, guilty of treason and were condemned.

According to Penruddock's account of his trial (the only one to survive), he faced a formidable tribunal: Lisle; Rolle; Nicholas; the Recorder of London, William Steele; and Sergeant John Glynne, who presided. The case lasted five hours, and Penruddock appears to have defended himself quite competently. He challenged Edmund Prideaux, the Attorney-General, over the unfairness of being allowed neither counsel nor a copy of the indictment. Under the 1351 Act, rather than any Commonwealth extension of it, he argued that the Lord Protector was not covered by a law that applied exclusively to protect a king.

He maintained that he and his comrades had surrendered at South Molton only on Unton Croke's explicit promise they would be spared. He argued that his activities amounted to no more than the non-capital offence of causing a riot. Despite his efforts, however, the jury took a quarter of an hour to find him guilty. Four days later, on 23 April, Glynne condemned him and the other twenty-five rebels to death.

Arundel continued her efforts to save her husband, following up his petition to the judges on 26 April with one of her own. Back in London, she addressed herself once again to the Protector and his son, and probably delivered Penruddock's two final petitions on 1 or 2 May. But a reprieve was out of the question if Cromwell's authority was to remain credible. The most that could be wrung from him in the warrant of 3 May was that John Penruddock should be beheaded rather than hanged, and not be drawn and quartered. It was the day that Arundel made her final, desperate plea for him, only to be 'turned out of doors, because I came to beg mercy', as she told him in her farewell letter that evening. Her thoughts concentrated by an unfixed execution date, she wrote an articulate and deeply moving love letter, which deserves wider recognition as a piece of literature than it has yet received. Despairingly affectionate and grief-stricken, its theme of Christian reassurance may have afforded some comfort to her doomed spouse. In fact, John's execution was not until 16 May 1655, so he was able to send her an equally devoted reply.[9]

Confiscation of much of the Penruddock property followed, and the family would have sunk into penury but for their mother's determination and the support of John Martin. Appointed vicar of Compton by Colonel John's father, Sir John, in 1645, Martin was one of Colonel John's trustees. Ejected for refusing to turn Nonconformist, he rented a farm at Tisbury, where he lived as a grazier during the Commonwealth years, and enjoyed widespread respect. According to Anthony Wood's *Athenae Oxonienses*, he managed to preserve at least some of the Penruddock estates from sequestration and 'was in a condition to cherish his distressed family, and take his children under his roof'. Ravenhill believed the Penruddock family accounts immediately following John's death were in Martin's handwriting, so he would appear to have discharged his trust conscientiously.[10]

For Arundel, the task of bringing up seven children at Tisbury cannot have been easy in her reduced circumstances. Despite this, she was as energetic in attempting to retrieve the family fortunes as she had been to save her husband. She wrote to her uncle, John Trenchard, to Cromwell and his son, and to her cousin, Colonel Fitzjames. Her persistence was rewarded, if parsimoniously, in 1657, by an order in council of 23 March: 'A sum of £200 out of John Penruddock's personal estate is granted to Arundel, his widow, for the benefit of the younger son and five daughters of the said John.'

The fact that Thomas and his sisters had preference over George, the eldest son, indicates that the situation may have been less severe than Arundel claimed. John's life tenancy of much of his Wiltshire property, with the freehold already vested in George, meant that his death simply enlarged George's existing rights, leaving them unencumbered. In thus creating a contingently 'nil' estate, John's foresight had averted disaster. The report by the Whitehall officials in February 1657 shows they accepted this situation, which means that the heir's exclusion would have been because he was adequately provided for rather than because the government wished to discriminate against him.

The family's fortunes had improved by 1660. George was up at Oxford, and that November Arundel offered the restored monarch £500 a year for a monopoly in glass-making, although there is no indication as to whether or not it was granted. Thereafter, the family record during Charles II's reign is sparse. George died unmarried in 1664, aged 20, two years before Arundel. Thomas succeeded George as heir, and in 1672 married Frances Hanham, who bore him eight children. In 1681 the king acknowledged the family's loyalty by making Thomas colonel of the Wiltshire militia. By James II's accession in 1685 the family fortunes were fully restored. Thomas was a deputy lieutenant of the county under the Earl of Pembroke, a justice of the peace and back in the family seat at Compton Park. Aged 39, his Stuart loyalty was unquestionable, securely rooted in memories of his father's martyrdom thirty years before, of the judges who had condemned him and of the hated Protector who had so heartlessly refused a reprieve.

*   *   *

Cromwell felt few inhibitions about his Protector's oath to 'govern . . . according to the laws, statutes and customs', notwithstanding the law-abiding reputation he sought to cultivate. For him, the law was there to be manipulated according to political need. If little complaint could be made about its enforcement against John Penruddock in the West, it would be difficult to imagine a more flagrant abuse than the treatment simultaneously handed out to George Coney in London. Coney was a merchant who had withheld customs duty on the ground that Parliament had not authorised it. When the collector took the money by force, Coney sued for its return. Fearful of the implications of such a precedent, Cromwell intervened personally. But Coney stood firm, and was promptly imprisoned. From there he instructed Sergeant Maynard, Sergeant Twysden and Mr Wadham Wyndham to apply to the Upper Bench (the renamed King's Bench of the Commonwealth) for release by habeas corpus. According to Clarendon, Maynard performed with great confidence, arguing that both the tax and the imprisonment were self-evidently illegal. The judges felt compelled to agree, but gave opposing counsel a day's adjournment to prepare a reply.

Cromwell, however, had no time for legal pedantries. On 18 May 1655, two days after John Penruddock's execution, all Coney's counsel found themselves in the Tower for having even dared to argue his case. Clarendon, sensitive to his readers' feelings, described what followed:

> The judges were . . . severely reprehended for suffering that licence; when they, with all humility, mentioned the law and Magna Carta, Cromwell told them, with words of contempt and derision, 'their Magna F**** should not control his actions; which he knew were for the safety of the Commonwealth'. He asked them who made them judges? Whether they had any authority to sit but what he gave them? . . . and so dismissed them with caution, 'that they should not suffer the lawyers to prate what it would not become them to hear'.[11]

In 1656, the High Court of Justice was reintroduced with 'An Act for the Security of the Lord Protector's person, and continuation of the nation in peace and safety'. Cromwell's spies were still at work, the measure asserting 'it hath manifestly appeared that divers wicked plots and means have been of late devised . . . to the great endangering his Highness's person'.

To ensure that Cromwell, though not king, was fully protected by the law of treason, the Act prevented the point taken by John Penruddock being raised again. It also confirmed and extended the embargo on dealings with royalty in exile: it was treason to 'proclaim, declare or promote Charles Stuart . . . or aid or assist the said Charles Stuart, his brothers or mother'. Trials by commission were reintroduced, and 140 commissioners were appointed, any seventeen of whom formed a quorum. Like its predecessor, the statute was to expire 'at the end of the last session of the next Parliament', which meant the end of July 1658.

John Lisle resumed the reins as President in the summer of 1658 and presided over another ten treason trials. On 2 June, the royalist Sir Henry Slingsby was charged with trying to persuade his captors to change their allegiance. Despite his arguments that he was 'a declared enemy, and therefore by the laws of war free to make any such attempt' and that he had only done it in jest, the commission convicted him.

Dr John Hewett, the royalist preacher at St Gregory's by St Paul's in London, appeared next and was impeached for 'holding correspondence with Charles Stuart'. He tried to follow the late monarch's example by wearing his hat in court, but the tribunal was established by law, and he was no king. While the impeachment was being read, John Lisle 'commanded his hat to be taken off; which the Doctor observing, took it off himself'. Hewett claimed ignorance of the law – 'I am better acquainted with a pulpit than a bar, better read in St Austin than my lord Coke' – but this was plainly disingenuous. His two-hour challenge to the commission's jurisdiction brought repeated warnings of the automatic conviction that would follow if he refused to accept it.

In the end, John Lisle had no alternative:

> Lord President: I must take you off, you have been required to answer, often required; and having refused, in the name of the Court I require the Clerk to record it; and pray take away your prisoner.
> Hewett: My lord –
> Court: Take him away, take him away.

Hewett and Slingsby were both executed on Tower Hill on 8 June.

John Mordaunt's trial followed Hewett's. Similarly charged with 'holding correspondence with Charles Stuart', he had the narrowest escape imaginable. According to Clarendon, Mordaunt's wife managed to bribe some members of the commission, who told her that they would have to convict her husband if he persisted in refusing to recognise the court; and that the principal, though extremely unwilling, witness against him was his accomplice, Colonel Mallory. She then bribed Mallory's guards, who allowed him to escape on his way to Westminster Hall, and she got a note to her husband on the second morning of the trial about what was happening. He accordingly pleaded not guilty, and, without Mallory's evidence, the case against him was weak and vague.

The *State Trials* report shows he summed up his own defence quite powerfully. One of the commissioners fell ill during the trial, leaving the remainder equally divided on the question of his guilt. John Lisle held the casting vote. Thus, continued Clarendon, 'the determination depended upon the single vote of the president, who made some excuses for the justice he was about to do, and acknowledged many obligations to the mother of the prisoner, and, in contemplation thereof, pronounced him innocent for aught [that] appeared to the Court'.

Cromwell was so infuriated that he kept Mordaunt in the Tower for a while afterwards, and wanted him retried on Mallory's recapture. It was one of the few occasions when he accepted advice that that was both legally impossible as well as politically unwise, and Mordaunt had to be released. The remaining seven conspirators were convicted of treason on 2 July, and three were hanged in the city on the 7th.

These cases in the summer of 1658 saw John Lisle's fortunes begin to fade. Six months earlier, Cromwell had appointed him to the Admiralty Court of Hampshire and to the newly created House of Peers, which brought Alice Lisle the courtesy title of 'Dame' after his death. Now he faced Cromwell's anger over Mordaunt's acquittal, while Cromwell himself had to bear the burden of accelerating his favourite daughter's death by refusing Hewett a reprieve. Sick and with children of her own, Elizabeth Claypole pleaded with her father on behalf of Hewett's pregnant wife, Mary. Cromwell would not listen, and, according to Walker's *The Compleat History of Independency*, 'the increase of her sickness made her rave in the most lamentable manner, calling out against her father for Hewett's blood . . . the violence of which extravagant passions . . . carried her into another world'. Her death on 6 August was followed by Cromwell's a month later.

Family misfortune also overtook John and Alice Lisle. Their sons, Beconsaw and William, died successively in 1653 and 1654, and their eldest daughter, also Alice, was deserted three weeks after her wedding. An attractive girl of 17, she was married at St Margaret's, Westminster, in July 1657 to the 19-year-old, and equally immature, Edward Zouch, heir to extensive estates in northern Hampshire. Edward, however, quickly decided he preferred his rakish fellow royalists' company in the Faubourg St Germain in Paris, where he died the following year. Selfish to the last, he must have destroyed for ever any spark of affection Alice may have cherished for him by his dying declaration: he directed that she should have none of his assets. Disillusioned, she avoided matrimony for a while, and it was not until October 1663 that she married Richard Glanville. Her younger sister Elizabeth fared better initially: in December 1659 she married Robert Gurdon, a 44-year-old bachelor from Suffolk, when John Lisle made over £3,000 to her. But she eventually went mad, and in her later years was looked after first by her sister Alice Glanville, and then by Robert Whitaker, the widower of her younger sister Margaret.

*   *   *

Richard Cromwell, 'Tumbledown Dick', was a mere shadow of his father, and John Lisle, although he had been made an Admiralty Commissioner in January 1660, recognised all too clearly what for him were the gathering storm-clouds of the Restoration. His leading role in Charles I's trial, the royalists he had condemned, the unswerving loyalty he had given Cromwell and the prosperity he had achieved – all these things made him a prime target for royalist vengeance.

For the fortnight before Charles II's landing at Dover on 25 May, Parliament was mainly concerned to decide on exclusions from the general pardon, and on 12 May, the more notorious candidates were required to defend themselves before the Commons. But time was up for John Lisle. It can have come as no surprise, when the bill reached the Lords, to hear that two widows, Arundel Penruddock and Mary Hewett, had personally urged his exclusion. Sooner than risk arrest, he submitted a written petition to the Commons, but this was not read out. His exclusion was later confirmed, so that he would certainly have shared his fellow Regicides' barbaric fates on the Charing Cross gallows had he not escaped before the ports closed on 15 May. Rumours flew – he had been arrested at Dover, he had taken refuge in a French monastery – but with other exiles he eventually reached Switzerland, where the group settled at Vevey, on Lake Geneva. They were joined there in the autumn of 1662 by another royalist enemy, Edmund Ludlow, who, after making his own way out from England in August 1660, had felt he was at risk in Geneva and Lausanne.

For the next three years they tried to live unobtrusively, moving on whenever they seemed threatened. Early in 1664, however, John Lisle got wind of serious royalist plans to kill him, and he moved to Lausanne, where the inhabitants were said to have been 'charmed by his devotion'. Records there show he sought anonymity under the name of 'Mr Field', though this was hardly helped, according to Anthony Wood (*Athenae Oxonienses*), by his habit of wearing his English Lord Chancellor's robes in public. Another reason he gave for moving was the visit Alice was planning the following May, and he felt she would be at risk on her return if it became known she had been to Vevey.

John Lisle's belief that he was a hunted man proved correct. Ludlow gives a detailed account of his assassination, and does not shrink from suggesting the cantonal government's complicity:

On Thursday, 11th August 1664 . . . Mr Lisle going that morning to . . . the church . . . was shot dead by a person on foot who had a companion waiting for him on horseback with a led horse in his hand, which the murderer having mounted and cried 'Vive le Roi', they immediately rode away together . . . The villain that murdered him had waited his coming at a barber's shop where he pretended to want something for his teeth, till seeing Mr Lisle at a distance he stepped out of the shop, and as he came by, saluted him. Then following him into the churchyard, he drew a Carabine from under his cloak, and shot him into the back. With the recoil of the piece the villain's hat was beaten off, and he himself falling over a piece of timber, dropped his gun . . . The Government of Lausanne was so remiss in pursuit of the assassins that it was suspected they had friends among them. And of this the villains themselves seemed to give proof; for before they had advanced half a league on their way, calling to some men who were working in the vineyards, they bid them give their service to the governors of Lausanne and tell them they would drink their health.[12]

The assassins were hired by English royalists. Most accounts suggest there were three of them, and that one was called, or masqueraded as, Thomas MacDonnell. Ludlow, however, was visited shortly afterwards by a traveller returning to England, and he relates what he learned:

> I think it necessary to insert in this place the true names of those assassins who were employed by the court of England, and others, to take away our lives, as I received them from an English gentleman well acquainted with their affairs, who made me a visit at Vevey on his return to England from Italy. He assured me that the villain who murdered Mr Lisle, by shooting him into the back, is an Irishman, and named O'Croli; that the name of his companion, who waited with a fresh horse to carry him off, is Cotter, and that he is a native of the same country; that the assassin who goes under the name of Riardo is also an Irishman, and his true name MacCarty . . .

Crowley and McCarthy are common enough Irish names, and there is nothing to establish their identity. But their leader was named in July 1700 by the Irish writer William MacCartain. He composed a poem praising Sir James Fitz-Edmund Cotter as John Lisle's direct assassin – the 'hit-man' rather than the individual who had simply held the horses – and it was apparently Cotter who had to adopt the 'MacDonnell' alias in place of his otherwise distinctive name. Knighted by Charles II, he was the owner of extensive family estates in Cork. As MP for Cork and the city customs collector, he would have been delighted to be of service to the monarch who had honoured him.

TWO

The Nonconformist Widow

John Lisle's assassination was the most crushing of the three blows Alice suffered in the wake of the Restoration. The first was his flight into exile once exclusion from the general pardon was inevitable; and, while he escaped with his life, he left her pregnant with their youngest, Anne, who never saw her father. This was swiftly followed by the second blow: his attainder and the forfeiture of his estates, with no shortage of royalist vultures for the pickings. William Chamberlain's three daughters, 'ruined by their father's loyal service in the late wars', petitioned for a low-rental lease of Crux Easton Manor; Anne Duke, widowed when her husband died in the East Indies after transportation for his part in the Penruddock rising, wanted Ellingham Manor and the Abbey Lands at Christchurch; and 'Katherine Hide, widow', asked for the income-producing assets of John Lisle's estate 'that she may . . . testify her kindness to . . . William Lisle and . . . obtain a better subsistence to herself'.[1] There were others besides. How many of these petitions were granted is not known, but much of the more valuable property was divided between the king's brother, James, and John's younger brother, William.

At the end of these ordeals, Alice found herself with little besides her own inheritance of Moyles Court (as this was her 'jointure', settled on her by her parents before her marriage, John had only a life tenancy of the property), probably secured to her on the petition of Lady Mary Howard (Appendix Three). This was all she had to support and educate her seven unmarried children: John, Bridget, Tryphena, Margaret, Mary, Mabella and Anne.[2] The final blow was the news of John's murder, ending all hope of reunion or return.

His death could hardly have left her more isolated, not merely as a widow, aged 47, but as the black Cromwellian sheep in an otherwise royalist family. Her sister's husband, Sir Thomas Tipping, and John's younger brother, now Sir William Lisle, were both devoted supporters of the Stuart throne. Her faith made her even more of an outcast. Quite when she and John had turned to Puritanism is not clear. But the Temple Church entry of the birth and baptism of their daughter Margaret in 1643 discloses a considerable shift of loyalty since their Anglican wedding seven years before. Margaret was baptised on 3 July 'at Mr Lisle's chamber' in the Temple, in contrast to other baptisms in the Temple Church, and the ceremony was performed by 'Mr Pearson, curate'. He was probably the James Pearson licensed in 1672 as a Congregational chaplain to John Lisle's close friend Bulstrode Whitlock.[3]

*   *   *

While there is no reason to think the Lisles' conversion to Puritanism was anything but sincere, those with political ambition during the Commonwealth had to adopt that faith, or at least adapt to it. John and Alice joined the Dissenting congregation in Westminster Abbey, led by the Cromwell family, and the chapel at Moyles Court no doubt housed similar gatherings. But at the Restoration, Nonconformists became the largest religious minority, representing, if the 1676 return for the province of Canterbury was typical, around 4 per cent of the population. The discriminatory Clarendon Code legislation, passed rather against the sympathies of the Chancellor after whom it was named, made them the kingdom's poor and often homeless relations.

The disabilities bore heavily. The Corporation Act of 1661 limited government employment to practising Anglicans; between 1700 and 1800 ministers who rejected Church of England doctrines lost their livings under the Acts of Uniformity of 1660 and 1662; statutes of 1664 and 1670 penalised attendance at Dissenters' meetings, known as conventicles; and the Five Mile Act of 1665 forbade ejected ministers from coming within 5 miles of any town or borough, their former parishes or wherever they had preached illegally. Moyles Court became one of many refuges of these Nonconformist nomads, and Alice Lisle undoubtedly risked prosecution for those she sheltered.

The 1664 Conventicle Act expired in 1667, and for a while the outlook brightened: Dissenters could gather as they pleased, and

Charles began to discuss freedom of worship more earnestly with his ministers. But the Anglican prejudices of Parliament ran deep. The realisation that 'universal' religious freedom would include toleration of Catholics, and the extent of Nonconformity disclosed in the 1669 return, prompted the much more rigorous Conventicle Act of 1670.

Among the numerous conventicles reported, the 1669 return noted one at Moyles Court of 200 Presbyterians 'of the meaner sort, who come most of them from Ringwood and out of Dorsetshire'. Though not the largest in the Winchester diocese, it was one of the better attended. The householder responsible was 'Mrs Lisle, the Regicide's wife', and the 'Heads and Teachers' included 'Mr Crofts, chaplain to Mrs Lisle'. Sixteen years later, it was the use of his name as an alias that so nearly destroyed Alice Lisle's defence at her trial.

After losing his living at Mottisfont under the 1660 Act, Crofts is reported to have preached at Botley and at Swanmore. His position as 'Alice Lisle's chaplain' in 1669 implies his duties probably included tutoring her children. He left to take a similar post with Lady Frances Fiennes at Newton Tony in Wiltshire, where fines were levied in May 1671 for permitting a conventicle. Crofts was clearly popular. During the 'Indulgence' of March 1672 to March 1673, when Nonconformity was officially tolerated, he was granted preaching licences as a Presbyterian with Frances Fiennes, and as a Congregationalist at John Girle's house nearby.

Crofts was succeeded at Moyles Court by the Reverend Compton South, whose first ministry included a 'numerous auditory' at Odiham. South later moved to the Wiltshire living of Berwick St John, from which he was ejected in 1662, and suffered relentless persecution for the next ten years. Calamy described his life as 'a constant scene of suffering . . . he was many times obliged to leave his house and numerous family to preserve his liberty'. But from the 1672 Indulgence, during his ministry at Ringwood, he appears to have been left alone. Every week he made the 36-mile return journey from his home at Donhead St Mary to Ringwood and, according to Calamy, 'was constantly entertained at Moyles Court, the seat of the pious Lady Lisle' until her arrest in July 1685.

In Hampshire and Wiltshire rather more than a hundred ministers lost their livings on 24 August 1662 under the second Act of

Uniformity, passed a few days before the church tithes fell due. Ejection carried the additional penalty of a year's loss of income. The date of 24 August was also St Bartholomew's Day. The victims and their sympathisers drew parallels with the Catholic massacre of Protestants in France ninety years earlier, describing themselves as 'Bartholomeans' and the 1662 statute as the 'Bartholomew Act'. Alice Lisle knew and helped many of these ministers, two of whom became her sons-in-law. Leonard Hoar, ejected from his living at Wanstead in Essex, married her daughter Bridget and was later President of Harvard College in Massachusetts;[4] and in the autumn of 1672 Margaret Lisle married the Reverend Robert Whitaker, a scholarly churchman from Lancashire. Denied a Cambridge degree because of his Nonconformity, he preached as a Presbyterian from about 1662, when he set up an Academy for Dissenting Students for those refused entry to the universities. He and Margaret lived at Stucton, a village near Fordingbridge.

The applications in 1672 for meetings at Fordingbridge and Moyles Court were almost certainly made by Whitaker. Though there is no record of what happened to the first, 'the house of the widow Lisle, Moyles Court' was licensed for Presbyterian worship on 18 November that year. At the same time, an Alice Lisle is also recorded, puzzlingly, as having received a Presbyterian licence for 'Bagshot Park in Hampshire'. Bagshot Park was, and remains, Crown property, and is now the home of the Earl and Countess of Wessex following their marriage in June 1999. But it lies in Surrey, so that the 1672 entry could have been a clerical error misdescribing the county, or misattributing to Alice Lisle a licence granted to some unrelated individual bearing the same name in Surrey. There is no suggestion apart from this that she ever owned substantial assets outside Hampshire, except possibly her will of 9 June 1682, which disposed of property in Hampshire, Dorset 'and elsewhere'. However, it is unlikely that this last category included Bagshot Park.[5]

It was some time between 1673 and 1675, after Charles II had been forced to end the Indulgence in order to secure Parliament's vote for supplies for the Dutch War, that a very determined champion of Nonconformity joined Alice Lisle's circle of friends as a preacher in Portsmouth. Born in 1633 at Newsham in the North Riding, John Hicks was energetic, intelligent and sincere. Aged 40, he had been through many adventures in the cause of Presbyterianism, for which he could claim some success. A graduate of Trinity College, Dublin, he had his first ministry in the Yorkshire parish of Stonegrave, where he was described as 'a great enthusiast' and preached in grey, rather than the normal canonical black, to distinguish his religious allegiance. In 1659, he took the living at Stoke Damerel in Devon. On ejection at the Restoration, he went to Saltash, some 4 miles across the Tamar in Cornwall, where he led a group of six ministers, reported by the Bishop of Exeter in 1665 as being 'all notoriously disaffected to King and Church'. The Five Mile Act in October of that year drove him back to Devon, this time to the Salcombe estuary at Kingsbridge, where he appears to have been subjected to the same harassment as his fellow preachers.

The respite enjoyed by Nonconformist congregations after 1667 ended abruptly on 10 May 1670, with the passing of the second Conventicle Act. This re-enacted the 1664 statute, restricting meetings to four individuals or household groups, with fines for the house owner, preacher and all participants aged 16 and over if the maximum was exceeded. Now, house owner and preacher faced heavier penalties – £20 for the first offence, increasing to £40 thereafter – and the 1664 loophole allowing open-air conventicles was closed. The new Act introduced the principle of communal liability for fines, of up to £10 a head, forcing the affluent to make up what the indigent could not find. A third of the money went to the Crown, a third was assigned to poor relief and the remainder rewarded spies and informers who tracked down the conventicles. Additionally, troops could now be enlisted to assist the civil authorities.

This incentive of a reward, and the specific provision in the Act that it was to be 'construed most largely and beneficially for suppressing conventicles', heralded a determined persecution by those with scores to settle and pockets to fill, as John Hicks quickly discovered. His *Narrative*, a diary published anonymously in 1671, records how he and his friends were hunted round south Devon as they tested the boundaries of the law, while trying to keep one jump ahead of their pursuers. If its 'truths' and 'injustices' are seen essentially through the victims' eyes, the account nevertheless provides a vivid insight into the depths of religious bigotry.

On Sunday, 29 May 1670, a fortnight after the Act had come into force, Hicks's home was raided by a party under the local magistrate, Squire Reynell. While they tried to force the front door, Hicks's wife and the congregation saw him out at the back. Frustrated and abusive, the raiders took the names of those present. Without apparent evidence of the minister's presence, much less of his preaching, Hicks was fined £20, and two others £1 and £2. Similar raids followed, at Kingsbridge and elsewhere, on the next five Sundays. John Lucas, one of the raiders, was involved in a fight during another search at Hicks's home on 12 June, and Hicks himself narrowly escaped capture on 3 July when his open-air conventicle on Lincombe Hill had to disperse on the approach of Reynell with about thirty soldiers.[6] Fines for a conventicle held there on 26 July were imposed by John Bear, a newly appointed magistrate and one of Hicks's particular enemies. Although not mentioned in the *Narrative*, there was one place where a legal anomaly provided sanctuary: the Saltstone, a rock in the Salcombe estuary that is uncovered shortly after high tide, was recognised as both 'extra-parochial' and beyond any magistrate's jurisdiction. Nonconformist convoys crossed there as weather and tides allowed.

Two events at this time put Hicks under increasing pressure. The first was Bear's appointment: he had made no secret of his determination to have Hicks behind bars, and now he was a magistrate this was within his grasp. The second was John Lucas's death in January 1671, some seven months after the Sunday morning fight at Hicks's home in Kingsbridge. Despite the lapse of time and a post-mortem that found Lucas had died of natural causes, Bear had Hicks charged with murder. Hicks went into hiding, and although he successfully avoided many searches, the charge hung over him for the best part of a year. It was only through publication of the *Narrative* in the spring of 1671 that he was eventually able to get it lifted.

When the document came to official notice, Calamy tells how two messengers sent to arrest him met him by chance and disclosed the purpose of their journey without realising who he was. Hicks gave them the slip, rode straight to London and gained access to the king. Charles began by reproving him for his attacks in the *Narrative*, but Hicks stood by it. He told the king: 'Oppression . . . makes a wise man mad. The justices, beyond all law, have very much wronged your majesty's loyal subjects, the Nonconformists in the West.' By the end of the interview, Charles promised that Dissenters 'should have no such cause of complaint for the future', and remitted a third of the fines already levied. Hicks's murder charge was withdrawn as part of his general pardon in January 1672, and two months later he could justly claim much of the credit for the Indulgence. Immediately after the Indulgence had been published on 15 March, he drew up an 'Address of Grateful Acknowledgement' to the king on behalf of the Devon Nonconformists. According to Calamy, 'the king received it very graciously and asked him "if he had not been as good as his word?"'.

For the rest of the year, Hicks made applications on a country-wide basis, collecting and delivering many of the licences granted. But at over-the-counter level, royal benevolence became minimum compliance. Control was exercised through a double-licence system, under which both house and preacher had to be separately licensed before a conventicle could take place, and licences were not to be had just for the asking. Of some 500 applications in Hicks's handwriting, his receipts totalled eighty-six. But, since he was a religious leader, the authorities made a special effort to keep his goodwill. His general licence, 'to be a Presbyterian teacher in any licensed place', was dated 2 April, presumably so that he could receive it at his audience four days later. It was followed on the 11th by the two specific authorisations to preach under his own roof in Devon, where the congregation rapidly outgrew the house. This resulted in 'a new-built meeting house belonging to John Hicks in the Town of Kingsbridge', licensed in September. Because of his obligations in London, Hicks also took a house in Hatton Garden, where another congregation gathered. When he came to Portsmouth, therefore, he was an acknowledged Nonconformist hero, with a proven record of loyalty and achievement. Even if Alice Lisle had not met him before, she would certainly have known him by repute.

It was, however, a time of uncertainty, because although the Indulgence had officially ended in March 1673, nothing was said about the validity of existing licences. This was almost certainly deliberate, Charles II's skills lying in compromise and offending as few people as possible. If no new licences were issued and existing ones left in doubt, a damper would be kept on both sides. Fervour would evaporate and Nonconformity would lose momentum. While things did not turn out in that way, it was a reasonable political prognosis to make at the time.

Hicks's wife, Abigail, died on 13 May 1675. With two sons and a daughter to look after, he did not remain a widower for long. In 1676, he married Elizabeth, aged 21, the daughter of a Portsmouth maltster, John Moody. They had another two children, a boy and a girl. Later that year, the horizon darkened when Charles again came under pressure and declared all preaching licences issued since 1672 as officially revoked. This ending of the three-year truce must have been a bitter blow to Hicks, and the following year he was again the target of persecution.

Whatever conventicles he held during his time at Portsmouth, and they doubtless included meetings in Moyles Court chapel, he was up before the local bench on Sunday, 14 October 1677 for preaching earlier in the day 'in a seditious conventicle . . . at a certain place . . . commonly called the Gold-ball, being the house of Robert Reynolds of Portsmouth . . . baker', for which he and Reynolds were each fined £20.

At some stage during Hicks's Portsmouth ministry, Calamy records that 'the king and duke of York came thither . . . the governor . . . and many of the inhabitants of the town, went to meet him, and Mr Hicks was one of the company. As soon as the king saw him he took particular notice of him.' Neither the date nor the occasion is recorded. Otherwise, the record is bare: Calamy simply notes 'he was driven away by fresh persecutions', which suggests the October 1677 proceedings were not the only cases he faced.

Hicks moved to Keynsham in 1682 and three years later, when the rebel army reached Shepton Mallet on 24 June 1685, he joined Monmouth. According to the evidence at Alice Lisle's trial, it was the very next day, in the stables of Sir Thomas Bridges' house at Keynsham, that he committed an act of treason that has taken men to the scaffold before and since: he tried to persuade his fellow countrymen, Monmouth's prisoners of war, to change their allegiance.

*   *   *

For English royalists, May 1660 was a moment of deliverance, a dream come true, a homecoming. The welcome that greeted Charles when he landed at Dover was wildly exuberant: it carried the underlying theme of 'continuity from 1648', with a determination to expunge the shaming republican interruption. The monarch was returning to his kingdom, rather than arriving for the first time; he was being restored to an existing throne left vacant on his father's martyrdom, rather than resurrecting one that had been abolished.

Within days of his coronation, the constitution underwent a thorough spring-clean. The parliamentary calendar painted out the interim, designating 1660 as '12 and 13 Car. II', or the twelfth and thirteenth years of the reign, and chapters I and III of the new legislation confirmed Parliament's link with the past by officially dissolving the final session under Charles I. Thereafter the two Houses worked on the basis that all 'pretended Acts' of the Protectorate (significantly omitted from most subsequent printings of the statutes) were void unless retrospectively confirmed – inevitably some had to be, to prevent the country collapsing into legal and commercial chaos. While Parliament professed disdain at having to mention them at all, it afforded yet another opportunity to condemn the interlopers. Section 12 of the Act validating previous court decisions proclaimed:

> although in this confirmation of Judicial Proceedings, it was necessary to mention divers pretended Acts and Ordinances, by the Names and Stiles which those Persons then usurped who took upon them to pass the same, namely some by the Stile and Name of the Keepers of the Liberty of England by the Authority of Parliament, and others of the Name and Stile of the Protectors of the Commonwealth . . . Yet this present Parliament doth declare . . . that the Names and Stiles aforesaid, and every one of them, are most rebellious, wicked, traitorous and abominable Usurpations, detested by this present Parliament, as opposite in the highest degree to his Sacred Majesty's Right . . .

Charles received the customary income from Tonnage and Poundage. Chapter IX, the Act of Indemnity and Oblivion, pardoned the nation at large for anything that might be seen as potentially treasonable under the Protectorate, though it named the more notorious exceptions, with John Lisle heading the list. These also included 'any . . . who plotted, contrived or designed the great and heinous Rebellion of Ireland' against Charles I; and 'every offence committed . . . by any Jesuit or Romish priest' against the anti-Catholic legislation of Elizabethan days.

But, despite the acclamations and rejoicing, the Convention Parliament that summoned Charles in 1660 was primarily motivated by self-interest. With the king reinstalled, the instrument of government was firmly back on its lawful foundation. For the next fifteen years, the Cavalier Parliament of 1661 wielded a near-unchallengeable authority. An assembly of royalists, rulers by tradition and caste – the socially elevated, hereditary, Anglican class – it was as determined to retrieve what it had lost in eleven years of oppression as to secure its supremacy for the future. Pursuit of these objectives generated an increasingly tense relationship with Charles and was the origin of the constitutional controversy that continued throughout this and the next reign: where lay the balance of power between king and Parliament? It raised a series of issues. Who was to control public spending? Could the king arbitrarily extend membership of the House of Commons? Could he suspend the laws against religious minorities? Could the Commons veto ministerial appointments? Within such uncertain limits, the task of governing effectively required all Charles's political skill, and it was only gradually that he learned what the Commons would tolerate.

Perhaps his most crucial mistake was to underestimate the depth of anti-Catholic prejudice, a misjudgement compounded by his monumentally insensitive brother and successor, James II. This blind spot in Charles's otherwise perceptive character is surprising, because the evidence was plain: the discrimination against Catholic priests in the Act of Indemnity and Oblivion, the xenophobia in 1666 that unfairly blamed French Catholics for the Fire of London, and the evident aversion to Popery behind the Conventicle Act of 1670. But the reason for it was undoubtedly Charles's own, necessarily covert, Catholic leanings and his equally secret agreement with the French king, Louis XIV, to convert England to the Church of Rome.

The issue came to a head in 1673. The Indulgence declared the previous March coincided with the outbreak of a war in which England was France's ally against the Protestant Dutch; that, combined with the increasing number of Catholics at Court – the most notable being the heir to the throne, James – created a stench of Popery that turned even the steadiest of stomachs. By 1673, there were even Dissenters who saw their Indulgence as a charter of Catholic toleration.

Charles's revocation of the Indulgence and his acceptance of the Test Act of 1673 were dictated by his need for money. The Test Act and its successor in 1678 debarred anyone from civil or military office unless a communicant member of the Anglican Church. The consequences were far reaching: it brought the end of the pact with Louis XIV; Catholics were forbidden to hold public office for over a hundred years, and it laid the foundations of the controversy that ended James II's reign in 1688.

By 1678, the Catholic menace seemed like an approaching tidal wave, with Parliament in a state of near paranoia. In what was to be the Cavaliers' final session, nearly eighteen years after first assembling, Lords and Commons unanimously resolved that 'there has been, and still is, a damnable and hellish Plot contrived and carried on by Popish recusants, for the assassinating and murdering the King, and for subverting the Government and rooting out and destroying the Protestant religion'.

A plot there certainly was, but not the one people believed in. The real plot was designed to secure the Catholic succession of James, Duke of York, once it was clear that Charles's pact with the French king was foundering. Evidence of this pact can be seen in letters dating from 1675 between James's secretary, Coleman, and Louis XIV's confessor, Père la Chaise. When those came to light, Coleman was convicted of treason and executed. But the other plot, foisted on the imagination of a fearful nation, was the work of a one-time cleric, the self-styled 'Doctor' Titus Oates.

A corpulent and foul-mouthed propagandist, Oates is one of the most unsavoury characters of the seventeenth century. Beneath the spurious title lay a street-level trader in slander and lies. He knew exactly how to whet the appetite of human credulity and what confections of fact and fiction it would swallow, and was not in the least concerned with the lives and reputations he destroyed in the process. His particular skill, the nightmare of today's newspaper editor, lay in 'finding an interesting situation and attracting the facts towards it'.

The plot of his devising was total fantasy, apart from one rather vague but crucial fact: that on 24 April 1678 there had been a 'consult', or meeting, of Jesuits in London. The rumour reached Oates at the Catholic seminary of St Omer, now in France but then part of the Netherlands, where he had enrolled as a student the previous December. What he did not know was that the meeting was an extremely secret one in the Duke of York's apartments in St James's, and that knowledge of it had leaked, possibly from Whitehall. Shortly afterwards, Oates, expelled from St Omer without assets or income, returned to London, where he set about packaging and marketing his information for what it would fetch. Within six weeks he had embroidered a horrifying tale of a Jesuit conspiracy to overthrow the government. Huge sums had been offered to murder the king and replace him with the Duke of York; a Catholic administration would be established; the French were to invade Ireland; and all Protestants would be massacred. According to Oates, this plan had been put together on 24 April at the White Horse in Fleet Street. Why he should have chosen that particular tavern as the supposed meeting place is not clear, unless the words 'Whitehall's conspirators' were misheard or misconstrued as 'White Horse conspirators' when the rumour crossed the Channel.

The authenticity of his story depended on a flagrant, fundamental lie, which brought Oates a double flogging on perjury charges seven years later: that he had been present at the White Horse in April and had heard everything with his own ears. Naming names, he set out what had passed in a lengthy document and appeared before the Privy Council to confirm its claims, having first sent a copy for perusal to the Protestant magistrate, Sir Edmund Berry Godfrey. Of the Council, only the king was sceptical, after he had caught Oates out in one or two blatant discrepancies. While a painstaking investigation would doubtless have exposed him as a liar, there were too many people ready to believe him to make that a realistic possibility. Those he denounced were arrested, and his tale gained widespread credibility with Godfrey's unsolved murder: his corpse, strangled and run through with a sword, was found on Primrose Hill on 17 October. Oates became a national hero overnight. Housed in Whitehall, with a bodyguard (one of them the Duke of Monmouth) and an income from the state, he appeared as the principal prosecution witness against Coleman at the end of November. Though Coleman's own letters were enough to condemn him, Oates added the baseless rider that he had conspired to murder the king. Over the next eighteen months, Oates and his accomplices swore away the lives of more than thirty victims, mostly innocent Catholics. With the judicial process swamped by anti-Catholic hysteria, the accused's faith and Oates's accusations were enough to condemn them. The honest testimony that should have saved them, given by inmates of St Omer – that Oates was there in April 1678 and not in London, and was therefore lying from start to finish – was rejected on the same score; it fell from Catholic lips and was therefore not credible.

Despite the minor setbacks of one or two acquittals, Oates achieved his selfish ends. He was now affluent (on top of his official income he had claimed large and fraudulent expenses for uncovering the 'truth', which the Commons paid without question), and had comfortable lodgings, servants to wait on him, and, for the time being at least, the status of a national saviour. For as long as the Catholic threat seemed real, his reputation held. As he launched and lost a number of patently dishonest libel actions, it began to ebb, however, after which his enemies started to speak out against him. By the middle of 1682, his state pension had been withdrawn and he did not dare testify against Kearney, an Irishman he had originally accused of conspiring to beat the king to death. The £100,000 damages award he faced in 1684 for calling the Duke of York a traitor took him to prison for debt, followed a year later by his conviction and flogging for perjury.

Oates's tide of religious bigotry effectively decided the elections of February and October 1679. During the campaign his abuse of his enemies as 'Tories', in its original meaning of 'Irish robbers', became part of the political vocabulary. To this the king and the Cavaliers responded by dubbing their opponents 'whiggamors', after the murderous Scots Presbyterian rebels of the time. It was these Whigs who swept the polls in 1679 and 1681. Efficiently organised from the Green Ribbon Club, their political headquarters in the King's Head on the corner of Chancery Lane and Fleet Street, they directed their efforts in Parliament towards getting the Duke of York excluded from the succession and putting forward James, Duke of Monmouth, as the substitute successor. This was the ultimate test of Charles's political skill, but he managed to outwit them by adroitly manipulating a Lords majority and a number of judiciously timed prorogations and dissolutions. With the secret assurance of Louis XIV's financial support, he dissolved the final Whig assembly at Oxford in March 1681. From then until his death on 6 February 1685, his ministers governed without Parliament, wielding virtually unlimited executive power.

*   *   *

Alice Lisle's preoccupations at this time appear to have been primarily with her property and her family. She had been able to buy back some of her murdered husband's confiscated land at Ellingham from the Duke of York in 1674 and in February 1679 included Moyles Court in the marriage settlement set up in anticipation of her son John's wedding on 20 May that year. He married Catherine Croke, a first cousin of the Unton Croke who had captured John Penruddock in 1655, and the daughter of Charles Croke of Bonham in Somerset. For Alice Lisle, the event must have been overshadowed by an instance of the backlash against Nonconformity generated by the Popish terror. Her daughter Margaret's husband, Robert Whitaker, was prosecuted by the Fordingbridge church wardens in March 1679 for not attending church, and was excommunicated on 2 May.

An arrest warrant followed in September, and while there is no record of its being implemented, it is clear that Whitaker and his family suffered. Calamy noted: 'he was often much overcome with Melancholy . . . he hath . . . but very little of his own and hath been a Sufferer and has a wife and several children.' It was a large household. Their children, born between 1673 and 1686, were Tryphena, two Johns (the first died in infancy), James, Jeremiah, Mary, Daniel and Robert. It was presumably with a view to relieving their poverty that Alice Lisle gave Margaret a legacy of £70 in the codicil to her will of 9 June 1682. Margaret never received this money, though her family may have done so later: she was buried on 27 March 1686, a fortnight after giving birth to Robert.

Margaret was the only married daughter to be thus favoured, since the main provisions of the will provided for her spinster sisters, Mary, Mabella and Anne, against the day of their marriage.

*   *   *

The dissolution of the Oxford Parliament in 1681 gave the able, leisure-loving monarch what he valued most – more time to himself and his mistresses – but it left a dangerous political vacuum. While the Tories proclaimed their loyalty and extolled the virtues of absolutism, the Licensing Act, renewed annually since its introduction in 1663, lapsed for want of a legislature to renew it. This released a flood of subversive literature that was checked only by a more rigorous, and often unjust, enforcement of the laws of sedition and libel. It was not until the summer of 1685 that official censorship was reimposed.

A half-free press was small comfort to those who, despite their electoral successes, had neither power nor a forum in which to use it. Denied the fruits of victory, the Whigs became increasingly angry and frustrated. The temperature rose in 1682 as Charles set out to undermine the centres of their support, the town and city corporations. Invited to surrender their ancient charters, the corporations were threatened with forfeiture if they refused. Restoration became conditional on giving key council positions to the king's appointees, who would ensure the nomination of Tory candidates for Parliament should an election be called. In London, Tory sheriffs were appointed, and their control of jury selection helped safeguard the Crown's interests in litigation.

It was the spectre of this creeping despotism that provoked the plots of 1682; and their betrayal in 1683 finally settled the fate of the Whigs for the rest of the reign. The conspirators were led by the Earl of Shaftesbury, and their overall objective was to raise a rebellion. Shaftesbury's principal colleagues were the Council of Six: Algernon Sidney, the Duke of Monmouth, Lord Howard of Escrick, Lord William Russell, the Earl of Essex and John Hampden. According to evidence at Russell's trial, most of them knew about John Rumsey's and Richard Rumbold's proposal to begin by murdering Charles and James on the Newmarket road into London. But two opportunities to achieve this were lost in November 1682, after which Shaftesbury's nerve failed and he fled to Holland, dying there in January. Plans were shelved until the spring, amid endless argument and indecision. When the time came, it was only bad luck that thwarted the plot.

The place fixed for the assassination was Hoddesdon, where Rumbold's Rye House overlooked a narrow stretch of the main road, and it was planned for the first week in April. But the king and his brother unexpectedly returned to London a week early after a fire in Newmarket, so the plotters again missed their chance to 'lop' the monarchy, as they put it. Even then they might have remained undetected had all concerned held their tongues, but by June the secret was out. Waves of arrests followed and the less courageous began to confess. Many who escaped fled to Holland, to form the nucleus of Monmouth's returning adventurers who would try their luck again in 1685.

A proclamation for the arrest of the would-be assassins still at large was published on 23 June and read by town criers up and down the country. Those named included Rumsey, Rumbold and Richard Nelthorp as fugitives from justice. It continued with a dire warning that

> if any Person or Persons after this our Proclamation, shall directly or indirectly Conceal, Harbour, Keep, Retain or Maintain the said Offenders, or any of them, or shall Contrive or Connive at any means whereby they . . . may Escape . . . We will (as there is just cause) proceed against them . . . with all Severity.

There was a £100 reward for any who were caught. On 28 June a similar proclamation was issued against the bigger fish – the Duke of Monmouth, Lord Grey, Sir Thomas Armstrong and Robert Ferguson – the price on each of their heads being £500. The shires were put on the alert: the following day the Earl of Pembroke wrote to Thomas Penruddock, colonel of the Wiltshire militia, that

> there has been discovered a horrid design upon the lives of His Majesty and his Royal Highness that should have been executed

on His Majesty's return from Newmarket . . . I am desired to take special care that the officers of the Militia be in readiness . . . [and] require you to take immediate care in your Regiment . . . that the officers and soldiers . . . make a search for all arms that can be found in the houses of persons whom you suspect to be ill-affected . . .

Of those caught, most were charged with treason or sedition, while others survived by turning king's evidence. The ringleaders and their accomplices were dealt with in trials over the next eighteen months, in which an accomplished advocate, George Jeffreys, took an increasingly dominant part. In July 1683, Jeffreys appeared as one of a team of four, which included the Attorney-General and the Solicitor-General, to prosecute three Rye House plotters, and took a prominent role in the case against Lord Russell that followed immediately afterwards. All were convicted and executed, and Essex would have undoubtedly suffered the same fate but for his suicide in the Tower during Russell's trial.

Jeffreys' elevation to the position of Lord Chief Justice on 29 September 1683 was primarily to ensure that the remaining Rye House conspirators were also punished. Those who came before him included Sidney, Hampden, Braddon, Speke and Sir Samuel Barnardiston. Sidney was convicted of treason on 21 November 1683, being executed a fortnight later; and on 6 February 1684, John Hampden was tried for sedition. The son of Charles I's opponent of ship-money tax, Hampden faced this lesser charge only because the prosecution lacked a second witness to prove treason. Convicted on the evidence of Lord Howard, who had earlier testified against Russell, he was fined £40,000. Being unable to pay, he remained in prison, presumably as Jeffreys had intended. Two barristers, Laurence Braddon and Hugh Speke, were convicted the following day of trying to start a rumour that Essex's death was murder by his guards rather than suicide. Sentence was deferred until April, after Jeffreys' return from the Western circuit, when they were fined £2,000 and £1,000 respectively.

On 14 February, Sir Samuel Barnardiston was charged with sedition for his letters scorning the existence of the Rye House plot; like Hampden, he was imprisoned when he could not find the

£10,000 fine. Another two, convicted in their absence, were captured and subsequently executed: James Holloway, a Bristol tradesman who had fled to the West Indies, on 30 April, and Sir Thomas Armstrong, the London merchant captured in Holland, on 20 June 1684. The one remaining member of the Council of Six, Monmouth, surrendered to make a confession: but, as the monarch's favourite bastard child, he was spared and banished to Holland.

Many smaller fry were either implicated or confessed what they knew, with the legal profession well represented. Robert West, a Middle Temple barrister, made a confession; Robert Blaney, a Whig law reporter known for his tearaway behaviour as a Middle Temple student, was taken for questioning; their colleague, Richard Holford, was arrested and released on bail; and the chambers of Richard Nelthorp, the Gray's Inn barrister, were searched after he disappeared. Spurred on, perhaps, by the prospect of a share in the rewards, Sir Christopher Musgrave wrote to his friend Sir George Fletcher on 26 June 1683 with a description of two to look out for:

> Nelthorp and Richard Goodenough have gone northwards beyond Doncaster . . . watch for them in Cumberland. Nelthorp is a black [dark haired] man, high nosed, pox holes in his face, of a lower and leaner stature than myself. Goodenough is a fair man, lean, of low stature. The Borders should be watched, and all passengers at Whitehaven.

The impact of this hue and cry came home to Alice Lisle in a number of ways. The persecution of Nonconformity intensified much as it had done in the wake of the Popish terror, and she must have been deeply worried to hear that her daughter Tryphena's husband, Richard Lloyd, a London linen draper, was another of those brought before the Privy Council. On 6 July 1683, he denied an accusation that he had discussed the plot and the proposed assassination. Evidently he was believed, since he was freed the following day. More significant than the mere fact of his examination is the official record misdescribing him as 'Lisle, a linen-draper of Cornhill', the same name appearing in the note of his release.[7] A clerical error, maybe, but almost certainly explained by his association, in government eyes, with the family he had married into headed by 'Mrs Lisle, the Regicide's wife'.

Alice Lisle bore this *persona non grata* designation of royalist hatred from the Restoration until her death: had she heard about the misnaming of her son-in-law, she would hardly have been surprised. Perhaps it left her reflecting on the sad condition of her other son-in-law's family, the Whitakers, and wondering how far the Lloyds' situation might come to parallel theirs. Apart from any knowledge of the plot gained through personal tribulation, it is clear she either heard the proclamation read out against the Rye House fugitives, or was told about it shortly afterwards. After Nelthorp had been discovered 'in the hole by the chimney' at Moyles Court on the morning of Wednesday, 29 July 1685, her explanation for having harboured him was that she never knew his name, 'and if he had told it to me, I had then remembered the proclamation', as she said at her trial. Since she did not face any charge of treason in relation to Nelthorp, one can assume that the authorities accepted her claim to ignorance of his identity (even though they were far too credulous in doing so).

*   *   *

The autumn of 1684 brought great sadness for Alice Lisle. Catherine Lisle, her daughter-in-law, had given birth to her first son, Charles Croke Lisle, at the beginning of the year, but she died in childbirth with her second in October. She was buried at Dibden on 17 October, and her son, John Croke Lisle, who survived, was baptised the following day. John Lisle remained a widower until he married Ann Howe in 1702, his death leaving her a widow seven years later in 1709.

THREE

The Battle of Sedgemoor and
Alice Lisle's Arrest

Skilful politician that he was, Charles never surrendered an option until he had to, a lifebelt principle that he followed to the end. Nowhere is it better demonstrated than in his handling of religious issues. As monarch, he umpired the Anglican–Nonconformist conflict, fully appreciating each side's sensitivities, revoking the Indulgence only *in extremis*, and on terms that simply blunted mutual belligerence. Though he misjudged the English appetite for Catholicism, and bowed to necessity when the Test Acts were unavoidable, his attitude was primarily dictated by the need to remain friends with Louis XIV, his principal ally and banker. Only Charles could have prevented the creditor calling in the loans when he could not deliver on his promise to convert the kingdom. As an individual, his faith was probably little more than a security based on the observance of ritual, and within the disciplines of Christianity there was little room for his own and the court's immorality. It was only when he lay dying, and probably because he saw a difficult interview with his Maker ahead of him, that he came down off the fence as a repentant recruit to the Church of Rome.

His legacy to his brother James was a broadly peaceable nation, which, though governed without Parliament, had survived one or two jolts to its stability without relapsing into the civil war of his father's reign. There was a resigned tolerance, *faute de mieux*, towards a Catholic king as long as he kept his faith to himself and did not Romanise the succession with a male heir. Initially, the outlook seemed promising. Shortly after Charles's death on 6 February 1685, James held his first Privy Council, when he is reported to have said: 'I know the principles of the Church of England are for Monarchy and the Members of it have showed themselves Good and Loyal Subjects, therefore I shall always take care to defend and support it.'

The first Parliament, summoned in May, voted him a generous income and rallied strongly with a further £600,000 in June when the news of Monmouth's landing reached London. Anyone but James would have seen the national goodwill behind these gestures as a priceless asset, worth preserving at any cost; it is a measure of his insensitivity that he still failed to recognise it even with his father's and brother's examples behind him. Political flexibility was a concept he did not begin to understand. More a soldier than a statesman, he appears to have taken his subjects' loyalty entirely for granted, seeing it as a condition of his doing the job at all, instead of as a bonus for doing it properly. He seems to have been guided by two basic beliefs: the excellence of his own judgement and the virtues of firmness and discipline. Together they ensured his downfall.

He came to the throne convinced that a nation prepared to accept a Catholic monarch ought also to be prepared to accept universal toleration of his faith – and if it was not, it would have to be made to. A clear-cut soldier's assessment, it left no room for compromise. All too soon his comforting assurance about 'defending and supporting the Church of England' had become political cant, lip-service to a principle he had no intention of fulfilling. In November 1685, after Monmouth's rebellion was over, he prorogued Parliament when it refused to repeal the Test Acts; and he then followed Charles's example in his claim to suspend those provisions by means of the royal prerogative. When the Court of King's Bench confirmed the power as valid, James made indiscriminate use of it in favour of both Nonconformists and Catholics. The spectre of Rome loomed ever more threateningly, and the skies darkened dramatically on 11 June 1688 with the birth of a royal prince.

A Catholic succession assured, James pressed ahead with one of the most ill-advised prosecutions ever launched. Seven Anglican bishops, the primate among them, were charged with seditious libel for suggesting that the king's power to suspend the Test Acts was illegal. On 30 June, they were resoundingly acquitted by that ultimate barometer of English opinion, a common jury. Even the thick-skinned James had to take the hint, and by December he had fled to France, abandoning the throne to his daughter Mary and her husband, and the kingdom to the Glorious Revolution.

But this display of Catholic bigotry was trivial by comparison with the horrifying cruelty that preceded it in September and October 1685. Even in an age when retributive justice was the norm, and the hanging of criminals a form of public entertainment, the nation reacted with stunned, uncomprehending revulsion at the corpse-strung countryside the Bloody Assize judges left behind them in the West. It does not seem to have occurred either to them or to James that simple folk of simple loyalties, rebels for a day, could again be tomorrow's faithful subjects if treated with the right blend of firmness and encouragement.

The impact of Monmouth's arrival on the dull monotony of country life was exciting and unsettling, a first-ever taste of political awareness. Protestantism instead of Popery was an easily understood manifesto, gaining strength from Monmouth's warm personality and his reputation for kindness and compassion. The more impressionable felt drawn towards him as today's bored adolescents are to a cult, needing no more than his bidding to fall into line and follow. In place of anonymity, he seemed to offer identity, adventure and, if successful, some sort of reward. If the thought of treason crossed their minds at all, it was probably outweighed by the idea of comradeship and safety in numbers, and the belief that they could slip quietly back to their homes and crafts if things went badly. Defeat they could cope with, but the penalties of wholesale slaughter and transportation they never began to contemplate.

James's blind spot – his requirement for total obedience from his subjects – and the narrowness of the Sedgemoor victory called, in his eyes, for exemplary punishment. The lesson would be brutal and uncomplicated, in line with the military parallel – as battlefield deserters were executed for cowardice, so rebel citizens must either be hanged for treason or removed from the kingdom. As monarch he felt he had to be firm; if he were seen to be in the slightest degree forgiving, discipline could not be maintained. All those captured must suffer, not just the ringleaders. What happened after that, how the nation and the rest of the world might react, was irrelevant. The man chosen to implement this policy was ambitious and aware that judicial promotion depended on how he performed. Alice Lisle was the first of those to come before him.

* * *

Through twenty-first-century eyes, Judge Jeffreys is often seen as the ogre of the law, the embodiment of every judicial vice and excess, the man whose red-draped court offered no better hope of survival than Dante's Inferno. Drunk, sarcastic and brutal, the monarch's puppet rather than the people's champion, he disgraced the office of Lord Chief Justice, and the law itself, as no judge has done before or since. That he should nevertheless be promoted Lord Chancellor, but then fall amid political turmoil, eventually dying in the Tower of London (less as a prisoner than as a refugee from the mob) is poetic and divine justice on a man quite unfitted to administer it himself.

This thumbnail sketch of Jeffreys is offered by many popular historians, for whom the distance of three centuries adds only greater disenchantment. It is also a view widely held by the legal profession. Constitutional lawyers see his performance as underlining the need for a clear separation between the executive and the judiciary. For practitioners, his career sets the datum-line of infamy against which the excellence or otherwise of the bench can be measured today. His name still heads the list of former chairmen of Middlesex Sessions in Parliament Square, where it has occasionally provoked spirited and unflattering comparison from advocates smarting under judicial rebuke.

Though partly true, this image is overstated and incomplete: and the scrutiny of more serious historians takes the pendulum of assessment a long way in Jeffreys' favour. They point to his brilliance as an advocate, without which he would have gone unnoticed, leaving his career stillborn. His reported cross-examinations, rigorous and precise, display a wide forensic armoury of hyperbole, satire and scorn: they could not have been achieved had he spent as much time as his detractors suggest hobnobbing in taverns in search of work.

These historians also point to his meteoric rise through judicial office, which speaks for itself; the compassion he did display; and the intellectual quality of some of his more notable judgments. Born sometime in 1644, he was called to the Bar by the Inner Temple in

1668, and three years later, aged 26, he received his first judicial appointment as Common Sergeant. Thereafter, he was successively Recorder of London, Chief Justice of Chester, Lord Chief Justice and finally, in the autumn of 1685 aged 41, Lord Chancellor, one of the youngest incumbents of the office between the Reformation and today.

His cases at Chester showed a remarkable leniency towards Nonconformists, whom he generally fined rather than imprisoned for their religion. His judgment in 1685 in the East India case, confirming the Crown's power to grant trading monopolies, demonstrated his capacity to grapple with legal complexities. As Lord Birkenhead noted in *Fourteen English Judges* (1926), the law reports compiled by Bartholomew Shower contain pragmatic common-law decisions from him: *King* v. *Pierce*, that soap-boiling, an otherwise lawful activity, becomes a nuisance if carried on to the annoyance of the neighbourhood; *Rosewell's* case, where he suggested that oblique or 'innuendo' meanings could not be read into words to make them treasonable, and in passing drew attention to the unfairness of the rule disallowing defence counsel in treason prosecutions; *Brason* v. *Dean*, that penal legislation cannot be retrospectively applied; and *Roe* v. *Clarges*, that calling a Privy Councillor a 'Papist' was defamatory, since Catholics were then debarred from such appointment.

The cases noted by Thomas Vernon cover his three years as Chancellor, which took him into the recondite area of equity, covering trusts, estates, wills, mortgages and other matters dealt with in the Chancery division of the High Court today. If his contribution in this area was less incisive than that of more distinguished Lord Chancellors, his decisions were generally sound, and he was not above calling in other senior judges to assist where important issues were involved. He put a stop to some of the more flagrant procedural abuses that characterised Chancery practice, and was no sluggard: six months before his death on 19 April 1689, the reports show him dealing with three or four cases a day.

This, Jeffreys' defenders point out, is not the picture of a sadistic inebriate perverting justice at a whim, nor the dissolute spare-time carouser. Only intelligence and political awareness could have taken him so far so quickly. But success breeds envy and, say his defenders, it is the gossips who have sketched in the colourful but misleading detail of his private life. Jeffreys, in fact, led a very settled and steady home life. There was no whisper of matrimonial infidelity, and if he enjoyed good wine, he drank only in convivial company or to relieve the pain of the stone.

But rehabilitation can be carried only so far, and there are three main criticisms that cannot be dismissed as the overpainting of political legend. First, in most of the political trials he conducted, he was unable to discard the mantle of advocate. This is a considerable fault in any judge. Not merely does it undermine his authority and role as a referee, but it prevents litigants from putting their cases properly. Modern examples are not far to seek: in the 1950s and 1960s both Mr Justice Hallett and Mr Justice Paull were inveterate interrupters who had decisions set aside as a result, and Hallett is generally thought to have retired under threat of removal for his pronounced loquacity. Jeffreys' conduct of the trials of Algernon Sidney for treason, Braddon and Speke for suborning witnesses, and Titus Oates for perjury seems to have made the role of prosecutor almost superfluous. In Rosewell's case, having initially summed up the case against the prisoner, he then 'inclined for him' when he was brought up for judgment, apparently as a result of behind-the-scenes representations to the king that Rosewell had been convicted on unreliable evidence. Jeffreys allowed him counsel to argue various technical defects in the indictment and took care to see that the result went in Rosewell's favour. One cannot help feeling that in many of these cases Jeffreys consciously used his skill as an advocate to ensure that the result he wanted was achieved, regardless of whether it was justified by the evidence, or fair.

The second point against him, at least to the modern mind, is that he overtly allowed political considerations to influence the way trials were conducted, seeing his duty primarily to protect the Crown's interests. The following exchange from Braddon's case speaks for itself:

Mr Wallop: I am here as counsel for Mr Braddon, and I only ask questions as they are in my breviate.

Jeffreys: But sir, if you have anything in your breviate that reflects upon the Government, you ought not to vent it, nor shant be permitted to vent it so long as I sit here.

He carried it a stage further with Wallop in the trial of Richard Baxter for seditious libel: he suggested, if the report is accurate, that it was discreditable for counsel even to appear against the Crown in such cases: 'Mr Wallop, I observe you are in all these dirty causes; and were it not for you gentlemen of the long robe, who hold up these factious knaves by the chin, we should not be at the pass we are at.'

Such partisan zeal was the more glaring in treason and felony trials, where defence counsel was forbidden; and it made a mockery of the rule that the court was itself supposed to 'be of counsel for the prisoner' to safeguard his interests. No doubt the turbulent politics of the age – the Popish and Rye House plots in Charles II's reign, followed by the Duke of Monmouth's rebellion under James II – required decisive handling: stability could be maintained in an inadequately policed kingdom only if subversives were seen to be punished as they deserved. In contrast to the constitutional independence of the bench today, Stuart judges held office 'at the king's pleasure', and their concern was more to secure the monarch's supremacy than justice for his subjects if the two happened to conflict. No seventeenth-century judge took quite such flagrant advantage of this politically based status as Jeffreys; nor was it then as customary as some have suggested for the bench to adopt the prosecutor's role. Hale before him, and Holt even more after him, were both scrupulously open-minded judges concerned to see that both sides' rights were properly protected.

But by far the worst stain on Jeffreys' career is the Bloody Assize. The Sedgemoor defeat on 6 July 1685 left some 1,500 prisoners awaiting trial for having either proclaimed their support for Monmouth, fought in his army, or helped fugitives from the battlefield. Jeffreys' progress round the Western circuit that September resulted in 1,381 convictions and death sentences for treason. Between 200 and 300 rebels were executed, and were either left to hang where they died, or were dismembered, boiled and distributed as heads and limbs for display in the more deeply disaffected areas. About 850 were reprieved for transportation, and were sold into overseas slavery. Those who could afford it bought their pardons: in this way Jeffreys himself made £14,500 out of Edmund Prideaux, the son of Cromwell's Attorney-General, which he put towards purchasing his Leicestershire property. The remainder either escaped, turned king's evidence, died of smallpox or gaol fever, or were fined and whipped for the lesser offence of sedition.

A few, a very courageous few, were acquitted. It was they who played for the highest stakes in what was much more a lottery for survival than anything resembling due process of law.

Part of the charge against Jeffreys is that he punished the West with sickening brutality, when lesser penalties on fewer victims would have sufficed; and that for a judge, of all people, to condone slave-trafficking and pardon-mongering is unforgivable. Yet it can be said that seventeenth-century society tolerated, and even approved, such practices. If he was unduly severe, it was more a political than a judicial mistake, for which his unimaginative master, James II, was equally to blame. The more serious accusation is that he forced those on trial to gamble their lives on dice overwhelmingly loaded against them. The reason was strictly practical: five judges had four weeks, including travelling time and weekends, in which to dispose of not merely 1,500 cases from the rebellion, but another 300 or so of everyday crime. Speed was therefore essential, and some inducement had to be offered to make the guilty confess.

Word preceded Jeffreys' arrival in the West that, while rebels convicted after a plea of not guilty faced swift and certain execution, any who admitted guilt stood a 'reasonable chance' of reprieval for transportation. The prospect was scarcely inviting. The rigours of the voyage and seven years' bondage on a West Indian sugar plantation were ordeals only the fittest could hope to survive. Balancing the merits of a lingering, slave-driven, disease-ridden death against immediate oblivion or the outside chance of an acquittal was not easy to resolve. The number – well over half the total charged – of those granted the 'privilege' of transportation could be seen as underlining the widespread guilt of the self-confessed rebels, so that no substantial injustice was done.

But rough justice for the masses tends to obliterate precise justice for the individual, and serious questions remain. How many of those who pleaded guilty had valid defences? How many executed after pleading guilty did so believing they would be transported? How many who asserted their innocence were hampered in their defence by Jeffreys' determination not to fall behind schedule? The answers can never be known, because none of the trials in the West, apart from the one examined here, was reported. The only reliable record of the accused and their fates is the Gaol Book of the Western circuit and one or two execution warrants that have survived.

But the detailed report of Alice Lisle's trial, the first connected with the rebellion, is enlightening. Not only are there grounds for accepting it as accurate, but it portrays Jeffreys in all his brilliance as an advocate and with all his faults as a judge, setting the stage and pace for what was to follow when he moved further West. He conducted his own investigation into the case before leaving London, and effectively led the prosecution from the bench on the basis of what he learned. He started the trial at about five in the afternoon, and carried on without a break until the jury returned their verdict six hours later. His partisan interjections against Alice Lisle, which jar so heavily on modern ideas of judicial behaviour, clearly reflect what he saw as his primary duty: the expression of the king's affront at his subjects' disloyalty, and inflicting a punishment that would deter repetition once and for all.

*   *   *

James Scott, Duke of Monmouth, sailed with some eighty supporters from Holland on 24 May 1685. Delayed by bad weather, they landed at Lyme on 11 June. Their enthusiastic welcome was a response to Monmouth's personal charm, remembered from his tour of the West in 1680, and which all but obliterated the political issues – conveniently, perhaps, in view of his fraudulent claim to the throne. A man of little religious belief, he portrayed himself as a Protestant alternative to his uncle's Catholicism, adding the baseless accusations that James had started the fire of London and had poisoned Charles to make himself king.

Within two weeks, Monmouth led an army of over 6,000, which should have been heartening: yet John Whiting saw him leave Taunton 'very thoughtful and dejected in his countenance and thinner than . . . four years before'. The reason was that, despite modest successes against the local militia at Bridport and Axminster, the backing Monmouth so desperately needed from the middle and upper classes was conspicuously lacking. Without it, his campaign would lose momentum and his men their morale, and they would never be equal to the day when they had to face the king's regular forces. At Taunton, on 22 June, he made his bid to win over the powerful landowners by proclaiming himself king. This increased the stakes dramatically. If they joined him and he won, well and good; but if not, Monmouth knew as well as anyone the penalties for self-styled monarchs who were defeated.

That support never came. The lack of it, Monmouth's indecision, the bickering within his leadership and the appalling weather all contributed to the rebels' dispiriting progress. While their reception at Bridgwater was no less effusive than at Taunton, it was when Monmouth turned north-east for Bristol that the king's forces reaching the West began to make an impact. The rebels marched from Glastonbury to Shepton Mallet in pouring rain, where Hicks joined them on 24 June, and they were on the outskirts of Bristol early next day. Though it was not strongly defended, Monmouth decided against attacking the city when he learned that the king's forces numbered some 4,000, and mistook a ship ablaze in the harbour for their destruction of anti-royalists' property, which he said he did not wish to encourage. He therefore withdrew to Keynsham, briefly quartering himself at Sir Thomas Bridges' mansion, and then led his army down to Bath. Finding it strongly held, they returned via Phillips Norton and Frome to Bridgwater, which they reached on 3 July.

Three days later they marched out to Sedgemoor in a bold attempt at a night attack. But someone fired his pistol too soon, surprise was lost and the rebel cavalry under Lord Grey got bogged in a dyke. For a while, as dawn broke, the issue hung in the balance. But gradually, though they were outnumbered, the discipline of the king's forces told: by nine o'clock the rebels were beaten in the last pitched battle on English soil. Monmouth and Grey retreated westwards, leaving their defeated army to its less than merciful captors.

For all his political blundering, James II was a competent soldier. Recognising the strategic importance of Keynsham bridge for an assault on Bristol, he ordered his commanders to make its destruction their first priority. It was only because they failed to wreck it thoroughly that Monmouth came as close to the city as he did. Parliament's vote of £600,000 was followed by an Act of Attainder against Monmouth personally, offering £5,000 for his capture, dead or alive. James issued two proclamations to combat subversion and sap the rebels' strength. It became treason to print, publish or distribute copies of Monmouth's 'Declaration' in support of the invasion: on 15 June, four days after the Lyme landing, William Disney was caught with copies coming off his press in Lambeth, for which he was hanged a fortnight later. The second, on 26 June, promised a pardon to all rebels who surrendered within four days of its local publication.

On 20 June, directives also went out to the lords lieutenant for the arrest of all 'disaffected persons, especially dissenting ministers'. Two days later John Allison, a mason, found himself up before John Warner JP in Winchester for having expressed himself rather too exuberantly in favour of Presbyterians. On 24 June, he was bound over to appear at the next sessions. On the same day in London the Licensing Act was reintroduced, bringing all printing back under government control.

James gave immediate orders for a comprehensive round-up. Lord Sunderland, one of the two Secretaries of State, wrote on 7 July to the Earl of Abingdon:

> to prevent the escape of such of the Rebels as are not yet taken, His Majesty would have you give Strict Orders . . . for apprehending all persons whatsoever, who shall be found travelling up and down, and are not very well known, and also for searching all suspicious places and houses for any of the Rebels or their abettors.

Grey was caught on the 7th just north of Wimborne Minster, and Monmouth the following morning near Ringwood, both bound for the south coast. The sea lanes were also watched. On 9 July, Lord Gainsborough wrote from Portsmouth to the other Secretary of State, Lord Middleton, mentioning Monmouth's capture, and continuing:

> the Merlin yacht is gone out . . . to cruise about Lymington and the Forest coast, and has orders to search all creeks, and examine

all boats they shall meet with . . . having good ground to believe that some of the Rebels would endeavour to make their escape that way.

On Saturday, 11 July, national relief was reflected in that day's *London Gazette*. Sunday the 26th was proclaimed 'a day of thanksgiving for the suppression of the rebellions' in the West and Scotland, and for the 'capture of their chiefs'. This gave the Anglican clergy a fortnight in which to compose resonant, patriotic sermons about David and Goliath, the triumph of good over evil and the wicked receiving their just deserts.

But the blessings of victory were not unmixed. The burden of troops on a civilian population has seldom been popular. Despite James's directive that board and lodging were always to be paid for, there were tense exchanges. On 11 July, John Warner was again in court hearing of the brush-off Jerome Adams had given a group of soldiers who could not, or would not, pay. Like Allison, Adams was bound over to appear at the next sessions.

Throughout the rebellion, Alice Lisle was in London, probably staying with her daughter, Tryphena Lloyd. She was still there when Monmouth was beheaded on Tower Hill on Wednesday, 15 July, and did not return to Moyles Court until the following Monday or Tuesday. The week passed uneventfully until Saturday afternoon, the 25th, when her bailiff, William Carpenter, came in to say that two strangers on horseback had arrived, one of whom wanted to see her. He had a letter, which left Carpenter puzzled and uneasy. He would prefer her to deal with the messenger herself.

*   *   *

Two Sedgemoor fugitives who managed to avoid capture were Richard Nelthorp, the Rye House plotter and outlaw who had returned from Holland as one of Monmouth's junior officers, and John Hicks the preacher, Alice Lisle's Nonconformist friend from Portsmouth who had joined the rebel army barely a fortnight before the defeat. Together they made their way to Warminster, where they found refuge at the home of a Presbyterian baker, James Dunne. That Dunne knew he was taking a risk in sheltering them is clear from his efforts to conceal them. Knowing that house-to-house searches were usually between dusk and dawn, he kept them indoors during the day and left them to shift for themselves outside at night.

After a week with Dunne, they wanted to move on, and Hicks sent Dunne as his envoy to Alice Lisle, to see if she would put them up. With Hicks's letter of introduction, Dunne set out for Moyles Court on Saturday, 25 July, but on reaching Fovant, he found he did not know his way across Salisbury Plain. He eventually met a local man, John Barter, who agreed to guide him. Once at Moyles Court, Barter saw Dunne deliver his letter to Carpenter, whom he presumed had given it to Alice Lisle. In his evidence at her trial, Barter said he had then seen her laughing with Dunne, apparently at his expense. Riding back to Fovant, Dunne revealed to Barter that he knew just how dangerous his guests were, explaining why he had sheltered them during the day rather than at night. His joke with Alice Lisle had, he said, been over Barter's presumed ignorance of 'the business' – the arrangement, to which Alice Lisle had agreed, that Dunne should bring his guests to Moyles Court the following Tuesday. Unable to contain himself, Dunne told Barter how rich they were, and how rich they would make him for the risks he was taking. Dunne spent the Saturday night at Fovant, having arranged for Barter to act as his guide again on the Tuesday. He left it that they would meet between nine and eleven that morning between Fovant and Compton Chamberlayne, a mile and a half to the northeast. During the 26th, thanksgiving Sunday for the rebels' defeat for all law-abiding Anglicans, he made his way home to Warminster.

Back at home, Dunne told Hicks and Nelthorp of Alice Lisle's willingness to welcome them after nightfall on Tuesday. One can assume he also made a clean breast of his unwise disclosures to Barter because, according to his evidence at the trial, they did not leave Warminster until about eleven on the Tuesday morning, the time they were supposed to be meeting Barter north-east of Fovant, and tried to take a different route (via Sutton Mandeville, southwest of Fovant) from that previously agreed. This shows their concern to avoid Barter, given the danger of the leak they rightly feared. But because no one knew the way, they got thoroughly lost in unfamiliar countryside, and there was nothing for it but to find Barter to put them back on course.

Back at Fovant, they found Barter and asked him to see them over their new route. Though also unfamiliar with it, he accompanied them as far as Martin, getting there about mid-afternoon. Here Hicks called on an old village acquaintance named Fane, who knew the way from then on, which enabled them to dispense with Barter. Once it was dark, Fane saw them to within a mile or two of Moyles Court. On arrival, Dunne's horse was stabled but the others turned their mounts loose. Inside the house, Alice Lisle joined them for supper, and the turmoil of the past six weeks, if nothing else, must have been extensively discussed. Alice Lisle would also have had much Nonconformist and family gossip to catch up on with Hicks since they had last met. The meal was served by the Carpenters in an upstairs room, where the three travellers slept when Alice retired.

They were scarcely secure. Dunne's revelations had left Barter worried about his own position if it ever emerged he had helped rebel suspects without informing the authorities. He therefore rode over to Compton Chamberlayne on Monday morning, 27 July, to tell Colonel Thomas Penruddock of the next day's rendezvous north-east of Fovant. Though Penruddock's plan for an ambush there was frustrated when the travellers failed to materialise, their afternoon reappearance at Fovant, bound for Moyles Court and once again seeking Barter's help, confirmed Barter's belief in Alice Lisle's complicity. Having seen the fugitives on their way, Barter went back to Penruddock, who took him and a body of the Wiltshire militia to raid the house early the following morning. Penruddock's decision to arrest Alice Lisle was prompted more by her own and Carpenter's attempts to mislead him than by the simple fact that two of her guests were fugitive rebels. Alice Lisle, the three travellers and, probably, the Carpenters were taken to Fisherton gaol in Salisbury, where she remained until Wednesday, 26 August, the day before her trial in Winchester Castle.

News of the arrest reached London on 1 August, to be entered as an internal memorandum by a clerk in the royal palace of Whitehall. He was Henry Muddiman (a direct ancestor of J.G. Muddiman, author of *The Bloody Assize* (1929)), clerk to Lord Middleton, and his note summarised the political implications:

'Tis advised from Salisbury that Nelthorp out of those in the proclamation against the Conspirators, one Hicks a Non-Con Parson and Dunn were taken at the Lady Lisle's House and carried prisoners thither with the Lady, who was wife to Lisle, one of the Judges of that blessed Martyr King Charles I and one of the Commissioners of the Seal. They were taken by Col Penruddock, son of that Col Penruddock who was murdered in the cause of his late majesty . . . Nelthorp was pulled out of a chimney. Dunne was the guide from Warminster to the Lady's house.

This prompted an immediate search warrant from Lord Sunderland, presumably in the hope of flushing out other fugitives Penruddock might have overlooked in the regicide household.

In their haste, Sunderland or his clerk misapplied the name of Lisle to the property itself:

Warrant to search   Robert,
Mrs Lisle's house   Earl of Sunderland
Whereas there is great cause to suspect, that several Traitors and rebels are harboured and concealed at the House of Mrs Alice Lisle at Lisle's Court in the County of Southampton. These are in His Majesty's name to will and require you to repair to the said house of Mrs Lisle, and there to make strict and diligent search (with the assistance of a Constable) for the said Traitors and Rebels, and such as you shall there find, as likewise any other dangerous and suspicious persons, to bring before me to answer such matters as shall bee objected against them, and to be further dealt with according to law . . . Whitehall, the 1st of August 1685.

Sunderland

But August was holiday time. With the rising crushed, the nation relaxed. Parliament adjourned on 4 August until November, and the Lord Chief Justice went down to take the waters at Tunbridge Wells, to relax before what promised to be a busy autumn assize. At Windsor, the monarch's mind turned to traditional royal recreation. The *London Gazette* of 7 August announced:

His Majesty intending to remove to Winchester towards the end of this month or the beginning of next; and being unwilling to have the usual plates run for while the Court is there, has been graciously pleased to Order . . . that the 10 Stone Plate shall be run for the 15th day of September, and the 15 Stone Plate the day following; And His Majesty, further to encourage the Breeding of good Horses, and recreation on those Downs, has been pleased to add Ten Guineas yearly to what he formerly gave to those Plates.

Some people had to stay at work, however, particularly those concerned with the forthcoming assize. The rebellion had made a summer circuit impossible, leaving a backlog of around 300 prisoners awaiting trial. Now there were another 1,400 from Sedgemoor. While most would probably plead guilty if offered a reprieve and transportation, cases had to be prepared against any who did not. Witnesses had to be traced and decisions taken about offering pardons for turning king's evidence, where there was no other testimony available or it was politically important to secure a conviction; sheriffs had to be warned to summon juries; counsel had to be instructed. A constant stream of messengers rode between the assize towns and the capital, and prisoners were taken to wherever they would stand trial.

On 9 August, Nelthorp was moved from Salisbury to London, where he was one of fourteen rebels to be examined by the Privy Council on 11 August. Muddiman noted: 'Nelthrop [*sic*] who was taken at the Lady Lisle's house at Moyles Court was brought before them but would confess nothing. Also said he knew he had deserved it and must be hanged and would not bring any others into trouble.'

As a barrister, Nelthorp knew just how slim his chances were. By law, as he had avoided capture for more than a year, his outlawry was enough to send him to the gallows regardless of the offence that gave rise to it, or of any other offences he might have committed meanwhile (anyone voluntarily surrendering within a year of being proclaimed an outlaw – but not one who was captured – was entitled to challenge the conviction on which his outlawry was based). Despite that, he resolutely refused to cooperate with the authorities in their efforts to gather evidence against Alice Lisle. He successfully misled Jeffreys into believing that any charges based on her having sheltered him as an outlaw would almost certainly fail.

By 20 August, preparations for the assize were nearly complete. Most prisoners examined by the Privy Council had been returned to where they were captured, and Jeffreys was back from Tunbridge Wells. Two important matters awaited his attention: the final approval of prosecuting counsel nominated for the assize, and the need to review with his fellow judges the more difficult cases, one of which was Alice Lisle's. Though partly illegible, Muddiman's note indicates that this included interviewing certain prisoners still in London:

> Tuesday Aug 18 85
> The 5 Judges going (?) . . . (?) on Monday next and on the 25 will open their Commission at Winchester. Of the Counsell for the King are Sgt Luttrell, Sgt Thomas Strode, Sgt Mr Pollexfen and Mr Coryton. They sit in 5 counties, Hants, Wilts, Dorset, Somerset and Devonshire.

> Thurs Aug 20 85
> On the 20th the Lord Chief Justice, the Lord Chief Baron, Judge Levins, Judge Withins and Baron Wright who are constituted by their Commission of Oyer and Terminer for trial of Rebels in the West met at the Lord Chief Justices Chambers to adjust the places of sitting (?) . . . (?) drawn one of Newgate and 5 from the (?) . . . Jeffreys (?) to review their trials in the County.

The 'one drawn of Newgate' was Nelthorp. His interview with Jeffreys probably took place on Friday, 21 August, and while there is no record of it, clues can be gleaned from a number of questions Jeffreys put in court at Winchester. Given the difficulties in Alice Lisle's case and the importance of securing a conviction, it would have been natural for Jeffreys to have tried to persuade Nelthorp to turn king's evidence against her; and equally natural, if the £14,500 Jeffreys accepted from Edmund Prideaux for his pardon is anything to go by, that he should have offered a similar inducement to Nelthorp. This would tend to corroborate the otherwise unsupported assertion nearly two centuries later (*Gentleman's Magazine*, January 1866), that 'the notorious Judge Jeffries . . . would have spared him for a bribe of £10,000, but Richard

Nelthorp magnanimously refused to save his life by depriving his children of their fortunes'.

Such life-or-death alternatives must have put Nelthorp under immense pressure. But however confidential his meeting with Jeffreys was supposed to have been, one man with excellent contacts was Robert Harley, about to go to Tunbridge Wells. The very next day, Saturday, 22 August, he wrote to his father, Sir Edward Harley, about what he had heard: 'My wife intends for the Wells on Tuesday . . . Tuesday next begins the Western circuit. It is thought that the Lady Lisle will suffer, or at least be condemned. Some say Nelthorp, taken at her house, is distracted.'

Muddiman's entry of the same date records the timetable and itinerary decided on by the judges: 'The Consensus of the Judges Counsel held at Sergeants Inn the 20 was that they (?) . . . (?) on the 24th at Farnham Lodge whither the Lord Bishop of Winchester has given them an invitation. On the 25 their Commission at Winchester then other places and Salisbury Dorchester Exeter and Wells.'

In his anxieties over Alice Lisle's case, Jeffreys was not content merely to brief himself from whatever Nelthorp chose to tell him: he also sanctioned the instruction of no fewer than five counsel to appear for the Crown. In overall charge of the prosecution was Serjeant Henry Pollexfen, then aged 53, and leader of the Western circuit. Despite his predominantly Whig outlook, which his practice reflected, he and Jeffreys were close friends, to the point where he became an executor of Jeffreys' will. From Shorford in Devon, he was called to the Bar in 1658. More a lawyer than an advocate, he was briefed in the enormously intricate East India monopolies case, which lasted intermittently from 1683 to 1685, and he appeared as one of Lady Ivy's team in the litigation over her forged land deeds. He represented the Nonconformist preacher Richard Baxter at his trial for seditious libel in May 1685, as well as the seven bishops on similar charges three years later. As Member of Paliament for Exeter in 1688, he became Attorney-General the following year, and was Chief Justice of the Common Pleas for the two years before his death in 1691.

Of the four junior counsel, Edward Jennings was also a friend of Jeffreys; and it is likely that the *State Trials* version of what happened at Winchester was compiled by him. Aged 38 at the time of the trial, in later years he appears to have been largely concerned with petitions and private bills in Parliament; but he also enjoyed royal favour: James II leased him a house in Lincoln's Inn Fields, and appointed him Attorney-General for North Wales. In 1711, he sat on a Commission to investigate the need for new churches, and he died aged 78 in June 1725.

William Coryton was a Cornishman from West Newton Ferrars, of a strongly royalist family, and was called to the Bar in May 1675. By the time of the trial, he was 35 and of ten years' call. He appears to have had a varied practice, which from 1679 he combined with his parliamentary activities. With its forty-four, mainly 'rotten', boroughs, Cornwall was grossly over-represented in Parliament, and finding a seat was scarcely a problem. He sat for various Cornish constituences; but Callington, which he represented intermittently for some seventeen years between 1681 and his death in 1711, had two particular attractions, its proximity to Crocadon, the property he bought on his brother's death in 1690, and its easily manageable electorate of about forty.

Nothing is known of John Rumsey, except that he was called to the Bar in July 1669. James Munday was called in November 1678. He and his wife were probably childless, because they adopted a 'poor child', for whom the Inner Temple gave an allowance to pay for his apprenticeship. Munday died in February 1718.

In the event, this team had little to do at Winchester because Jeffreys conducted virtually the entire prosecution case himself. Their efforts seem to have been restricted to picking up occasional loose ends and putting behind-the-scenes pressure on the main witness, Dunne, to elaborate on the supper-time conversation he had heard at Moyles Court. But their presence alone was enough to underline the government's attitude to the occasion and the Crown's evident determination to win its case.

* * *

Since well before the seventeenth century, Winchester had been the first city on the Western circuit and by far the most popular among judges. The countryside is more pleasant, the weather warmer and the accommodation generally better than, for example, on the Northern or North-Eastern circuits. At Winchester, judges are now comfortably accommodated in the Cathedral Close, in a building of monastic origin that was largely remodelled in the seventeenth and eighteenth centuries. It is situated opposite the Deanery, with the only possible inconvenience being the need to borrow an ancient, cumbersome gate-key if one is returning late at night. It was on the western slopes of the city that Charles II planned his magnificent palace (a plan frustrated by his death in February 1685); and his grandfather, James I, moved to Winchester for a while after his accession to avoid the London plague. In November that year, 1603, Sir Walter Ralegh was one of ten defendants on treason charges in Winchester Castle Hall, an event described at some length by John Trussell in his *Touchstone of Tradition*. A local lawyer and twice mayor of the city, Trussell records how the College evacuated to Silkstead to make way for the legal profession, to the satisfaction of even the most discriminating:

> The Judges and Sergeants-at-law were pleasantly lodged . . . in the College of St Mary, situated close to Wolvesey . . . The one Sergeants Inn being kept within the second court of the college [i.e. Chamber Court], the other in the wardens lodgings in the first courts [i.e. Outer Court] . . . Provision for every one of wood, coal, candle and all other . . . necessaries whatsoever were stowed ready for every private chamber . . . After which time it was observed that in no one place out of Westminster, there could better accommodation be found . . . than in Winchester . . .

But travelling there was not easy and the road from London to Hampshire left much to be desired. On the Western circuit the previous year, Jeffreys had written from Winchester on 28 February: 'Last night we arrived here, the ways being very foul, but the remembrance of them was soon passed over by the happiness I met with in the conversation of a numerous train of loyal gentlemen in this county.'

No doubt the comforts of Farnham palace and the attentions of an equally loyal host helped relieve the rigours of the journey on Monday, 24 August 1685. Jeffreys and his four colleagues – William Montagu, Chief Baron of the Exchequer; Cresswell Levinz, a King's Bench judge; Francis Wythens, a judge of Common Pleas; and

Robert Wright, a judge of the Exchequer – were entertained by Peter Mews, translated from Bath and Wells on the death of the previous Bishop of Winchester, George Morley, towards the end of 1684. Taken prisoner at the battle of Naseby, where he was badly wounded, Mews acted during the Commonwealth as a cross-Channel envoy for the exiled Charles Stuart, for which he received lavish promotion after 1660. Aged 64, he followed the king's forces down to Sedgemoor, where his horses helped site their cannon. He directed their fire himself and was again wounded. Known as 'Old Patch' from the cover over a facial scar, he was doubtless able to give his guests an eyewitness account of the battle.

The assize opened in the Castle Hall on the morning of 25 August, with the judges dealing with everyday crime for most of the first three days. The Whitehall authorities were primarily interested in the only case connected with the rebellion, but the first despatch left them disappointed. Though it arrived at the weekend – by which time, as they realised, the trial must have finished – the news it contained only covered events up to the 26th. Recalling once again Alice Lisle's status as a political outcast, Muddiman concluded on a note of evident impatience:

Sat Aug 29
85
They write from Winchester date 26 that the Judges were then there only to give a general gaol delivery. The Lady Lisle so called by courtesy to the Rebellion (her husband who was one of the Kings Judges and Commissioner of the Great Seal to Oliver having been lorded by him) was brought thither by Habeas Corpus from Salisbury but was not to be tried till the morrow so that we will await till next Post for an account.

FOUR

The Report of Alice Lisle's Trial

A part from the summarised and slanted Whig version in *The Bloody Assizes* first published in 1689[1] (which nevertheless bears out the main thrust of the story), no report of Alice Lisle's case was available until 1719, some thirty-four years after the event, when Thomas Salmon brought out his first four-volume folio edition of *State Trials*, costing seven guineas. That report, the one used here, ran virtually unaltered through all four subsequent editions. Since its source material is not identified, its authenticity has been questioned in a debate in which there is a sharp division of views.

Alice Lisle's case seems to have been very much a last-minute 'scoop'. It is reported in volume III, and appears in its correct historical sequence for 1685. Having occurred at the end of August, it lies between Titus Oates's second trial in May and John Fernley's in October. The penultimate page of the Oates trial, a right-hand page, is numbered 487 and is in sequence with the preceding pages; the final page, however, is numbered 576. The facing page, on which Alice Lisle's trial begins, is unnumbered (though designated in the index as 489) and her case then occupies a further twenty-seven pages numbered 490 to 516, each bearing an asterisk. But the next case, Fernley's, begins on page 577 and thereafter the pages run in sequence to the end. In addition, the 'printer's signature' (the alphabetical code indicating the order of the page bundles) appears at the foot of the page at regular intervals and, excluding Alice Lisle's trial, follows a regular sequence throughout the volume; but for her asterisked pages it is partially repeated, in square brackets. So far as one can tell from the binding, these pages have been sewn as a separate bundle.

The most likely explanation for this anomaly is that the printer did not know until a very late stage whether any of the Bloody Assize trials were available. He left an arbitrary gap, from 488 to

577, to accommodate them between the Oates trial in May and Fernley's in October. The news that none was to be had prompted him to try to hide the page gap by numbering the final, left-hand, page of Oates's trial 576, as if it immediately preceded Fernley's. When he got Alice Lisle's trial after all, it was necessarily a rushed job and had to be set separately – hence the asterisks and the one-off printer's signature. While sixty pages short, its overall length of twenty-eight pages, neatly divisible by four, meant he could have it printed and sewn for inclusion without single or blank pages over at either end. In addition, apart from the wrongly numbered final page of Oates, there was no objection to his making Alice Lisle run consecutively to the correctly numbered earlier pages. This he did: and, since the case finished on page 516, the cursory reader would be less likely to notice the hiatus between that and the 577 on the facing page, where Fernley begins. But he did not correct the final page of Oates from 576 to 488, because the unnumbered page opposite would almost certainly keep the reader ignorant of the interrupted sequence; and to have made a mess of correcting it would merely have drawn attention to what he wanted to hide.

In the preface, Salmon commends his work to the reader on the ground that 'several valuable manuscripts . . . buried in private hands, are here brought to light'. This is perhaps an overstatement: his index describes only two trials in this way, one being Alice Lisle's. Salmon adds that 'such care has been taken to avoid all mistakes [in the manuscripts], that the judges and counsel, who were concerned in such trials, and are still living, have been attended with their respective arguments and have been pleased . . . to correct whatever was amiss'.

Clearly, in 1719 there would have been no opportunity to ask any of the Bloody Assize judges to preview the work. Jeffreys and Wright died in 1689, Levinz in 1701, Wythens in 1704 and Montagu in 1706. Pollexfen, the leading counsel, died in 1691 as Chief Justice of the Common Pleas. Of the four junior counsel, Jennings is the only one who was definitely still alive in 1719: Coryton died in 1711, Munday in 1718, and there is no record of Rumsey's death. A last-minute rush to include the report, however, would confirm the description that it had indeed been 'buried in private hands' until then; and it also tends to suggest that there would have been little opportunity to amend it for publication until there was some firm prospect that it was going to be printed.

Jeffreys' defenders think otherwise. J.G. Muddiman[2] and Seymour Schofield[3] suggested that the abrasive language in the report was added after the Glorious Revolution by Whigs anxious to blacken his memory; and that the absence of any other reliable account of a trial recording comparable flamboyance makes it less probable Jeffreys spoke in the way reported. G.W. Keeton[4] (*Lord Chancellor Jeffreys and the Stuart Cause*) believes he would have felt inhibited in the presence of his four brother judges. He also considers that Pollexfen's conduct of the prosecution was in fact taken over by Jeffreys by arrangement, or that the report of it was subsequently curtailed, or transferred to Jeffreys' lips, through editing. Muddiman believed the report was compiled by Robert Blaney, the Whig barrister earlier implicated in the Rye House plot, from imperfect notes made by junior counsel which he 'powdered with oaths and exclamations Jeffreys did not use'. He concluded that the account was subjected to 'no authoritative revision at all', that 'as printed, the trial is a fraud', so that 'half the modern case against Jeffreys falls to the ground'.

In fact, the trial speaks convincingly for itself as it stands, and there is no reason to doubt it as a verbatim account. The existence of the named participants – judges, barristers, jurors, witnesses and court officials – is beyond question, and the reporter could hardly have identified them unless present at the hearing. Of greater significance are the points that particularly strike him, such as Jeffreys' direction that a jury 'of the best quality in the county' should be returned; that Barter, Dunne's guide, was 'a very lusty man' (that is, heavily built), to explain why Jeffreys confused him with someone else; the moment when a candle was 'still held nearer' Dunne's nose; and Alice Lisle's reference to one witness as 'that white-headed man'. Many such points are noted; and, regardless of their strict relevance to the narrative, they can only have come from eyewitness observation.

After three centuries, as one would expect, some things have changed – the language, certain place-names, judicial attitudes, and in particular the law of evidence, which barely existed at that time.

But one thing that has not changed is the method of forensic investigation and trial. The way this is brought out in Alice's trial evokes a convincing authenticity: the gradual unfolding of the evidence; the backtracking to pick up loose ends; the occasional misunderstandings and leads left unexplored; the increasing tension in the retreat of the principal witness, Dunne, over whom he saw, when, and how much he told them; the way Jeffreys drives him less and less gently from each successive refuge; to the moment of that final off-guard answer, the advocate's godsend, that traps him, and the more dramatically because it is so unnecessary, in the thicket of his accumulated lies – all this comes across today with total realism.

Beneath the surface of the evidence lie patterns and pressures that the modern lawyer can identify at once. Though the account is occasionally difficult to follow, a detailed examination of what the witnesses said highlights the obstacles they faced and the reasons for their reactions. It illustrates the well-established principle, as valid then as today, that the path to truth most often lies in exposing why people lie. These clues could hardly have arrived by accident, or have been edited in by a stranger to the case: that they have lain there unexplored and unexplained for three centuries is a strong argument against the claim that the account was the 'dramatised version' Muddiman believed it to be.

Given Dunne's persistent prevarication, Jeffreys' exasperation is understandable, and his castigation of him as 'you blockhead' and 'thou vile wretch' (there are about a dozen such instances during the trial) at no stage seems out of context or, indeed, anything but natural in one prone to the discomfort of gallstones.

The attempt to defend Jeffreys on the basis that words have been surreptitiously attributed to him is misconceived on two grounds. First, his recorded excesses are, on close examination, relatively infrequent; and, second, the language used, though certainly strong and hardly acceptable in court today, nevertheless falls short of coarseness or blasphemy. Muddiman's defence is little short of hero-worship, and seems to blind him to the forceful nature of the man and the pressures he faced. Away from London, unaware of the unseen scribe and with all printing under government control,[5] the fear of publicity would hardly have inhibited him, whatever his sensitivities about his brother judges.

Similar considerations apply to the attempt to explain why Jeffreys ran most of the prosecution case himself, on the ground that the anonymous editor has transferred to him most of what fell from Pollexfen, to portray a judicial monster concerned only to obtain a conviction. One is certainly left with the impression that this was indeed Jeffreys' purpose, and that he acted far more as an inquisitor than a judge. There can be no doubt that the extent of his interference alone would justify an appeal today: the modern view is that the arena is for the gladiators and that judges, no matter how sorely tempted, must remain above the dust of conflict. It is probable that such behaviour was barely acceptable in Jeffreys' day, but that does not mean it did not happen. On the contrary, there is every reason to believe it did, because the case occurred at a particularly crucial moment of Jeffreys' life. The acquittal of the first, and one of the more distinguished, prisoners connected with the rebellion was the last thing the authorities were looking for in bringing the West to heel, and even less would it help Jeffreys towards the goal of his career, the Lord Chancellorship.

It was therefore natural that Jeffreys should have prepared himself in detail for this case. The key to his knowledge was Nelthorp, brought up from Salisbury to Newgate gaol in London shortly after his arrest. As Jeffreys stated later in the trial, Nelthorp 'told me all the story before I came out of town'.[6] This prompted Jeffreys to 'give particular direction that the outlawry of Nelthorp should be brought down thither', that is, to Winchester, for he wanted to be certain that Alice Lisle could not avoid giving some explanation of how a former Rye House conspirator and outlaw came to be hiding in her house, even though she faced no charge relating to Nelthorp.

There were probably two reasons why Alice was not charged with harbouring Nelthorp. One was the need to concentrate men's minds on the rebellion, rather than on some half-forgotten plot against the previous monarch two years earlier. The other was the lack of any evidence suggesting that Alice Lisle knew anything about him. As it turned out, it was Nelthorp she had to thank for this, for he was able to mislead Jeffreys over the implications of the alias he adopted and what it meant to her. Many of the issues Jeffreys pursued, and his angles of approach, can only have been based on information he had obtained from Nelthorp, thus leaving the use he made of it exclusively his own. It is this more than anything that underlines the authenticity of the *State Trials* account, and destroys the argument that it has been edited to blacken Jeffreys because, had Nelthorp's information been available to Pollexfen, it is inconceivable he would not have exploited it to the full in opening and building the prosecution case.

These considerations apart and despite his ailment, at 41 Jeffreys was at the height of his powers. His calibre for forensic debate had in no way diminished, and the complexities of the case offered a challenge he would have welcomed. While Pollexfen was certainly a prominent lawyer, his political sympathies lay more with the Whigs, and it was probably a relief to him to hand Dunne's examination over to Jeffreys. More significantly, there is no reported case showing Pollexfen to have been anywhere near in the same class as Jeffreys as criminal advocate. The whole thrust of the cross-examination – its incisiveness, attention to detail, its essentially 'whiplash' quality – bears the stamp of one who was past master of his trade. It is difficult to avoid the conclusion that it was indeed the work of Jeffreys, not merely because he felt impelled to it and had prepared for it, but because he, and he alone, was capable of it.

If there are passages in the report that sit uneasily on Jeffreys' lips, they are his monologues against Nonconformists and Dissenters, his repeated threats of damnation for the main witness as a penalty for lying, and the first part of his summing-up, which reads like a thanksgiving sermon for deliverance from the rebellion and contrasts sharply with his subsequent evaluation of the evidence. That is not to suggest these passages are fabrications, simply that they might have been embroidered. There could be two reasons for this. First, a speech lends itself to amendment much more readily than cross-examination. Second, the trial did not finish until eleven at night, and the judges had to be in Salisbury the next day. It seems inherently unlikely that Jeffreys would have indulged himself at greater length than the time available would warrant.

Since the source material is no longer extant, one can only speculate over possible amendments to the record. In what follows, those passages that might have been edited are identified as such, and it is for the reader to decide whether this is correct. Nor do we know who compiled the original record, but its quality seems clearly to disclose a lawyer's familiarity with courtroom procedure, suggesting it was almost certainly compiled by one of the four junior counsel. If the author compiled his notes at the time, it is hard to believe his memory would serve him thirty-four years after the event to make accurate additions or amendments, or that he would have wished to do so. Whoever took the original note has, in this writer's view, wisely refrained from attempting to interfere with the examinations of the witnesses, which flow consistently and convincingly.

Of the four junior counsel, Jennings, the one documented survivor, is the most likely author. He was living in London in 1719; and, if the report is in fact his contemporary note, which he transcribed and gave to Salmon to rush into volume III, it is hard to see how any Whig propagandist could have interfered with it before publication. If Jennings amended the record, it is clear that his editorial loyalties would have lain far more with the judge than against him. He had been close to the Jeffreys family for many years and had often acted professionally for them. He was present when Jeffreys died in the Tower in April 1689. Briefed in an important case before a judge he knew well, he would have taken a personal as well as a professional interest; and the proper conduct of the prosecution would have required someone to take a note.

Whatever amendments Salmon might have made after obtaining the author's script, in the preface to the fourth edition of *State Trials* (1775) the then editor, Francis Hargrave KC, had this to say:

it may be of use to observe, that however indebted to [Mr Salmon] the public may be for his industry in first forming a Collection of State Trials . . . he is frequently betrayed . . . into a false notion of characters and opinions . . . [But] candour and justice require us to add, that notwithstanding the faults which may be justly imputed to his critical review, it is in many respects a useful work . . . for it must be confessed, that on those trials which were foreign to the basis of his political tenets, [they] are frequently pertinent, and accompanied with suitable illustrations from this history of the times . . . some of the animadversions which he makes under the malignant influence of party-spirit may be deemed not altogether without foundation and therefore . . .

they ought not to be wholly disregarded, where it is possible to discriminate the shades of truth from the tinge of exaggeration with which they are disguised.

Born in 1679, Salmon was a writer of wide-ranging interests and intellect. His work was translated into French, Dutch, German and Italian before he died, aged 88, in 1767. His main interest in the cases he included reflected the fact that he was predominantly a historian. Whatever his political views on William III's accession, his commentary on Alice Lisle's trial in the *Critical Review*, a one-volume abridgment of the 1719 work, published in 1738, amply demonstrates his capacity for objective analysis for which Hargrave allowed him grudging credit.

Salmon is at pains to discredit the exaggerations in Bishop Burnet's defence of Alice Lisle in his *History of his Own Time* (Appendix Five). His most significant argument is that it is difficult to see why Burnet went out of his way to embellish when the truth would have done no harm:

This trial . . . manifests the little care Bishop Burnet used to inform himself of the truth . . . even in instances where he might have done it with all the ease imaginable. Either he thought it beneath him to ask a question . . . or he designedly relates facts directly contrary to the truth, for the sake of his party; or purely for the sake of lying; it not being easy to conceive why he should misreport some passages, where the truth would not have been at all disadvantageous . . . if it had appeared in its proper colours.

Speaking of this trial, he says, that the night after Monmouth's defeat, Hicks and Nelthorp escaped from the army, and came to Mrs Lisle's house for shelter; that Hicks told her the occasion whereupon she immediately ordered a servant to give an information against them to a Justice of Peace, and in the meanwhile to suffer them to escape but on a sudden the house was surrounded by a party, who took both them, and her for harbouring them . . . That there was no proof she knew the persons were rebels; nor were they in any proclamation; but Jeffreys charged the jury in a violent manner; and turned them back twice, threatening them with an attaint . . .

Now, in the first place, Hicks and Nelthorp did not come to Mrs Lisle's house the night after Monmouth's defeat; for the battle of Sedgemoor was fought on the 6th July, and Hicks and Nelthorp did not come to her house till the 28th . . . Mrs Lisle says in her defence, that she was at London at the time of the battle, and when the Duke of Monmouth was beheaded; and did not come into the country above a week before these two gentlemen were taken at her house; which was three weeks after the battle of Sedgemoor: how the Bishop therefore, came to say they fled to her house the night after the battle or for what reason he forged this tale, I cannot conceive.

It is equally true, that they were not in any Proclamation; for Mrs Lisle herself says in the trial, she knew Nelthorp was in a Proclamation.

He says also, that Jeffreys gave evidence himself, that they confessed they were with Monmouth: but I cannot see what occasion there was for this, when there were three witnesses, that swore positively Hicks was in Monmouth's army; and would have persuaded them to join the rebels.

As to Mrs Lisle's sending to inform a Justice of Peace, that Hicks and Nelthorp were at her house, as soon as they came; it appears, they supped and lay all night in her house, and were not taken till the next morning: nor did she ever mention her sending to inform a Justice of the Peace of their being there, as she certainly would have done, in her defence at the trial, if she had ever given any of her servants such orders . . .

As to . . . the Chief Justice's menaces, these, possibly, were thrown in by friends. I do not find the Chief Justice used any threats, either to the jury or witnesses; unless when he examined Dunne, who notoriously prevaricated, and forswore himself at this trial, by his own confession, and from whom the truth was extorted with the utmost difficulty.

This is the reasoned approach of a historian anxious to sustain his account factually and impartially. He naturally assumes the correctness of his own version, which, if it stood alone, would certainly leave room for the argument that he had edited it to suit his purpose. But it does not stand alone. On 5 September 1685, a week after the trial was over, Robert Harley wrote again to his father from Tunbridge Wells (Appendix Six). He related his own hearsay summary of what had happened at Winchester, and, apart from minor details as to Alice Lisle's age and the time the case finished, his account reflects the *State Trials* account remarkably accurately. As corroboration, its value lies in the fact that it was written within a week of the events it describes; and that it is a letter to which Salmon could not have had access in 1719, since it remained in private hands from the time it was written until published by the Historical Manuscripts Commission in 1894.

The inferences Salmon seeks to draw in his comparison with Burnet carry none of the 'animadversions . . . under the malignant influence of party-spirit' ascribed to him by Hargrave. Salmon's approach is balanced and precise, and at no stage overstates Alice Lisle's defence; and his discussion of the law, which will be examined later, is equally convincing. Whatever his political allegiances, one cannot help feeling he was sufficiently disciplined a historian not to give way to them.

Although mildly disapproving of Jeffreys' handling of Dunne, Salmon regards the issue as insignificant: in fact, to treat it otherwise leads to a distorted perspective. Later historians have argued, justifiably, that Jeffreys' recorded behaviour as a judge leaves much to be desired. But both his supporters and his detractors are on dangerous ground when they take the further step and suggest that the record must be wrong: in Muddiman's case, arguing that he actually behaved a good deal better than the transcript depicts; or, in Burnet's case, very much worse. Both are the prisoners of their prejudice in a way that Salmon never was, and make the mistake of trying to dress their emperor in ill-fitting clothes he never wore.

FIVE

The Law of Treason – Then and Now

In England, twenty-first-century traitors share the historic distinction of prosecution under the same enactment as their fourteenth-century predecessors, the 1351 Statute of Treasons.[1] The last person convicted under this law was William Joyce, 'Lord Haw-Haw', for his anti-British broadcasts from Germany during the Second World War. While the species of his offence was legally different from Alice Lisle's, and his indictment less colourfully phrased, the underlying accusation was the same, that of breaking the citizen's duty of allegiance to the Crown. As required by law, Joyce was hanged in Wandsworth prison on 3 January 1946.

A remarkable feature of Joyce's case was that he could have been beheaded had the monarch and the government so wished: it was not until July 1973 that the royal prerogative to substitute the axe for the rope as the penalty for treason was abolished by Act of Parliament. The last man to die at the block in Britain was the Scottish Lord Lovat, for treason, on Tower Hill in 1747, after his capture in 1745 at the battle of Culloden.[2]

Though the law of treason seeks to protect the monarch, and to maintain national stability by requiring the people's allegiance, the 1351 statute was in no sense prompted by a moment of national peril. Passed during a period when the criminal law was developed almost entirely in the courts, it arose out of a financial struggle between Edward III and his lords. The more serious criminal offences in the Middle Ages were either 'felonies' or 'treasons', and, while both were punishable with execution and confiscation of the offender's assets, a felon's property 'escheated' to the lord of the manor, whereas that belonging to a traitor became 'forfeit' to the Crown. It was thus in the monarch's interest to extend the categories of treason, which by the middle of the fourteenth century was leaving the lords seriously out of pocket. The statute set out a series of definitions, and concluded by making Parliament henceforth the sole arbiter of what amounted to treason.

The lords in fact conferred lasting longevity on their statute, because its general lack of ambiguity made it an ideal instrument for safeguarding the monarch and his kingdom even in the changed conditions of later centuries. At the same time, Parliament's right to extend the categories of treason allowed a swift response in times of national crisis, one example being the embargo on possession or publication of Monmouth's first Declaration after he landed. (By proclaiming himself king in his second Declaration, at Taunton on 22 June, Monmouth may also have hoped to confer on his followers the benefit of Henry VII's Treason Act of 1495, which is still in force today, that 'service in war under the king de facto is not an act of treason against the king de jure'. But he never achieved sufficient success to make his 'royal' status a reality, and none of those charged in the course of the Bloody Assize saw fit, or dared, to raise it as a defence.)

On 23 May 1940, however, instead of extending the original enactment, Parliament passed the Treachery Act which lasted for the duration of the Second World War. This made it a capital offence for British subjects to do anything that might frustrate the war effort, but there were two reasons it did not cover Joyce. First, although he had lived in this country for many years and had claimed, more mistakenly than fraudulently, to be 'British' when obtaining a British passport, his birth in the United States actually made him an alien. Second, the main broadcasts relied on by the prosecution were made before the Act came into force. (Even if Joyce had been treated as notionally 'British' by virtue of his passport, he would have been at risk under the Treachery Act only for the six weeks between the day it came into force and the expiry of his passport on 2 July 1940. By implicitly accepting that this was when his allegiance ended, the Crown could hardly have argued that he continued to be a British subject, or that his later broadcasts could have put him in jeopardy. Charges the Crown had prepared under this Act were dropped when the jury convicted him of treason.)

It was therefore Joyce's British passport that put him under the duty of allegiance envisaged by the 1351 statute. Despite his twenty-four years' residence in Britain or in British dominions overseas, the

Crown evidently considered that, apart from his passport obligation, his continuing American nationality was enough to prevent any duty of allegiance arising.

This concept of allegiance, exclusive to the law of treason, casts its obligations on a wide variety of people entering the United Kingdom, principally those of British citizenship or nationality. Foreign nationals and diplomats apart, the duty is generally owed by anyone 'ordinarily resident' here, regardless of occasional absence, and it includes current British passport-holders wherever they may be. Joyce therefore owed allegiance to George VI, to whose enemies he had 'adhered . . . giving them aid or comfort in the realm or elsewhere' by broadcasting German propaganda.

Francis Bacon pointed out in *Cases of Treason* (1641): 'In treason there be no accessories, but all are principals.' In other words, the extent of an individual's involvement, however slight, is irrelevant. Since the statute makes it treason to 'violate the king's companion or the king's eldest daughter unmarried or the wife of his eldest son and heir', queens and princesses who consent to their own 'violation' are equally at risk if they commit adultery with those owing allegiance. Henry VIII took this point against Anne Boleyn, on the basis of indiscretions more presumed than proven, once he decided she was superfluous to his requirements. It remains the position; and, though the penalties are scarcely appropriate today, there is no doubt that the late Diana, Princess of Wales's affair with James Hewitt, to which they both admitted in 1995, left them equally guilty. However, the presumed infidelity between 1814 and 1817 of Princess Caroline, the wife of the Prince Regent, later George IV, with the Italian Signor Pergami, could not have put her in jeopardy. Pergami was an alien who had never lived in Britain. Because he owed no allegiance to her father-in-law, George III, there would have been no treason in which she could have been implicated. When Parliament cleared her of adultery in 1820, it did so more in response to public opinion than on the evidence. Since the statute is mainly to protect the royal succession, it in no way restricts or penalises the monarch's or his sons' philandering.

In the Middle Ages, traitors were generally executed with greater barbarity than ordinary criminals, to emphasise the seriousness of the offence and to achieve maximum deterrent impact. Until the implementation on 30 September 1998 of the Crime and Disorder Act 1998 (which, apart from certain provisions of service law in time of war, abolished the death penalty altogether) this distinction was preserved. Treason was one of only two remaining offences to carry the death penalty, the other being piracy with violence. Convicted traitors do, however, remain subject to automatic disqualification from positions in the armed forces and the civil service.

Despite the lords' interest in limiting the categories of the offence, both the 1351 enactment and later legislation took it into many areas now dealt with under separate statutes, some of them far beyond the modern concept of treason. While modern terrorist and official secrets legislation would certainly have been included, the old law covered counterfeiting and clipping coin; refusing the oath of supremacy; becoming, regardless of hostilities, a foreign national; and, from a century before Alice Lisle's trial, setting foot in England as a Jesuit priest.

In contrast to other areas of the criminal law, trials for treason attracted wide publicity. Not only were they generally reported at length, but by the middle of the seventeenth century there was enough published material for two distinguished lawyers to produce their own independent reviews of the law. Francis Bacon, Viscount St Albans and Lord Chancellor under James I, was a lawyer of formidable intellect. His prolific literary output included proposals for codifying the law, one part of which, *Cases of Treason*, was first published in 1641, some fifteen years after his death. In the same year, Sir Robert Holbourne, shortly afterwards Attorney-General to the then Prince of Wales, delivered his *Learned Readings on the Statute of Treasons in Lincoln's Inn* (1642). Presumably because both publications were thought to represent an accurate statement of the law, they were combined in a single volume, which appeared in 1681.[3] The detail gives an insight into how the law actually operated at the time of the Bloody Assize.

Holbourne explained the legal uncertainty that gave rise to the 1351 enactment:

Before the statute, trespasses were made felonies, and felonies were made treasons; and we could not judge which were felonies and which were treasons, but it did rest in the breast of judges that were in those days. For the preventing of which mischief this statute, which I now read upon, was made, which hath two parts: a Declarative part; and that doth declare what shall hereafter be judged treason . . . [and] . . . the Directive part [which] directs the judges how far to proceed upon a fact that is not within the statute.

Bacon started with the four main categories of the offence under the statute:

Where a man doth compass or imagine the death of the king, the king's wife, the king's eldest son, and heir apparent, if it appear by any overt act, it is treason.

Where a man doth violate the king's wife, the king's eldest daughter, unmarried, the wife of the king's eldest son, and heir apparent, it is treason.

Where a man doth levy war against the king in the realm, it is treason.

Where a man is adherent to the king's enemies giving them aid and comfort, it is treason.

Having been declared a traitor by a separate Act of Parliament, Monmouth's position under the third head was academic, and he was lawfully executed without trial. But there is no doubt that his followers 'levied war' against James II in exactly the same way as John Penruddock did against Cromwell. In his concern to clarify as well as codify, Bacon in fact simplified the fourth category, the full text of which reads:

When a man is adherent to the king's enemies in his realm, giving them aid and comfort in the realm, or elsewhere, it is treason.

The grammatical permutations in the double reference to 'the realm' followed by the phrase 'or elsewhere', and the impact of the punctuation, raise serious problems of construction, which Bacon probably recognised and for that reason preferred to avoid.

But the definition was directly in point in 1916, nearly three centuries later, in the trial of Roger Casement. Casement had gone to Germany shortly after the start of the First World War, where he tried to persuade British prisoners-of-war of Irish origin (Ireland then being still part of Britain) to join the Irish Brigade and with German support to fight against England in the cause of Irish nationalism. Casement was found guilty of treason and hanged.

Bacon gave various examples of the 'overt acts' of treason that might justify a conviction under one or other of these four categories. Two were to be of particular relevance to the issues in Alice Lisle's trial.

> Where a man doth persuade or withdraw any of the king's subjects from his obedience or from the religion by his majesty established, with intent to withdraw any from the king's obedience, it is treason.
>
> Where a man relieveth or comforteth a traitor, and knoweth of the offence, it is treason.

The first of these was precisely what Hicks did in the stables of Keynsham House on 25 June 1685, the words 'obedience' and 'allegiance' being virtually interchangeable for the seventeenth-century lawyer. In Jeffreys' view, the fact that he had also long since 'withdrawn from the religion by his majesty established' made his position substantially worse. It was also the act of treason committed by the royalist Sir Henry Slingsby in 1658 when he tried to win over his Cromwellian captors in Hull; and by Casement in Germany in 1915. The second was the basis of the accusation against Alice Lisle, the crucial issue being whether or not she realised Hicks was a traitor. If her actions in feeding and sheltering him seem much more like 'adherence to the king's enemies' than the 'levying of war' or 'compassing the king's death' actually recited in her indictment, the reason she was not charged with adhering was the curious distinction, still recognised today, between 'enemies' and 'rebels'. In elaborating the point, Holbourne unconsciously anticipated how it would apply to Casement and Joyce three centuries later:

This word Enemy cannot extend to Subjects, for they are Rebels and no Enemies . . . and therefore the aiding of Rebels cannot [mean] . . . the aiding of the Kings Enemies within this Law . . .

A Subject *rationae originis* cannot be an enemy, although he doth Levy War (in respect of his Obedience) but a Rebel he shall be.

A Subject *rationae loci*, during his residence here, can be no Enemy either, but if he goeth over Sea, and then Levy War against this Kingdom . . . then he is an Enemy within this Law, and no Rebel.

Though less severe, coinage offences were classified as treason under the statute on two grounds: they undermined economic stability,[4] and to counterfeit or deface the monarch's effigy seemed tantamount to attacking him personally. Henry V's statute of 1415 added the offence of clipping. While Holbourne explained the scope of these provisions in detail, Bacon contented himself with a summary:

Where a man bringeth into this Realm false money, counterfeited to the likeness of English . . . and knowing it to be false money, it is Treason.

Where a man counterfeiteth any Coin current in payment within this Realm, it is Treason.

Where a man doth clip, waste, round or file any of the King's money, or any foreign Coin, current by proclamation, for gains sake, it is Treason.

In both treason and felony, the defendant was severely handicapped: he was allowed neither bail nor a copy of the indictment; he could not be represented, except on points of law; and, though he might speak in his own defence, neither he nor his witnesses could be sworn.[5] The law allowed two concessions, presumably in recognition of the seriousness of the offence: the accused could challenge up to thirty-five jurors 'peremptorily' (that is, without giving a reason), as opposed to the twenty allowed on a simple felony charge; and from 1547, he had the benefit of one of the earliest rules of evidence, which remained the law for nearly four centuries. A statute passed in Edward VI's reign set a more rigorous level of proof:

> Treason ought to be fully proved, as it appears by the words of the Statute, and that is to be by two witnesses, for the proving of every Treason . . .

The consequence of producing only one prosecution witness was that the accused was either acquitted, or convicted of the lesser, and non-capital, offence of sedition. It was not until the Treason Act of 1945, passed specifically to cater for the perceived weaknesses in the case against Joyce, that the two-witness rule was abolished.

Because of the Magna Carta requirement that a man should be judged by his 'peers', or equals, trial procedures in treason and felony differed according to the status of the accused. Whereas commoners were always tried by a judge and jury, peers could be tried only by fellow peers in the House of Lords.[6] Because it came to be felt that this 'jury' was more amenable to pressure from the king than the body of the whole house, the Treason Act of 1695 required all peers to attend whenever treason charges were heard. Bacon highlighted the difference:

> In Treason, a Trial of a Peer of the Kingdom is to be by special Commission before the Lord High Steward [the Lord Chancellor] and those that pass upon him to be none but Peers: the Proceeding is with great Solemnity, the Lord Steward sitting under a cloth of Estate, with a white rod of Justice in his hand, and the Peers may confer together, but are not any ways shut up; and are demanded by the Lord Steward their Voices one by one, and the plurality of Voice carries it . . .
>
> The Proceeding in case of Treason, with a common subject, is in the King's Bench.

The severity of the law lay in its publicly inflicted penalty. The ultimate deterrent was the spectacle of the traitor's agony. That put the offence in a class of its own, driving home the lesson of allegiance and setting stakes that only the most desperate would play for. While felons were simply hanged, traitors suffered the

greater disgrace of being dragged on a hurdle to the scaffold. Bacon
outlined the ritualistic barbarity that followed:

> In Treason, the Corporal Punishment is, by drawing on a hurdle
> from the place of the prison to the place of Execution, by hanging
> and being cut down alive, bowelling, and quartering, and in
> Women burning.

Evisceration seems to have originated in the ancient belief that the
body's main organs were the seat of the emotions. Jeffreys alluded
to this in the course of examining Dunne; and at The George in
Salisbury,[7] where three of Monmouth's former prisoners stayed
overnight when they went to identify Hicks as the man who had
tried to dissuade them from their loyalty, an exposed beam still
carries this fifteenth-century admonition:

> Have God before thine eyes,
> Who searcheth hart and raines [the kidneys],
> And live according to his law
> Then glory is thy gaines.

The idea emerges more clearly from the sentence passed on
Andrew Harcla during Edward II's reign, that

> for your treason you be drawn hanged and beheaded, your heart
> and bowels and entrails *whence come your treacherous thoughts*
> be torn out and burnt to ashes and that the ashes be scattered to
> the wind.

The concept can be traced still further back to classical literature,
where the Latin word *stomachari* meant 'to become angry'.

There were two categories of traitor for whom the extremities of
this punishment were relaxed. For peers, as Bacon recalled: 'it hath
been an ancient Use and Favour from the Kings of this Realm, to
pardon the Execution of hanging, drawing and quartering; and to
make Warrant for their beheading'.

Holbourne also mentioned the concession allowed to non-
subversive traitors, such as coinage offenders: 'for treasons that do

not immediately concern the person of the King, the judgment ought to be, That he shall be drawn and hanged only; and not that he shall be quartered'.

The punishment nevertheless extended beyond the individual, with far-reaching consequences for his family. Bacon summarised what a traitor's 'attainder' involved:

> In Treason there ensueth a corruption of blood in the Line ascending and descending . . . Lands and Goods are forfeited, and Inheritance, as well entailed as Fee-simple, and the profits of Estates for Life . . . the Escheats go to the King, and not to the Lord of the Fee . . . the Land forfeited shall be in the Kings actual possession . . .

PART TWO

SIX

Winchester Assize, August 1685

Alice Lisle, hold up thy hand. (Which she did). Thou standest here indicted . . . as a false traitor against the most illustrious and most excellent prince, James the Second . . . King, thy supreme and natural lord, the fear of God in thy heart not having, nor weighing the duty of thy allegiance; but being moved and seduced by the instigation of the Devil, the love and true, due and natural obedience, which a true and faithful subject . . . of right ought to bear, wholly withdrawing, and with all thy might intending the peace and common tranquillity of this kingdom of England to disturb . . . the 28th day of July . . . at the parish of Ellingham . . . well knowing one John Hicks . . . Clerk, to be a false traitor . . . the said John Hicks in thy dwelling-house . . . secretly, wickedly and traitorously didst entertain, conceal, comfort, uphold and maintain . . . and meat and drink unto the said John Hicks then and there, maliciously and traitorously didst give and deliver . . . against the duty of thy allegiance . . . and against the form of the statute in that case made and provided. (Clerk of Arraigns, Winchester Castle, 27th August 1685)

Lying in the hollow of the Itchen valley, Winchester is best seen from the upper slopes of St Giles's Hill to the east. From here, the High Street divides it neatly into two: the red-brick profusion of the northern half, increasingly overshadowed by the office-block architecture of the past four decades, is in striking contrast to the open lawns and pale stone of the ancient buildings to the south. The city's anchor-points with the past, the cathedral, the college and the Bishop's Palace, are too spaciously set to dominate, except within their own precincts. At the south-eastern limit of the city, they lead into water meadows and open countryside, where the Itchen continues past the almshouse foundation of St Cross and finally disappears beyond the shoulder of St Catherine's Hill.

Older than any of these, but now obscured by the modern court building next to it and the Royal Green Jackets former barracks behind, is Winchester Castle. Today it is represented by 'the Great Hall', all that remains of a much larger and more impressive medieval fortress overlooking the valley from the south-western corner of the city wall. The approach up the side of the Westgate gives it dignity and independence: the open forecourt emphasises its heavy, Gothic construction and diverts attention from the featureless municipal offices on the right. It was built between 1222 and 1236 for Henry III, with an interior that is spacious and well proportioned. The high, timbered roof rests on parallel stone arcades supported by slender marble columns: these form a wide central aisle flanked by two narrower ones. Looking west, they focus attention on the end wall where the legendary King Arthur's Round Table, a huge emblem in green and white, hangs high above the remains of a dais. The upward sweep of the arcades, the breadth of the beams and arched braces between them, the long, transomed windows, the massive flintstone walls, all combine to create an atmosphere of permanence and established authority in a 'hall . . . where the general Assizes, Quarter Sessions and County Courts, for the general county, have for many hundreds of years constantly been kept'.

John Trussell was giving an eyewitness account of an important occasion there in November 1603. At 'the Bar: which was made at the west end of the hall', eleven conspirators stood trial for treason, of whom the most distinguished were Sir Walter Ralegh, Lord Gray and Lord Cobham. In an age when politics came before justice, trials for treason were intended more to proclaim than to investigate guilt, and the legal process simply added authority to the desired result. Ralegh's conviction by a prosecution-packed jury from Middlesex was as certain as the death sentence that followed from Chief Justice Popham.

The castle's demise as a fortress followed Ogle's surrender to Cromwell's forces in October 1645. Musket-fire echoed inside the hall as the Roundheads celebrated their victory: the Round Table, with its painting of King Arthur at the top, was an irresistible target, and marksmanship seems to have been excellent: most of the shot removed in recent restoration came from the area of the king's head and crown. The castle was then 'slighted': Cromwell's gunners systematically destroyed the ramparts and outer fortifications, reducing everything except the hall to a heap of rubble.

Despite this treatment, the hall was clearly a significant landmark on Charles II's accession in 1660. Twenty-five years later, the ruins cleared, it was already in the shadow of the northern wing of Charles II's most ambitious, but unfulfilled, project, a palace to rival Versailles, planned by Sir Christopher Wren, with tree-lined avenues running directly down to the cathedral. It was abandoned on his death in February 1685 and later destroyed by fire.

The hall came into its own again as a single chamber in 1974. For the previous thirty years it had housed two assize courts, which made it an acoustic disaster. Walls and partitions destroyed every perspective and the wooden panelling so deadened speech as to make trials virtually inaudible to all but those immediately involved. These were removed when the new court building opened next door, and it now appears much as it would have done 300 years ago.

In his *Commonwealth of England*, Sir Thomas Smith, one of Queen Elizabeth's Secretaries of State, describes the impressive scene of a Tudor assize trial:

Upon the highest bench sit the judges . . . Next them on each side the justices of the peace according to their degree. On a lower bench before them, the rest of the justices of the peace and some other gentlemen or their clerks. Before these judges and justices there is a table set beneath, at which sitteth the . . . keeper of the writs, the escheator, the under sheriff, and such clerks as do write. At the end of that table there is a bar made with a space for the inquests, and twelve men to come in when they are called, behind that space another bar, and there stand the prisoners which be brought thither by the gaoler.

The discharge of judicial business there in 1685 would have been much the same as in Westminster Hall. Courts would have sat with the participants close enough to each other to hear what was said. The modern concept of a single judge presiding in a single chamber had not then emerged. In contrast to the majesty of the main tribunal at the western end, these other courts would have seemed relatively informal. Under guard but freed from his chains, the prisoner would stand at the 'bar', a simple barrier at waist height. Between him and the judge would be a table for counsel and clerks, and the all-male jury would be grouped to one side. Subject to official supervision, the public could come and go more or less as they pleased.

The list for that autumn assize at Winchester was heavy. Bartholomew Shower, a busy London barrister and law reporter, noted: 'in Trinity Term, Monmouth's rebellion in the West prevented much business. In the vacation following, by reason of that rebellion, there was no assizes held in the Western circuit, but afterwards five judges went as commissioners of Oyer and Terminer, and gaol delivery.' Though the judges' main task was to deal with the rebels, they could expect little respite if they were also to clear the backlog of everyday crime. Some seventy prisoners awaited trial in Winchester Castle when the assize opened on Tuesday, 25 August. In the course of that and the next two days, fifteen contested cases were heard. This gives a rate of disposal of roughly one case per judge per day, not unreasonable given that they were all trials for treason, murder or felony in which defence counsel were not allowed. In its curious mixture of English and Latin, the ancient script of the Gaol Book recites the same catalogue of human weakness and depravity – murder, rape, house-breaking and theft – as can be heard in any Crown Court today. But the details are tantalisingly brief: the book sets out no more than the defendant's name, the victim, the charge and its criminal category, the plea, verdict and sentence. It is a record and in no sense a report. There is nothing about which judge presided, the defendant's background, who the witnesses were or what was said.

Frustrating as this is, the reasons are clear. Opportunities for appeal were limited to judicial scrutiny of the record, so there was no need for a transcript. In addition, with the reimposition in June 1685 of the Licensing Act to control printing (after six years of axe-grinding scurrility), the government would be unlikely to tolerate accounts for public consumption that reflected discredit on the administration of justice. The account we have of Alice Lisle's trial would for this reason have stood little chance of contemporary publication. Perhaps the reason we have it at all is because it was not published until the events it recorded had passed harmlessly into history and had lost most of their relevance.

Local crime was a local affair, seldom aired in print. For the humble and illiterate it was the drama of the trial itself, and even more what happened afterwards, that caught the imagination. The spectacle of the convict suffering on the gallows or in a pillory, or being flogged 'at the cart's tail', doubtless repeated and exaggerated in the taverns, was the deterrent face of justice that the masses turned out to watch. It made an impact far preferable, in the government's view, to the predominantly seditious pamphleteering of the past six years, so dangerous for simple minds.

Cursory as the official record may be, its detail gives an insight into the mechanics of criminal justice, and confirms the law's barbaric penalties. The severity of the punishment for theft, for example, depended on the value of the goods stolen. If worth more than twelve pence (a figure fixed nearly four centuries earlier in the reign of Edward I, when it was taken as a labourer's weekly wage) it became the capital offence of 'grand', as opposed to 'petty', larceny, and this was the principal reason indictments included a valuation of each article taken.[1]

At first sight it seems extraordinary that anyone should have been so desperate as to risk his neck for trivial gain, but this assumption overlooks the abiding philosophy of the criminal mind. Even today, penalties seldom deter if other considerations, such as profit and the risk of detection, seem to make the gamble worthwhile.

The first prisoner before the court was John Carter, charged with murdering Anne Kitchiner. The abbreviated Latin entry against his name shows he defended himself successfully: 'po: se non cul nec rec' – this means he pleaded not guilty; he puts himself (on his country) ('ponit se'); was found not guilty ('non culpabilem'); and, of equal importance on an acquittal, 'he did not fly for it' ('nec recessit'). Those who took to their heels when pursued by the law were liable to be penalised even if innocent.

Hercules Hayes faced two charges, housebreaking and theft. The first was: 'Breaking the dwelling howse Ricardi (of Richard) Young in the day time nulla persona (with no one present) et furavit (and he stole) a Cloth Coat value xii shillings, a Cloth Wastcoate value ii shillings, v Dowlas (old English for coarse linen) shirts value x shillings et alia bona predicti Ricardi (and other goods of the said Richard).'

The second alleged he had helped himself elsewhere: 'Breaking the dwelling howse Ricardi Daw in the daytime nulla persona & furavit a Brasse Kettle value iii shillings, a stuffe petticoate value i shilling vi pence, a laced Coife (headdress) value ii shillings vi pence et alia bona predicti Ricardi.'

According to the record, Hayes pleaded not guilty, was found guilty and possessed no chattels ('catella nulla'). This finding was the first step towards enforcing the law of forfeiture of goods on conviction of felony.[2] In the margin, a large asterisk and the letters 'SS' ('suspensus') indicate he was sentenced to be hanged. In common with others destined for the gallows on this occasion at Winchester, Hayes was not sentenced until the final morning of the assize, Friday 28th, while the rest were, as far as one can tell, informed of their fates as each trial ended. Despite being well above the petty larceny limit, he seems to have been shown mercy: the note continues 'Reprivatus transportandus' ('Reprieved for transportation'), which meant to the West Indian sugar plantations, so he presumably survived for a while at least.

William Parris was charged with stealing a sheepdog belonging to John Caplin valued at fifteen shillings. The jury found him guilty, and he would doubtless have been sentenced to death but for the fact that he availed himself of the privilege of 'benefit of clergy'. This originated in the twelfth century as a claim by clerics to be dealt with in the ecclesiastical courts, where penalties were non-capital, after conviction in the king's courts. Proof of status depended on the ability to read (or more probably learn by heart) and was eventually confined to that condition regardless of any connection with the Church. By the end of the sixteenth century, those allowed the privilege were discharged without being handed over. Thus it became a device designed to mitigate the severity of the criminal law in favour of first offenders, as it could be claimed only once. Though treason was never clergyable, subsequent legislation bridged the enormous gap between felonies and misdemeanours by subdividing felonies into clergyable and non-clergyable offences. The privilege was not abolished for commoners until 1827, or for peers, because of their inadvertent omission from that statute, until 1841.

The note against Parris reads 'clergie petit librum legit et uritur', meaning 'Clergy: he asks for the book, reads and is branded'. The Bible passage was verse 1 of Psalm 51, known as the 'neck verse', followed by branding in the hand with the letter 'C'.[3]

For Robert Bateley there was no mercy. He was convicted of robbing Ann Pledger on the highway and stealing a shilling, a penny and a farthing, together with a gold ring valued at ten shillings. There is no note that he was reprieved, and he is probably the individual later recorded as being hanged at Portsmouth.

Maria Stephens pleaded not guilty to stealing five gold rings worth four pounds belonging to Robert Griffen. The jury found her guilty 'ad valorem viii shillings viii pence' and she was sentenced 'uritur T' ('let her be branded as a thief'). This indicates she was a first offender claiming benefit of clergy under the statute that had extended the privilege to women, passed sixty years earlier.

By the afternoon of Thursday, 27 August 1685, it is probable that only the principal court remained in session at the western end of the hall. Following the grand jury's finding of a 'true bill of indictment', that there was enough evidence to justify prosecution, the final case was called at about five o'clock. The previous day, there had been a last-minute rush to cover a potentially serious gap in the prosecution evidence, which involved sending three witnesses, Monmouth's ex-prisoners of war, to Salisbury to identify one of their former captors. The charge was one of high treason against an elderly lady. She was asked to raise her hand, and Lawrence Swanton, Clerk of Arraigns, began to read the cumbersome verbiage of the indictment.

The significance of the occasion was underlined by the number of those involved. Five Crown counsel were in court, the prosecution being in the hands of the most senior, Serjeant Henry Pollexfen, the leader of the Western circuit. The jury panel, many from well-known Hampshire families, and nine prosecution witnesses, were waiting to be called. The lawyers, their clerks, the guards, the prisoner's family and friends, and the public would all have been watching anxiously for this trial to start. The assize at Salisbury was due to open next day, and the court would be under pressure to get through in time.

The accused, brought over from Salisbury gaol the previous day, was Dame Alice Lisle, twenty years a widow and approaching her sixty-eighth birthday. For her, everything was at stake: if convicted, she faced being burned at the stake and confiscation of all she possessed, with disgrace and deprivation for her dependants. The judge was George Jeffreys, whose appointment as Lord Chief Justice two years earlier at the age of 39 was far from his ultimate ambition. The importance of the case to him was that it was the first of those connected with the unsuccessful rebellion in the West, and the king was looking to him to mark the royal displeasure. With Lord Guildford, the Lord Keeper, close to death, it could not be long before the position Jeffreys coveted most, the Lord Chancellorship, fell vacant, and he was the obvious successor. Yet the choice was bound to depend to some extent on the monarch in whose gift that office lay, and how effectively the West was reminded of its allegiance.

Swanton finished reading the indictment and then turned to the prisoner:

> Clerk of Arraigns: How sayst thou, Alice Lisle, art thou guilty of the high-treason contained in this indictment, or Not Guilty?
> Lisle: Not guilty.
> Clerk: Culprit,[4] by whom wilt thou be tried?
> Lisle: By God and my country.
> Clerk: God send thee a good deliverance.

SEVEN

The Jury

Because Alice Lisle had pleaded not guilty, a jury had to be sworn. The panel was therefore summoned:

> Proclamation was made for the jurors empanelled to try the issue between our sovereign lord the King, and the prisoner at the bar, to appear. And the prisoner desiring, by reason of her age and infirmities (being thick of hearing), some friends of hers might be allowed to stand by her, and inform her of what passed in the court; one Matthew Browne was named, and allowed of by the court to give her all assistance that he could in that matter.

It was scarcely an equal contest. Old, deaf and unrepresented, Alice Lisle must have looked a forlorn figure against the five Crown counsel ranged against her. It would have seemed most unfair to have refused her plea, yet the law was clear: those charged with treason or felony were not allowed counsel. Jeffreys compromised by limiting the assistant's role to 'informing her of what passed in court'. But she was fortunate in having Browne allotted to her. Besides being, as the report states, a 'friend of hers', he was also Deputy Clerk of the Peace, a post for which a legal qualification was necessary and one he had held since 1675. His experience at assizes and Quarter Sessions would have given him an extensive knowledge of criminal law and procedure, so that 'all the assistance he could give' could go well beyond merely repeating to her what was said.

Jury selection is a two-stage process and follows the same procedure today as it did then. A sufficient number of properly qualified candidates are summoned to court, to form the 'panel' from which twelve are selected for each trial.[1] The accused has a double right of challenge: first, though rarely used, 'to the array', to have the whole panel dismissed if he can show bias in its selection;

and second, 'to the polls', when he can object to individuals before they are sworn. In Alice Lisle's time, this second challenge was 'peremptory' (in other words, no reasons had to be given) up to a maximum of thirty-five in cases of treason, and thereafter 'for cause', when reasons had to be shown and adjudicated on by the court.[2]

Jeffreys' charge to Sir John Mill, the sheriff, 'that a very substantial jury should be returned, of the best quality in the county' leaves him open to criticism if he was trying to have the panel packed against Alice Lisle. But he may only have been trying to secure the protection due to her by Magna Carta, which required that she should be tried by those of equal status. This direction was followed by the 'Proclamation for Information and Evidence in the usual manner', a formal call by the crier that those summoned as witnesses should 'come forth and be heard'. This was followed by the selection of the all-male jury. Then:

> the Prisoner was bid to look to her challenges, and the jury was sworn in this order:
>
> Sworn: Gabriel Whistler, Henry Dawley, Francis Morley, Francis Paulet, Richard Godfrey, Thomas Dowse, Dutton Gifford
> Challenged: Robert Barton, Godson Penton, William Taylor, Thomas Wavell, Anthony Yalden
> Sworn: John Cager
> Challenged: Robert Forder, Thomas Lloyd, Thomas ----, Philip Rudsby
> Sworn: Thomas Crop, Richard Suatt
> Challenged: Lawrence Kerby, John Fletcher, William Clarke, John Haily, Richard Sutton, Richard Snatt, Robert Burgess
> Sworn: Matthew Webber
> Challenged: George Prince, Stephen Steele, Thomas Merrot
> Sworn: John Feilder
>
> So the twelve sworn were: Gabriel Whistler, Henry Dawley, Francis Morley, Francis Paulet, Richard Godfrey, Thomas Dowse, Dutton Gifford, John Cager, Thomas Crop, Richard Suatt, Matthew Webber, John Feilder.

The charge being high treason, Alice Lisle had thirty-five peremptory challenges, of which she used nineteen. Some clues as to how she made her choice may be gathered from what is known of the individuals concerned.

The main distinguishing feature of those she accepted appears to have been their lack of political involvement. Of Gifford and Webber, little is known. Whistler was sheriff in 1682. Dawley, Morley, Paulet, Crop and Suatt had become freemen of the city in years gone by.[3]

Dawley owned Lainston manor near Sparsholt, but was probably better known to Alice Lisle as MP in 1680 and 1681 for Lymington, the coastal town about 14 miles from Moyles Court. After the 1688 Revolution, Morley was a member of the Convention Parliament. Crop was city chamberlain in 1668, and later served three terms as mayor. Suatt was a freeman in 1677, and two years later was elected a member of 'the twenty-four', the body of senior citizens who formed the mayor's inner council. He was chamberlain in 1683, and in May 1685 acquired a house and garden in the part of the High Street known as the Pentice. There are contemporary Quaker records of a family of Caigers at Froyle, three of whom were called John, and of a John Feilder who lived at Alton. If they were on Mill's panel, their faith would have commended them to Alice Lisle as sympathetic jurors.

More is known about Paulet. He was the Honourable Francis Paulet of Amport, a village 5 miles east of Andover and close to Thruxton in north-west Hampshire. Alice Lisle almost certainly knew him: his mother, Lucy, was the daughter of Sir George Philpot, whose family owned land at Thruxton. In late medieval times the manor of Thruxton had come to a collateral branch of the Lisles by marriage, and the two families would have been close neighbours over a long period.

Broughton lies 10 miles south of Thruxton, and Thomas Dowse, as lord of the manor, would certainly have qualified for the panel. He was Alice Lisle's neighbour, and during pre-Commonwealth days had owned the manor of Bramshaw, also some 10 miles from Moyles Court.

By contrast, the nineteen she rejected contained a fair proportion of extremely active local figures. Most were freemen and members of the twenty-four, and a number had served as mayor. In 1676, Penton, Taylor and Wavell became trustees of the castle and were serving aldermen in 1685. In 1682, Taylor, Wavell and Yalden led the opposition in blocking the efforts of the then mayor, Thomas Coward, to co-opt the king's nominee, Edward Harfell, to the corporation. The son of a former chapter clerk, Harfell was a lawyer who practised in the Cheyney Court in Winchester. His first wife, Abigail, and their only son died a few days after Alice Lisle's trial was over, and on 1 March 1686, he married Alice's youngest daughter, Anne.

Wavell was aged 52 at the time of the trial, a linen draper and a direct ancestor of the Second World War field-marshal of the same name. His family has been connected with the city and Winchester College since the fifteenth century. He lived in the parish of St Lawrence in the middle of Winchester, was city chamberlain in 1663 and mayor in 1671 and 1679.

So far as one can judge, Alice Lisle seems to have made her choice on the basis of friendship, lack of political involvement and religious affinity, and rejected any whose affiliations were plainly royalist or who might see such a reputation as a help to their careers. The failure of the rebellion was still vivid in the public mind, and although Hampshire was only marginally involved, few would wish to be too closely identified with the losing side. It would need integrity and independence of mind to make a fair assessment of a case carrying political and religious overtones. In view of what happened, Alice Lisle's choice seems to have been percipient and wise.[4]

When they had been sworn, Swanton 'gave the prisoner in charge to the jury', telling the latter briefly of the charge the accused faced, and of their duty to decide the question of guilt, a procedure largely similar to today's. He concluded:

> If you find her guilty, you are to enquire what goods or chattels, lands or tenements she had at the time of the high-treason committed, or at any time since: If you find her not guilty, you are to enquire whether she did fly for it; if you find that she did fly for it, you are to enquire what goods or chattels she had at the time of the flight, as if you had found her guilty. If you find her not

guilty, nor that she did fly for it, you are to say so, and no more, and hear your evidence.

With the abolition of forfeiture of goods for felony in 1870, this part of the charge to the jury became obsolete and was withdrawn. Before 1870, however, the jury's obligation to investigate not merely guilt on the main charge but also the extent of the prisoner's assets and the question of his 'flight' gave the Crown a double chance of winning. Lord Mansfield summarised the law of flight in the trial of John Wilkes in 1770: 'Flight in criminal cases is itself a crime. If an innocent man flies for treason or felony, he forfeits all his goods and chattels.' While an acquittal of having fled was necessarily an end of the matter, a conviction on either that or the main charge put the whole of the individual's estate at risk.

With the formal process of arraignment complete, the prosecution opened its case. This consisted of a simplified explanation to the jury of the indictment, followed by an outline of the evidence. The first stage fell to Mr James Munday, junior counsel for the prosecution, who summarised the indictment. The outline of the evidence the Crown proposed to call was given by Serjeant Henry Pollexfen, the leader for the prosecution. In any criminal trial, this is an important stage, not merely because it gives the defence their first indication of how the prosecution intend to play their hand, but also because it becomes a yardstick by which the strength of evidence can be measured. Every experienced prosecutor knows his review will be scrutinised as much for what it includes as for what it omits; and he also knows the hostages to fortune given by 'opening too high' or 'too low', for the wider the gap between what he asserts his witnesses will say and what they actually say, the greater the scope for the defence to criticise his case as lacking credibility and to suggest that the witnesses lied either when giving their accounts before the trial or when on oath in the witness box.

The task was left to Pollexfen, who was ultimately responsible for the prosecution, and the detail of his speech is worth bearing in mind in relation to what his witnesses said. He addressed the jury as follows:

May it please your lordship and you gentlemen of the jury, I am of counsel in this case for the King. The prisoner . . . Alice Lisle, is the widow of one Lisle, who was in his life time sufficiently known: The person mentioned in the indictment to be entertained and concealed by her, John Hicks, is a conventicle preacher, and one, that for bringing the traitorous purposes intended in this late horrid rebellion to effect, was one of the greatest and most active instruments; for he was personally in this rebellion, and did persuade and exhort some loyal persons, that happened to have the misfortune of being taken prisoners by that rebellious crew, to quit their duty and allegiance to the King, their sovereign lord, and become partakers with them and the rest of his traitorous accomplices, in taking arms . . . This, my lord, we shall prove to you by plain, evident and undeniable testimony of those very persons whom this seducer thus applied himself to. Gentlemen, after it pleased God, by his blessing on the victorious arms of the King, that the rebels were defeated, their pretended prince and head with some of the chief of his accomplices, were taken prisoners, and that in a place near the house where the prisoner lived, when all the country was full of hurry in pursuit after those wicked rebels, thus, by God's blessing and providence, dissipated, and forced, like vagabonds, to skulk up and down; then does this Hicks, having got from the battle as far as Warminster in the next county, send a messenger, one Dunne, to the Prisoner's house, to desire her and request her, that she would receive and harbour him and his friend (who that was will appear by and by). Mrs Lisle returns an answer by the messenger, that she would receive him, but does withal give particular direction, that the time when they did come should be late in the evening. Accordingly he comes in the beginning of the night, at 10 of the clock, booted and spurred, and brings with him another arch rebel, one Nelthorp, that stands outlawed for a most black and horrid treason. When they came to the prisoner's house, they turn their horses loose, for the danger was so great, and their apprehensions of being taken so urgent upon them to conceal and shift for themselves, that they thought it convenient to let their horses go where they would. When they came there, the messenger, as we shall prove by himself, was conveyed away to a chamber: but Mrs Lisle caused meat and drink to be set before Mr Hicks and Nelthorp, and they supped with her, and afterwards they were lodged by her particular order and direction. The next morning colonel Penruddock, who had some intimation, in his search after the rebels, that some persons lay concealed in Mrs. Lisle's house, comes thither, and tells her, after he had beset the house, 'Madam, you have rebels in your house, I come to seize them, pray deliver them up'. She denied that she had any in her house; but upon search Hicks, and Nelthorp, and, that other fellow, the messenger, were all found there, and she thereupon secured with them.

Pollexfen's case against Hicks was firm and direct, and he put it in two ways: Hicks was 'personally in this rebellion', and he 'did persuade and exhort some loyal persons to quit their allegiance'. With neither fugitive present at court, the evidence against them was in every sense 'undeniable'. Pollexfen could safely paint Hicks as 'one of the greatest and most active instruments' in the rebellion, and Nelthorp as 'another arch rebel', without fear of contradiction. But his case against Alice Lisle was mainly circumstantial. Monmouth's and Grey's capture at Ringwood, barely 3 miles from her home, and the hue and cry in pursuit of the defeated army, were matters of general report of which she could hardly claim ignorance, and they should have alerted her against befriending destitute vagabonds. Despite that, however, she agreed to shelter two such individuals – one of whom, had she known his name, she should instantly have recognised as a traitor and outlaw – and told them to come under cover of darkness. She fed them, though not, apparently, the messenger, and lodged them overnight. When challenged the next morning, she denied she had any rebels in the house. Yet there they were, in hiding, along with the messenger.

Forcefully put, the charge certainly called for an answer. But proof depended principally on 'a very unwilling witness', and Alice Lisle's defence had yet to be heard. What Pollexfen may not have realised, however, was the help he would get from the bench in building his case, and for the most part on information not available to him.

EIGHT

Opening of the Prosecution

Pollexfen concluded with an indication of how he would develop his case. 'The method wherein we shall give our evidence, will be this; we shall first begin with this piece of evidence, that we shall prove, that Hicks was actually in the army, and in the rebellion; and then we shall prove the several subsequent facts as have been opened. We desire Mr Pope, Mr Fitzherbert and Mr Taylor may be sworn.'

But he was interrupted by Alice Lisle. As frequently happens in criminal trials, this is the point at which the unrepresented defendant feels the tide at its height against him, and is driven to protest.

> Lisle: My lord, as for what is said concerning the rebellion, I can assure you, I abhorred that rebellion as much as any woman in the world –
>
> LCJ (Lord Jeffreys): Look you, Mrs Lisle, because we must observe the common and usual methods of trial in your case, as well as others, I must interrupt you now.

Jeffreys then outlined the trial procedure, emphasising that Alice Lisle would be able to make her defence once the prosecution case was concluded. His suggestion that he was doing this because she might be 'ignorant of the forms of law' appears almost patronising given she was the widow of a lawyer and judge under Cromwell. High-mindedly proclaiming his accountability as much to the monarch as to 'the great judge of heaven and earth', Jeffreys was anticipating the Anglican–Nonconformist conflict he knew would overshadow the trial, and was obliquely telling the jury to put aside their religious loyalties.

The evidence opened with three witnesses against Hicks, prisoners-of-war captured in the early stages of the rebellion.

Monmouth seems to have kept prisoners to a minimum, presumably on economic as well as political grounds: they had to be guarded and fed, and the popularity of the rising would suffer if he were seen to be taking too many. When he reached Keynsham, he requisitioned Sir Thomas Bridges' home, Keynsham House, as a temporary headquarters and put his prisoners in the stables there.

A descendant of the Chandos family and a devoted royalist, Bridges was unscrupulous and unpopular. As governor of Bath during the Civil War, he and his deputy, Henry Chapman, had required heavy financial sacrifices of the inhabitants, only to surrender their city virtually without a fight to Fairfax in July 1645. In August the following year the corporation sued Bridges for the recovery of a 'forced loan' of £100, and he had to pay heavily to retrieve his confiscated estates from the Parliamentarians. In the post-Restoration elections of 1661, he and Chapman dishonestly and unsuccessfully tried to eject Bath's two properly elected Members of Parliament in favour of themselves; later in the year they also tried, equally unsuccessfully, to take over the corporation by having nine of its members arrested just before the municipal elections. Bridges' forebears had built Keynsham House from the ruins of Keynsham Abbey after the dissolution of the monasteries, and he lived there until his death in 1706, aged 90.

The ex-prisoners described what had happened in the Keynsham House stables when Hicks and Monmouth's domestic chaplain, Nathaniel Hook, approached them and tried to win them over to the rebel cause.

Mr Pollexfen: Swear Mr Pope, Mr Fitzherbert and Mr Taylor. (Which was done).

LCJ: Who did you begin with?

Mr Pollexfen: Mr Pope, pray will you tell my lord and the jury, what you know concerning this Hicks? Pray tell your whole knowledge.

Pope outlined his capture while 'going about some business of my own'; and some days later, when the rebel army reached Keynsham, he found himself in Sir Thomas Bridges' stables. Hicks and Hook visited him and appeared solicitous for his welfare. They said they would 'speak to the King (meaning, as I suppose, the late Duke of Monmouth) who is a good king and a Protestant; and a great deal to that purpose, with some reflecting words on the government, and upon the person of the king; and he wondered what we had to say for ourselves, being Protestants, that we did in serving a Popish prince, and not obeying a Protestant one'.

About two weeks after Sedgemoor, one of Monmouth's battalion commanders, Nathaniel Wade, was captured. In return for his life he agreed to dictate a detailed account of the whole expedition, from its planning stage in Holland until his capture. It took him a fortnight, more than a month after Alice Lisle's trial was over, to complete what became known as his Narrative.

In the course of the account, he twice mentions the taking of prisoners by the rebels. The first capture was made four days after the landing at Lyme, while preparing to attack Bridport: 'We marched all night in great secrecy and by the way met with information that the forces in the town were 1200 foot and 100 horse strong at the least . . . We carried the person prisoner that gave us the account.'

The fight at Bridport had taken place on 14 June, and it was not until Tuesday 23rd that the rebels reached Shepton Mallett, where Hicks joined them the following day. Two days later they were at Keynsham, preparing to attack Bristol, where they took one prisoner before repairing Keynsham bridge; they captured another three during inconclusive skirmishing on the retreat to Sir Thomas Bridges' house nearby. According to Wade, it was the information obtained from these three, putting the king's forces at some 4,000, that decided Monmouth against attacking Bristol. Fitzherbert did not say how he was captured, but Taylor's reference to Hicks 'wondering . . . that they should take up arms' suggests they were both soldiers, and were probably two of those taken in the vicinity of Keynsham.

Pope's evidence that the prisoners 'were about four or five in number' thus coincides with Wade's estimate of the total taken by the time they got to Keynsham. Having at that stage 'been taken some days', Pope was almost certainly the non-combatant captured just before Bridport. To have told the court the reason given by

Wade for taking him prisoner, which virtually amounted to spying, would doubtless have invited fearsome judicial wrath, if not also prosecution; and therefore simply 'going about business of my own' enabled him to underline his loyalty as well as the apparent injustice of his capture.

In reply to Jeffreys, Pope confirmed that the man he had seen in Keynsham was the same individual that he had seen at the George in Salisbury the day before the trial had started, 'that goes by the name of Hicks', and added that Hicks had at first been reluctant to concede they had met previously.

Hicks was in Fisherton prison, the Wiltshire county gaol near the street that bears its name today, and within walking distance of the George Inn, built some three and a half centuries earlier, in the reign of Edward II, on the east side of the High Street leading to the Cathedral Close. As a hostelry, it was well known, and maintained a high standard of comfort for those who could afford it. Though much to his taste, Samuel Pepys found it distinctly overpriced on his visit in June 1668:

> 10th – come to the George . . . where lay in a silk bed, and a very good diet . . . 11th – Up and down the town, and find it a very brave place . . . to Stonehenge . . . and so home to dinner, and that being done, paid the reckoning; which was so exorbitant . . . that I was mad, and resolve to trouble the mistress about it and get something for the poor.[1]

Pope concluded with the comment that he did not remember having seen Hicks armed. The next witness, Fitzherbert, recalled that 'at Keynsham, on 25th June, I saw this man, John Hicks, who held a discourse with Mr Pope near an hour's time, disparaging the government and his majesty, and extolling the duke of Monmouth, what a brave prince, and how good a Protestant he was . . . and I saw him yesterday at Salisbury'. Taylor likewise confirmed Hicks's assertions at Keynsham 'that he wondered at us that we should take up arms against so good a prince and Protestant as the duke of Monmouth, and hold up with Popery; Saith he, York is but a papist; and a great many such words'. He also confirmed he had seen Hicks at Salisbury the previous day.

As witnesses of Hicks's and Hook's rebel sentiments, and of their efforts to dissuade the prisoners from their loyalty, these three ex-prisoners were specific and direct,[2] though they were less willing to be drawn on the question of Hicks's status as a combatant. Pope had only seen him in the army a day or two before the battle, when he was unarmed.

Whether it was fair to convict Hicks 'behind his back' will be considered later. For the purposes of Alice Lisle's trial, however, this evidence of Hicks's treason was regarded as sufficient.[3]

Pollexfen then moved on to the main part of his case, and stressed the significance of the sequence of events:

Mr Pollexfen: Next, my lord, we come to prove the message and correspondence between this same Hicks, and the prisoner Mrs Lisle.

Mr Jennings: Swear Mr James Dunne. (Which was done).

Mr Pollexfen: If your lordship please to observe, the times will fall out to be very material in this case: the battle at King's-Edgemore was the 6th July; three or four days after was the taking of Monmouth, and my lord Grey at Ringwood; upon the 26th July, ten or twelve days after the taking of Monmouth, was this message sent by Dunne to Mrs Lisle; so we call Dunne to prove what message he carried upon the 26th, and what answer was returned; he will tell you, that Tuesday was the time appointed for them to come, in the night, and all the other circumstances.

This outline was marginally inaccurate. Grey was captured on 7 July, and Monmouth the following day; and Dunne's first visit to Moyles Court took place on Saturday, 25 July.

Pollexfen then turned to the issue at the root of the case, and which would dictate the whole course of its development. 'But withall, I must acquaint your lordship, that this fellow, Dunne, is a very unwilling witness; and therefore, with submission to your lordship, we do humbly desire your lordship would please to examine him a little the more strictly.'

This introduction of the principal witness suggests he had been given no clear promise of immunity or merciful treatment in return for testifying, and the invitation to Jeffreys to examine him probably carried the veiled warning to Dunne that his salvation would depend on his performance.

From the prosecution's viewpoint, the case against Alice Lisle was far from straightforward. It had to allege and prove at least one 'overt act' of treason, that is, some clear instance of rebellious behaviour, which by statute had to be corroborated: a single witness to it was not enough. That standard of proof had to be satisfied against two defendants, one of whom was not before the court. So far as the absentee, Hicks, was concerned, this was quite simple, for there was nothing to contradict what the three ex-prisoners had said about his assertions at Keynsham. But against Alice Lisle, their testimony was irrelevant – and would today be treated as hearsay and inadmissible – on the question of what she knew about him. Alice Lisle wisely and properly refrained from challenging it. That the jury, to its credit, disregarded it is clear from the foreman's request for guidance towards the end of the trial: 'My lord . . . we have some doubt upon us, whether there be sufficient proof that she knew Hicks to have been in the army.'

Under the procedural rules of the day, Hicks, although not convicted, was disqualified as a Crown witness: first, since he was to be charged, he could not be put on oath to testify, which was obligatory for prosecution witnesses; and second, he had an obvious interest in the outcome. On any view, he was far too big a fish to be allowed to escape, and there was considerable risk he would hinder rather than help the Crown's case. Dunne was therefore indispensable, for without him there would hardly have been a case for Alice Lisle to answer. He had set up the arrangement with her, had brought Hicks and Nelthorp to her house, and eventually admitted he had heard her conversation with them. That was the only direct testimony as to what she must have known about their involvement in the rebellion; and it is an open question whether the Crown ever satisfied the legal requirement of a second witness to her 'overt act' of knowingly harbouring a rebel. Whatever the implications of Dunne's conduct in guiding the fugitives in return for their promised reward, the Crown could not charge him if they wanted him as a witness; and in any case he was adamant, for what it was worth, that he never gave them shelter in his house as Alice Lisle did in hers.

The tenacity with which he held to this assertion seems to demonstrate not merely his self-deluding belief that it made all the difference between his own guilt and innocence, but also its falsity. Lurking in the early part of his account is the 'short black man . . . that came to my house and desired me to go of a message to my Lady Lisle's for one Mr Hicks'. Jeffreys' later comments show that he took the point, even though he may not have appreciated it initially; and he probably realised that to expose the messenger's phantom existence from the outset would risk a point-blank refusal by Dunne to testify at all.

Dunne made it clear that the 'short black man' was not Nelthorp. He is unnamed and otherwise unidentified and, according to Dunne, is last seen when he and the two fugitives begin the final journey to Moyles Court. His function was simply to conceal the fact that the two rebels had spent ten days at Dunne's house before they set out for Moyles Court. His eventual exposure as a mythical figure was to prove a useful pressure-point on Dunne.

Letting Dunne keep to his assertion during the early stages was probably convenient for the Crown and linked to the decision over how Hicks should be dealt with. He, Dunne and Alice Lisle had all been imprisoned at Salisbury during the month between their arrest and Alice's trial on Thursday, 27 August. She and Dunne were brought to Winchester the previous evening: and earlier that day, the Wednesday, the three witnesses to Hicks's treasonable attitudes were taken to Salisbury to see him, to be certain of his identity when they gave evidence. At first sight it seems odd, both on the grounds of convenience and in the interests of justice, that Hicks was not tried at Winchester as well, either before Alice Lisle or on a joint indictment with her. All the witnesses against him were there; and his prior conviction as a traitor would have made the Crown's position far more secure. Yet he did not stand trial until three weeks later at Wells, where he pleaded guilty. Why?

The Crown would probably have argued the procedural point that since Hicks's offence had occurred in Somerset, that was the appropriate venue for his trial – although it was not an inflexible rule in cases of treason that offenders should be tried in the place of their offence. Whatever the legal position, Hicks's absence from court at Winchester in fact amounted to a substantial tactical safeguard in the Crown's favour. As the advocate who had prevailed on Charles II to grant the 1672 Indulgence, there was no knowing what effect he might have on a jury. There were three main considerations. First, had he been charged at Winchester and pleaded not guilty, and made a determined challenge to the evidence about his assertions at Keynsham, he might conceivably have been acquitted, which would necessarily have meant the end of any case against Alice Lisle. Second, he was a devout Nonconformist, a 'fanatic' in contemporary parlance. With an overwhelming case against him, there was a fear he might do his utmost to bolster the defence of a friend and fellow Nonconformist, and claim that she knew him only as a preacher and not as a rebel, regardless of any consequences for himself. Third, there was the risk that he would explode the myth of the 'short black' emissary between himself and his guide. Such a denial would have devalued the credibility of the recalcitrant Dunne still further, and a jury might hesitate before convicting one harbourer of rebels on the evidence of another who was both corrupt and going unpunished.

The deal with Dunne was probably that he could have his life and whatever advantage he thought might accrue from trying to distance himself from the fugitives, provided he gave evidence against Alice Lisle and told sufficient of the truth to convict her. Otherwise, he would be charged with treason as well. Though also a Nonconformist, martyrdom was not one of his aspirations. When it was put to him, he was probably quite sincere in denying the suggestion that he was lying to protect her. Much more compelling was the threat of the hangman's noose around his own neck, and the need to convince the court that, whatever she might have done, he had not harboured anybody.

NINE

The Evidence: Dunne Visits Moyles Court

Pollexfen's introduction was primarily for the jury's benefit. Jeffreys was probably already aware of Dunne's uncomfortable position and of the need to turn both it and the information he had obtained from Nelthorp to maximum advantage. He took the reins from Pollexfen without more ado.

> LCJ: You say well: Hark you, friend, I would take notice of something to you by the way, and you would do well to mind what I say to you. According as the counsel that are here for the King seem to insinuate, you were employed as a messenger between these persons, one whereof has already been proved a notorious rebel, and the other is the prisoner at the bar, and your errand was to procure a reception at her house for him.
> Dunne: My lord, I did so.

Put in this way, Jeffreys had glossed over a small but important gap in the prosecution's chain of proof. Dunne's errand was, as he agreed, to 'procure a reception' with Alice Lisle for someone, but there was no evidence as yet to show it was the person who 'had already been proved a notorious rebel' by the first three witnesses, nor was Dunne in any position to confirm it: he had not attended the identification session in Salisbury the previous day, and Hicks was not in court.

Jeffreys continued with a stern warning, designed to intimidate a Nonconformist conscience, of the temporal and spiritual penalties any departure from the truth would involve.

> LCJ: Now mark what I say to you . . . Consider that the Great God of Heaven and Earth . . . will call thee to an account for the rescinding his truth . . . and make thee drop into the

bottomless lake of fire and brimstone, if thou offer to deviate the least from the truth, and nothing but the truth . . . Now . . . tell us, how you came to be employed upon such a message, what your errand was, and what was the issue and result of it?

Despite this admonition, Dunne launched straight into his account of the arrival of the mythical 'short, black' messenger at his house on 'a' Friday evening. Deliberately vague about the date, he had to conceal the fact that he had sheltered Hicks and Nelthorp in his house for about a week, thus committing treason himself, before arranging to take them to Moyles Court. He implied he made the journey to Moyles Court, to see if Alice Lisle was prepared to put Hicks up, the day after the messenger had first appeared.

Barter later contradicted this statement, saying that, on 25 July, Dunne had told him he had concealed two men he 'took to be rebels' in his house ten days before, adding that he 'did keep them in a chamber all day, and they walked out at night, for the searches of the houses was usually at night'. Dunne's own claim that he 'never knew any of their names' was also highly improbable: he could hardly have entertained them at his home for a week without knowing them by some name or other.

The cracks were already there, because Dunne had just committed himself on three important points: that his initial dealings with 'one Mr Hicks' had been conducted through a messenger; that the messenger had mentioned Hicks to him by name; and that he was to find out from Alice Lisle whether she would entertain Hicks.

But when Jeffreys went on to ask him about his arrangement with Alice Lisle, it became apparent that Hicks was not the only person who wanted accommodation. When the bailiff, William Carpenter, took him in to see her, Dunne at first said she told him she might be prepared to entertain Hicks; but he added he had later informed the messenger of her willingness to entertain 'them'. Instantly alert to this discrepancy, Jeffreys pressed Dunne to explain. All he could say was that it was Alice Lisle who had increased her invitation from one guest to two.

The reason for this damaging assertion was Dunne's wish to conceal his letter of introduction from Hicks to Alice Lisle; and he was probably trying more to protect than to implicate her. But the complications of the task were beyond his simple mind. As a stranger, there would have been no reason for her to see him or to trust a word he said unless he had something by way of a credential. But either because he did not know whether the document had been found or, if it had, because he was afraid of being asked about its contents, he felt it safer to avoid mentioning it at all.

When Barter, Dunne's guide across Salisbury Plain to Moyles Court, came to give evidence, he said he saw Dunne produce a letter to Carpenter. According to Barter, Carpenter refused to have anything to do with it, and Barter said he presumed Dunne had then handed it to Alice Lisle. But Dunne, Alice Lisle and Carpenter all denied the very existence of any letter, from which it would follow that the only information about the expected guests came from Dunne.

It was Dunne's failure to appreciate this last point that tripped him up. Having started by denying all knowledge of a possible second guest, he should have kept to that. Or he could have said he was acting from the outset for two people, one of whose names he did not know; and this was what Carpenter, presumably in an attempt to repair the damage, later testified. Or, if Dunne had been prepared to admit to bringing the letter, he could have said what was almost certainly the truth: that Alice Lisle learned about the second guest only when she read the letter.

Jeffreys was unable to get to the bottom of this because so far there had been no mention of a letter, and Barter had yet to give evidence. In the event, Barter's reference to the letter was subsequently contradicted by Carpenter, after which the point was dropped. For the moment, however, Jeffreys clearly appreciated the implications of Dunne's account, because he was about to repeat what he had said back to him.

LCJ: Prithee, friend, mind what thou has said, and recollect thyself, I will repeat it to thee, because thou shalt see that I remember it all very well. It seems that a man, a short black man, came to your house in Warminster parish to get you to go for a message to Mrs Lisle's, to know whether she would entertain one Hicks; and that you went upon the Saturday, and first you met with Carpenter and asked him that question, whether his lady would entertain one Mr Hicks? and he told you he would have nothing to do with it; and thereupon you went to Mrs Lisle, and asked her the question, and she told you that you should tell the man that they should come the Tuesday following, and come in the evening and she would entertain him: Is not this what you have said?

Dunne: Yes, my lord, it is.

LCJ: Well then, now let us know what other discourse you had with her.

Dunne: My lord, I do not remember anything more.

Dunne was probably thinking that perhaps it had not been such a good idea not to have mentioned the letter, because in the absence of a letter he would have explained everything by word of mouth. As counsel picked up on the point, Dunne took refuge in ignorance and a bad memory.

Mr Pollexfen: Pray, Mr Dunne, did she ask you any questions, whether you knew Mr Hicks or no?

Dunne: Nothing at all of that, that I remember.

Mr Coriton: Did she believe that you knew Mr Hicks?

Dunne: I cannot tell, my lord.

Mr Coriton: Do you believe that she knew him before?

Dunne: I cannot tell truly.

LCJ: Why, dost thou think she would entertain anyone that she had no knowledge of merely upon thy message? Mr Dunne, Mr Dunne! have a care, it may be more is known of this matter than you think for.

Dunne: My lord, I tell you the truth.

LCJ: Ay, be sure you do, do not let me take you prevaricating!

Dunne: My lord, I speak nothing but the truth.

LCJ: Well, I only bid you have a care, truth never wants a subterfuge, it always loves to appear naked, it needs no enamel, nor any covering; but lying and snivelling, and canting and Hicksing, always appear in masquerade. Come, go on with your evidence.

In the sense that Jeffreys used it, the word 'hick' has now disappeared from the English language. In the seventeenth century, to 'hick' meant to hiccough, but its secondary meaning was to hesitate or falter in speech. Jeffreys was unable to resist the pun, as the reporter clearly recognised.

The cross-examination continued:

Dunne: My lord, I say I went back again and returned my answer to the same man that brought the message to me.

LCJ: Pray, let me ask you one question; were you got to your house before you found him, or was he waiting there for you?

Dunne: He came to my house after I came home.

LCJ: It was the same man, you say?

Dunne: Yes, it was.

LCJ: Had he no company with him neither time?

Dunne: No.

LCJ: Well, and what answer did you return him?

Dunne: I told him, my lady said she would entertain Mr Hicks: he asked when he might come up; I told him upon Tuesday and upon Tuesday they came to my house.

LCJ: What time did they come to your house?

Dunne: About seven of the clock in the morning.

LCJ: What day of the month was it?

Dunne: Truly, my lord, I cannot readily tell what day of the month it was.

LCJ: Was it one or two that came to thy house?

Dunne: My lord, there were three in all.

LCJ: Who were those three, prithee?

Dunne: My lord, there was the little black man, that brought the message, and two other people.

LCJ: Prithee, describe what two other people these were.

Dunne: One was a full fat black man, and the other was a thin black man.

LCJ: Who was that thin black man?

Dunne: My lord, I did not know him.

LCJ: Did you not fancy which was Hicks?

Dunne: My lord, I never knew any of their names.

Dunne realised that, if he admitted to knowing one of his companions' names, he could hardly deny he must also have known the others'. But because of Nelthorp's previous outlawry (and for another, and potentially much more incriminating, reason no one else yet knew about) the one thing he could never admit to was knowing who Nelthorp was. It could hardly have been a more precarious refuge, for apart from its sheer improbability the messenger, so he said, had come on behalf of 'one Mr Hicks'. Dunne had then discussed Hicks by name with Alice Lisle, and had returned with a message to pass back to him. He could hardly have set out for Moyles Court the second time without making sure he had the right man.

Jeffreys pursued Dunne about his companions' names later, but there were probably two reasons why he held back at this stage. First, the ignorance Dunne was affecting was so transparently false as to make it unnecessary; and second, there was more to be had from the witness on the point, which could only be extracted by degrees. Jeffreys therefore left things where they were for the moment, aware, as Dunne himself was almost certainly unaware, that he had him on the edge of a quicksand.

TEN

The Travellers Arrive at Moyles Court

Jeffreys was about to get Dunne to trace their route to Moyles
Court to probe what looked like another weak point in his
story: why had he sent word to Hicks to join him at seven in the
morning, if they were not due at Alice Lisle's until late in the
evening? Fourteen hours to cover 26 miles on horseback was very
slow going. Even if they had left later and it had taken only ten
hours, as Dunne was about to suggest, they had travelled at barely
walking pace.

But there were gaps in Jeffreys' knowledge that had to be filled.
He had assumed that Dunne had spent the Saturday night at
Moyles Court, and he was also unaware that Dunne did not know
his way across Salisbury Plain (the area now known as Cranborne
Chase) and that he had had to find a guide when he got to Broad
Chalke, then known simply as Chalke. There Dunne met John
Barter, who showed him the way and agreed to do so again when
he came the second time. Jeffreys also had mistakenly identified
Barter as the 'messenger' who first made contact with Dunne on
behalf of Hicks.

His error was understandable. Pollexfen had not mentioned
Barter in opening and Dunne had not yet been asked to explain his
role. It is also unlikely that Nelthorp would have told Jeffreys much
about Barter beforehand: he had met him only on the second
journey, and to have passed on Dunne's account of his first
encounter with him would have been extremely damaging to Alice
Lisle. The point had to be clarified.

LCJ: How long did they stay at your house?
Dunne: About three hours.
LCJ: When did you go away from thence?
Dunne: About eleven of the clock.

LCJ: Which way did you go then?

Dunne: We went through Deverel, and from Deverel to Chilmark, and from Chilmark to Sutton, and from Sutton to the Plain, and then one Barter met me; I knew the way no further, and he was to show me the way from thence.

LCJ: Prithee hold, before thou goest any further, I desire to be satisfied about a question or two: dost thou say thou didst not know the way?

Dunne: No, my lord, after I came to the Plain.

LCJ: How didst thou find the way when thou wentest on thy message first?

Dunne: My lord, after I came to Salisbury Plain, I met with one Barter, and he showed me the way.

LCJ: Where is that Barter?

Mr Pollexfen: My lord, we have him here; we shall examine him by and by, there he stands.

LCJ: Sure that was not the little man thou spokest of. (Being a very lusty man)

Dunne: No, my lord.

LCJ: Prithee let me understand thee then, if I can. Thou didst say at first there was only a little man with a black beard, that was concerned with thee about that message; now thou talkest of some guide that thou hadst, prithee who did guide thee, let us know?

Dunne: My lord, I say I went so far as Fovant, and so to Chalke, but when I came upon the Plain, I did not know my way . . . at last I spoke to one John Barter to go with me to my Lady Lisle's, and he and I did agree to go together, and he showed me the way and carried me to the house.

LCJ: Thou shouldst have told us this before, man, that we might have understood it. Where did you lie upon the Saturday night?

Dunne: At Fovant.

LCJ: I thought you had said, you had come to Mrs Lisle's on Saturday?

Dunne: Yes, my lord, I did so, and came back to Fovant that night.

LCJ: And where did you lie on Sunday night?

Dunne: I lay at my own house on Sunday night.

LCJ: And Barter came along with you when you came on Tuesday?

Dunne: Yes, my lord.

LCJ: And did you go the same way upon the Tuesday that you went upon the Saturday?

Dunne: Do you mean, my lord, the same way I came at first?

LCJ: Ay.

Dunne: No, my lord, we came to Sutton, not to Fovant.

LCJ: Why did you not go the same way upon the Tuesday that you went upon the Saturday?

Dunne: Because I had appointed to meet him at such a place.

Dunne's account of the timing, and of their reasons for following the routes they did, discloses the same muddled attempt to conceal incriminating facts as his efforts over the letter. His last answer, that they went via Sutton Mandeville, west of Fovant, on the Tuesday because he had arranged to meet Barter there, was a lie; the truth was they went that way to avoid meeting Barter. Colonel Thomas Penruddock would later say how Barter came to his house at Compton Park on the Monday, to tell him of his arrangement to meet Dunne close by on the Plain north-east of Fovant, towards Compton Chamberlayne, between nine and eleven the next morning. To keep that appointment, the travellers would have had to leave Dunne's house between seven and eight. By delaying their departure until eleven and taking a different route, they made certain they would miss Barter. Why should they want to do that?

The most probable explanation is that, when he got home, Dunne gave Hicks and Nelthorp a full account of his dealings with Barter and Alice Lisle. This alerted them to the possible consequences of his loose talk and, as Barter would later testify, some of it had been very loose indeed. Rightly fearing a leak, they decided to make the journey on Tuesday without Barter; and to avoid him they left late and tried to take a route none of them knew. Instead of going east of Fovant, as arranged with Barter, they went west of it. But the task of finding their way in unfamiliar countryside got them thoroughly lost, and the only thing to do was to try to find Barter to put them back on course. They eventually met him in the early afternoon, and passed through Fovant, according to Dunne, between two and three.

Penruddock later told Jeffreys of their failure to meet Barter as arranged. With his plan for a mid-morning ambush thwarted, Penruddock decided to search Moyles Court early the next day. The three continued their journey with Barter for about 10 miles, but mutual suspicion and mistrust increased as they refused to discuss or divulge their names, and insisted on taking roundabout routes; they eventually parted company at Martin. It was there that Fane took over as guide, probably sheltering them until nightfall, and then saw them to within a mile or two of Moyles Court.

Conscious of the need to explain these time-consuming meanderings and to fit in with whatever Barter might say, Dunne began to flounder, blurting out the first thing that came into his head. Having said he 'left word with the messenger' for Hicks and Nelthorp to join him at seven (the time they would, presumably, have returned anyway from their nightly excursions), he had gone on to claim they did not leave until eleven. Why not? Fortunately for Dunne, Jeffreys was too preoccupied with sorting out Barter and 'the messenger' to put that extremely awkward question, and he forgot about it when Barter and Penruddock outlined the timing of the arrangement.

Dunne continued by saying the reason they made the detour via Sutton Mandeville was that he had arranged to meet Barter there. Not merely was this untrue, but he went on to undermine it by claiming he thought it was the shorter route, as Jeffreys was swift to point out. Later, while Jeffreys was laying the ground for the most incriminating answer of the whole trial, he contradicted this with the truth when he said he had arranged to meet Barter east of Fovant, towards Compton Chamberlayne.

These matters apart, Dunne now sought to put the burden of the decision over their route on the second journey squarely on Hicks's and Nelthorp's shoulders. In doing so, he made clear that the 'small black' messenger did not accompany them. He also said he told Barter when they first met that Hicks was the person he was acting for (which Barter later denied, asserting that he knew neither of Dunne's fellow travellers' names until after their arrest). Jeffreys then pressed Dunne over what each had paid Barter for showing them the way, but his underlying purpose was to see whether Dunne would go any further in admitting knowledge of their identities.

Dunne held to his original theme that he 'never knew any of their names until after they were taken', but his guard slipped slightly in answer to Jeffreys' question:

> LCJ: What name did he go by before he was taken?
> Dunne: Were I to die presently, my lord, I cannot tell it.

Jeffreys simply wanted to establish that Nelthorp had used an alias, and since this was the more probable construction of Dunne's answer, he left the point for the time being. Alice Lisle must have been relieved because she realised it had laid the foundation for something far more damaging – to which Jeffreys would return later, and more insistently, to prevent Dunne slipping the leash. For the moment, however, he concentrated on the final stage of the journey to Moyles Court.

Dunne said they left Fovant in mid-afternoon, reaching Moyles Court after nine in the evening. He added that at Martin, about 8 miles short of the house, Barter was discharged and replaced by Fane. Dunne was the man who contacted Fane, and Jeffreys used the incident to establish Dunne's awareness of Hicks's identity.

> LCJ: Well, what didst thou say to him (Fane)?
> Dunne: I told him I came from one Mr Hicks.
> LCJ: And what didst thou desire of him?
> Dunne: I told him that one Mr Hicks desired to speak with him; and when he came out to Mr Hicks, Mr Hicks did desire him to show him the way to Mrs Lisle's.
> LCJ: Now tell us what kind of man that was, that desired this of Mr Fane?
> Dunne: My lord, it was the full fat black man.
> LCJ: Now we have got him out, now we know which was Hicks: Now go on.
> Dunne: My lord, this man went and rid along with them as far as the new house that is built there, within a mile of that house Fane went along with us; and afterwards, whether Hicks or Nelthorp, or who knew the way, I cannot tell, but to my lady Lisle's we went.
> LCJ: Who directed you the way when Fane left you?

A miniature of Alice Lisle by John Hoskins the elder (d. 1664). *(© copyright National Museum of Sweden, Stockholm)*

The regicide John Lisle, Alice's husband, who fled to Switzerland, where he was assassinated in August 1664. *(© copyright the Trustees of The British Museum)*

Jeffreys as Lord Chancellor in 1686. *(Photograph: Sally Soames, by kind permission of the Masters of the Bench of the Inner Temple)*

Sir Peter Lely's painting of James II, which now hangs in the Royal Hospital, Chelsea. *(Author's collection)*

An etching of E.M. Ward's imaginary depiction of the arrest of Alice Lisle. A similar fresco adorns a lobby wall in the Houses of Parliament. (*Witt Library, Courtauld Institute of Art, London*)

Underground tunnels at Moyles Court that were probably used to smuggle Hicks and Dunne from the house, where Nelthorpe was discovered, to the Great Granary. (*© copyright Richard Dean, headmaster, Moyles Court School*)

Above: The Great Granary (right), where Hicks and Dunne were found, with (left) the chapel where Hicks was a visiting preacher and (centre) Moyles Court. *(From a drawing c. 1813, in* The Gentleman's Magazine, © *copyright The British Library)*

Right: Keynsham Stables, where Hicks tried to persuade Monmouth prisoners to change sides. *(Photograph of Remains of Offices at Keynsham House, 1828, by John Buckler, Pigott Collection of Drawings, by courtesy of the Somerset Archaeological and Natural History Society)*

Moyles Court today. *(Author's collection)*

A drawing of John Hicks, the man Alice Lisle was convicted of harbouring after the Battle of Sedgemoor. The drawing is in Calamy's *Nonconformist Memorial*. (*© copyright the Trustees of The British Museum*)

John Penruddock with his wife Arundel. He was executed after leading the 1655 rebellion against Cromwell. John Lisle was one of the judges at his trial. *(Private collection)*

Thomas Penruddock, Deputy Lieutenant of Wiltshire under Charles II, who arrested the fugitives at Moyles Court. *(Private collection)*

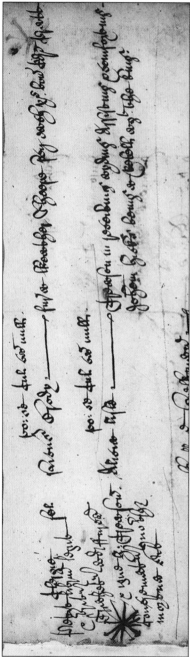

Extract from the Gaol Book of the Western circuit, recording Alice Lisle's conviction and sentence. *(The National Archives, Public Record Office)*

Winchester from the slopes of St Giles's Hill, from a drawing by William Schellinks, mid-seventeenth century. *(Austrian National Library in Vienna)*

Dunne: My lord, I cannot tell; For my part I did not know the way.

LCJ: Who went with you?

Dunne: None but Hicks and Nelthorp.

LCJ: How far from my lady's house was that place where Fane left you?

Dunne: My lord, I cannot directly tell.

LCJ: Then Hicks knew the way, it seems, from thence?

Dunne: So he might, my lord, for aught I know, for I did not.

Jeffreys had started here by pursuing points that had been covered or may have seemed unimportant, or to which truthful replies could do little harm, and then to ask for an explanation that, if it incidentally included the fact he was looking for, Dunne could not then withdraw. It was presumably Nelthorp who had told Jeffreys that Fane had replaced Barter as the guide on the final leg of the journey from Martin. But by expressing surprise when Dunne told him and inviting him to elaborate, Jeffreys got Dunne's confidence and caught him unawares.

Dunne was in the trap before he realised his predicament, and dug himself deeper as he described how Fane greeted 'Mr Hicks' (it was too late to revert to 'the man I discovered to be Mr Hicks after his arrest') and how 'Mr Hicks' asked him to be their guide to Moyles Court. By getting the name, and then making Dunne tie it to the individual described, rather than the other way round, Jeffreys left him no option but to identify Hicks as the man he must already have known him to be. This exposure left Dunne feeling, and no doubt looking, extremely chastened. It prompted Jeffreys' next comment.

LCJ: Thou art strangely stiff; but now we are come thus far with you, tell me what entertainment you had at my lady Lisle's and look to it that you should be sure to tell me truth, for I know it to a tittle, I can assure you that.

Dunne: They went in before me, my lord.

LCJ: Who went in before you?

Dunne: Hicks and Nelthorp.

LCJ: But the door was shut when you came, was it not?

Dunne: My lord, I cannot tell truly.

LCJ: Then tell me what entertainment you had there?

Dunne: For my own part, my lord, I carried a bit of cake and cheese from my own house, and that I eat.

LCJ: What became of your companions Hicks, and Nelthorp, I pray you?

Dunne: I never saw them again till after they were taken.

LCJ: How is that, prithee recollect thyself?

Dunne: Sure, my lord, I did not see them till then.

LCJ: Who came to the door to you?

Dunne: A young girl my lord, I knew not who nor what she was.

LCJ: Did they go directly into the house?

Dunne: It was dark, my lord, I did not see what they did.

LCJ: Was there never a candle there?

Dunne: No, my lord.

LCJ: It was dark, very dark, was it not?

Dunne: Yes, my lord, it was so.

LCJ: Was my lady stirring then?

Dunne: I did not see her.

LCJ: And this is as much as you know of the business?

Dunne: Yes, my lord, this is all that I remember.

LCJ: Well; and what hadst thou for all thy pains?

Dunne: Nothing but a month's imprisonment, my lord.

Cautious and wary, Dunne had clearly decided that tight-lipped ignorance was the safest course for the moment. The less he knew about Alice Lisle's dealings with her guests, the better for all concerned. If he had only had the intelligence and courage to keep to that, he would have saved himself and her a great deal of trouble.

ELEVEN

Dunne's Overnight 'Isolation'

For Jeffreys, these questions were a preliminary skirmish over a crucial issue on which the prosecution could stand or fall: what had happened when the party arrived at Moyles Court. Thus far, the Crown's position was not promising. Proof that Alice Lisle had sheltered those she knew to be rebels depended almost wholly on suspicion – the night-time arrival, the release of the horses, and her supper with two of the guests – and it stopped there. Dunne had obviously lied about one or two earlier matters, but mainly to protect himself; and, according to Pollexfen's opening, he had been 'conveyed away to a chamber' on his own at this point, so could add nothing. The other point on which Pollexfen had laid such emphasis, the discovery of rebels in the house after Alice Lisle's specific denial to Penruddock that any were there, now looked as if it might backfire. Hicks, according to Pollexfen, was a 'conventicle preacher', so why should Alice Lisle betray a fellow Dissenter if she had no reason to suspect him of anything worse? What was lacking was clear evidence to contradict this, and the gap it left was by no means small. The offence of treason required at least two witnesses to support a conviction; and if Dunne refused to incriminate her, as he showed every sign of doing, the chances of an acquittal were considerable. With nothing else to go on, the jury might easily forgive an act of charity towards someone Alice Lisle knew only as a persecuted preacher and his friends.

Despite what the prosecution were saying, however, Dunne had not spent the night on his own. As he was eventually to admit, he had remained 'above stairs' throughout. Jeffreys' cross-examination from now on demonstrates he was aware of this; and, since Pollexfen had asserted the opposite, Jeffreys' knowledge can only have come from Nelthorp. Jeffreys realised this point contained the key to saving the prosecution, despite Nelthorp's anxiety to protect Alice Lisle.

As a lawyer, Nelthorp would have seen that telling Jeffreys the truth, that they had all dined together, could do Alice Lisle little harm. Having arrived as a group of travellers, and with nothing to hide, it was natural they should remain as a group. On that basis, Nelthorp reasoned, both Alice Lisle and Dunne would be able to say how innocuous their conversation had been. Things only began to look suspicious if Alice Lisle had felt obliged to exclude Dunne from the supper table. But the frightened and dim-witted Dunne could not see it like that. His first concern was his own survival, and he preferred to deny having heard any conversation rather than risk questioning on whether it was incriminating. He took refuge in another fabrication, no doubt imagining it as safe as the mythical messenger between himself and Hicks. He said he had stayed 'below stairs', hearing nothing.

With neither Nelthorp nor Hicks there to contradict him, Dunne could be forgiven for thinking he could ride through unscathed. But he had reckoned without Jeffreys' forensic determination. Jeffreys decided he would have to try to 'break' Dunne as a witness purely by cross-examination. On Dunne's performance so far, little ingenuity was required to expose him as a liar; the problem was to get him to admit the fact and tell the jury what he was holding back. It was an ambitious target, and Jeffreys could hardly have foreseen the path he would have to follow. For the moment, he simply changed gear, and began by expressing incredulity at Dunne's account, which had become progressively less convincing. Dunne began to offer even more improbable explanations for his conduct.

> LCJ: Thou seemest to be a man of a great deal of kindness and good nature; for, by this story, there was a man that thou never sawest before (for I would fain have all people observe what leather some men's consciences are made of) and because he only had a black beard, and came to thy house, that black beard of his should persuade thee to go 26 miles, and give a man half a crown out of thy pocket to shew thee thy way, and all to carry a message from a man thou never knowest in thy life, to a woman thou never sawest in thy life neither; that thou shouldest lie out by the way two nights, and upon the Sunday get home,

and there meet with this same black-bearded little gentleman, and appoint these people to come to thy house upon the Tuesday; and when they came, entertain them three or four hours at thy own house, and go back again so many miles with them, and have no entertainment but a piece of cake and cheese that thou broughtest thyself from home, and have no reward, nor so much as know any of the persons thou didst all this for, is very strange.

Jeffreys began by scorning Dunne's trust in the messenger's claim that Hicks would reward him for his pains, given that he had never met either of them in his life; he was equally scathing that the messenger agreed to lend Dunne his horse for his first journey to Moyles Court. On his second visit, on his own horse, he said he stabled the animal while the others left theirs at the gate. He said he lived at Warminster, 'near my Lord Weymouth's',[1] but did not believe there were any fugitive rebels nearby. Nor did he make any effort to establish his visitors' names, whether any were rebels, or why they wanted to go to Moyles Court. Hicks merely said it was because he was in debt. Dunne then changed his story, saying that it was the messenger, not Hicks, who told him this.

Whether through terror or incompetence, Dunne was answering without thinking. A promised reward from a man seeking refuge from his creditors was about the worst financial risk he could undertake, but he took it, via an anonymous messenger, with a named individual he neither knew nor bothered to identify when they met. Yet it was of supreme importance for him to know who Hicks was, not merely to secure his reward and ensure he was taking the right man to Moyles Court, but also to avoid getting involved with fugitive rebels. Having blundered through this series of self-evident fabrications, he ended up by forgetting (because he had never existed) that it was the messenger, rather than Hicks himself, who allegedly had told him they were in debt.

Dunne could have aligned his story with Alice Lisle's defence at this point and have said he took Hicks for what he held himself out to be, a Nonconformist minister 'that used to preach and not to fight', as she was to describe him, rather than a defaulting debtor. But there were dangers along that path, for, if he knew Hicks, it would raise questions about what he knew of Nelthorp. The difficulty there was not simply that Nelthorp was an outlaw, which meant he could never admit to knowing him by that name, but the complications inherent in the name he had known him by, which were bound up with Hicks's clerical status. The truth on that issue was potentially far more incriminating for both himself and Alice Lisle than anything else that had emerged hitherto, so it was safer to avoid it altogether.

Jeffreys' purpose in pouring such scorn on Dunne's unreliability was primarily to shame him into the truth. But it also laid the ground for the next, and more abrasive, stage if the first one failed, as it had: he had twice asked Dunne to say just how much he did remember of what had happened at Moyles Court. Against that background, sparse though it was, he interrogated Dunne according to the age-old precept that telling lies is a great deal easier than remembering them afterwards.

Jeffreys pursued Dunne over what had happened to the horses when they arrived. Dunne said he did not know. A girl showed him into the house on his own. He could not decide whether he took his horse to the stable alone, or whether Carpenter did and fed him hay.

Today, friendly advice to witnesses about to give evidence is often 'Tell the truth, but don't elaborate. The best answers in cross-examination are "Yes", "No", or "I don't know".' Dunne was clearly trying to follow this course, and so far he had performed not too badly. But as a juggler he was slow, and had too many balls in the air. His main concern, because it was obviously where the questions were leading, was to avoid having to recount what was said when Carpenter greeted them at the gate, for there might be all sorts of allusions and innuendos – about their plans, the letter, their adventures en route, relief at their safe arrival, Nelthorp's identity and, in particular, about turning Hicks's and Nelthorp's horses loose – that could be deeply incriminating. So he said he went round to the stables alone.[2] He first said he had 'plucked up the latch' himself, but then claimed Carpenter had done so.

His lies blinded him to the inherent improbability of what he was saying. Despite having been to the house once before in daylight, it would require an unusually retentive memory to find his way to the stables in the dark and get his horse in before Carpenter arrived.

To say he 'plucked up the latch', and remembered doing so a month after the event, was as improbable as it was unnecessary, as was also the fact that, although Carpenter had joined him with a candle and fed his horse, it was not he, but 'the girl', who took him indoors. As the pressure increased, Dunne missed his catch on both points, thereby inviting a justifiable tirade of judicial wrath.

For the moment, Jeffreys was not making much headway, so he began to lay the ground for what had happened inside the house. He pressed Dunne over who he had seen, and returned five times to the most improbable detail of all, that at no stage had Dunne had anything to drink with his picnic. But he had still not finished with the point about where Carpenter greeted them.

> LCJ: Now prithee tell me truly, where came Carpenter unto you? I must know the truth of that . . . assure thyself I never met with a lying, sneaking, canting fellow, but I always treasured up vengeance for him: and therefore look to it, that thou dost not prevaricate with me . . .
>
> Dunne: My lord, I will tell the truth as near as I can.
>
> LCJ: Then tell me where Carpenter met thee.
>
> Dunne: In the court, my lord.
>
> LCJ: Before you came to the gate, or after.
>
> Dunne: It was after we came to the gate, in the court.
>
> LCJ: Then tell me, and I charge you tell me true, who was with you when Carpenter met you?
>
> Dunne: Hicks and Nelthorp.
>
> LCJ: Was there anybody else besides them two in the court?
>
> Dunne: There was nobody but Hicks and Nelthorp, and I and Mr Carpenter.
>
> LCJ: You are sure of that?
>
> Dunne: Yes, my lord.
>
> LCJ: Consider of it, are you sure there was nobody else?
>
> Dunne: Truly, my lord, I do not mind that there was anybody else.
>
> LCJ: Recollect yourself, and consider well of it.
>
> Dunne: Truly, my lord, I do not know of anybody else.
>
> LCJ: Now upon your oath tell me truly, who it was that opened the stable-door, was it Carpenter or you?
>
> Dunne: It was Carpenter, my lord.

Successful as it was, the forensic tactic that produced this contradiction, reverting to the point after Dunne's mind had been on something else, barely advanced the prosecution case, because Jeffreys' fury made him forget what he was after. As a concession from Dunne, it was of some significance, because, if Carpenter had 'plucked up the latch', it could mean only that he had seen Dunne round there instead of letting him find his own way; and that in turn, presumably, after Carpenter had met all three of them, and had turned Hicks's and Nelthorp's horses loose. Dunne would have seen and heard all that, and it pointed to the conclusion that his denial of being present was because he knew how incriminating the conversation had been.

Having established that Carpenter met the party 'after we came to the gate, in the court', Jeffreys should have gone on to ask how they greeted each other, what they discussed and what was said about turning the horses loose. Instead, he told Dunne what he thought of him, and then concentrated on the rather less important issues of Carpenter's presence in the stable, of the hay being pulled down and who took Dunne into the house.

LCJ: Why thou vile wretch, didst not thou tell me just now, that thou pluckedst up the latch? Dost thou take the God of heaven not to be a God of truth, and that he is not a witness of all thou sayest? . . . Jesus God! there is no sort of conversation nor human society to be kept with such people as these are who have no other religion but only in pretence . . . did you not tell me that you opened the latch yourself, and that you saw nobody else but a girl? . . . Answer me one question more: Did he pull down the hay, or you?

Dunne: I did not pull down any hay at all.

LCJ: Was there any hay pulled down before the candle was brought?

Dunne: No, there was not.

LCJ: Who brought the candle?

Dunne: Mr Carpenter brought the candle and lanthorn.

LCJ: It seems the saints have a certain charter for lying . . . You see, gentlemen, what a precious fellow this is, a very pretty tool to be employed upon such an errand, a knave that nobody would trust for half a crown between man and man, but he is the fitter to be employed about such works . . . A Turk has more title to an eternity of bliss than these pretenders to Christianity, for he has more morality and honesty in him. Sirrah, I charge you in the presence of God, tell me true, what other persons did you see that night?

Dunne: My lord, I did not see any than what I have told you already.

LCJ: Then they went out and brought word that thou wert come, and so he came out to meet thee. Very well; I would have everybody that has but the least tang of saintship to observe the carriage of this fellow, and see how they can cant, and snivel, and lie, and forswear themselves, and all for the good old cause . . .

The 'good old cause' was Cromwell's, and Jeffreys' allusion was to one of his earlier constitutional innovations, the 'Parliament of Saints' of 1653. Nonconformists of all denominations looked back to those days with nostalgia; and, as their fellowship gained strength under Stuart repression, their description of each other as Saints was an echo of that Parliament, as well as comparing their sufferings with those of the early Christian Church. Jeffreys underlined the religious identity between Alice Lisle and her guests, suggesting it was little more than a bond of mendacity and deception.

The effect of this verbal battering was simply to drive Dunne back to his original position, that he had been at the stable when Carpenter met the other two, and had therefore heard nothing.

Dunne may have reflected that, of all life's experiences, turning king's evidence was the least rewarding, and the sooner he could leave the witness-stand the better. But Jeffreys had not finished, because he wanted to explore something else Nelthorp had said. What followed had a particularly disturbing undertone.

TWELVE

A Question of Identity

If Alice Lisle felt the ice melting beneath her as pressure on Dunne increased, she must have heard it crack when Jeffreys returned to the issue of Nelthorp's identity. She had not been charged with harbouring him, but it was only two years since he had fled the country after being involved in the Rye House plot, convicted of treason in his absence and proclaimed an outlaw. There was a £100 reward for his capture, making it a treasonable act for anyone who knew him by name to help him, regardless of any part he may have had in the rebellion. Even if the jury was unaware of his status before the trial began, Pollexfen had reminded them of it in his opening, which meant that Dunne's and Alice Lisle's dealings with him could not be brushed aside.

Dunne was already heavily exposed over when he had first learnt Hicks's name; but he had asserted he did not know who Nelthorp was, or his name, until after his arrest. That had to be his and Alice Lisle's position from the outset: she was to say later that had Nelthorp told her his name, she would have remembered the proclamation. If this could be maintained, it was as safe a refuge as either could hope for. But it was not entirely secure, because of Dunne's earlier concession that he could not remember what name Nelthorp had gone by, rather than that he had never known him by any name at all before his arrest. Dunne now began by holding to his original claim, but suddenly undermined it with a further, and potentially damning, concession.

LCJ: Come, I will ask thee another question: When was the first time thou heard'st Nelthorp's name?

Dunne: Not till he was taken.

LCJ: What name did the fellow with the black beard tell thee he had?

Dunne: My lord, he never told me any name.

LCJ: Didst thou never ask him his name?

Dunne: No, my lord, that man that was afterwards found to be Nelthorp, I did not know to be Nelthorp until he was taken, nor what his name was, nor any name he had.

LCJ: No, prithee tell the truth, did not Nelthorp go by the name of Crofts?

Dunne: He did, my lord.

LCJ: Then prithee, when did he first go by that name in thy hearing?

Dunne: My lord, I only heard Hicks say he went by the name of Crofts.

LCJ: When was that?

Dunne: When they were taken.

Jeffreys' device for getting this admission was simple but effective. With Nelthorp's outlawry uppermost in Dunne's mind, Dunne would have been conscious that the one thing he and Alice Lisle could never admit to was knowing him by that name. If Nelthorp had used a different, innocuous name, there would be no reason to suspect him of anything. So when Jeffreys dangled the Crofts alias in front of Dunne, he grabbed at it, but forgot the barb it contained. A different name it was, and Nelthorp had used it. But Dunne suddenly remembered it was far from innocuous, and he tried to get off the hook by saying he knew neither of Nelthorp's names until after the arrest.

Those with long memories might have recalled Crofts as Monmouth's childhood name, after his guardian, Lord William Crofts; but in 1663 Monmouth discarded it when he married the 11-year-old Countess of Buccleugh. It was also the name taken by the four illegitimate children his mistress, Eleanor Needham, bore him in the early 1670s – good reason for a battlefield fugitive to avoid the name, unless so devoted to Monmouth as to wish to act as a decoy, diverting the search from his commander to himself. To take on such a name would also require a degree of self-advertisement, hardly the behaviour of a rogue seeking safe and secret conduct to a 'lurking-hole', where he could lie low until the hue and cry subsided. Therefore Nelthorp, probably ignorant of

Monmouth's earlier use of the name, had adopted it at random simply to hide his real identity.

Since Jeffreys did not pursue the point, one may assume he accepted this, and never knew the opportunity he missed. It was a chance no advocate, and Jeffreys least of all, could have failed to exploit. The two people for whom the name carried the utmost significance were Alice Lisle and, if he was in court, John Crofts himself. Whenever she first heard it attributed to Nelthorp – whether from the letter, or 'after they were taken', or before that – she would have instantly realised why it had been used. The Reverend John Crofts had been her private chaplain at Moyles Court in 1669, preaching at conventicles there and probably educating her children. He then took a similar position with the Honourable Frances Fiennes at Newton Tony, across the Wiltshire border, where he was licensed during the short period of Nonconformist toleration in 1672. A popular preacher, he later moved to Allington, about a mile away, where he 'had a considerable estate', and later died. Hicks had moved from Devon to Portsmouth between 1673 and 1675, where his ministry lasted until 1682. During that time he was a visiting preacher at Moyles Court, and would have met Crofts many times.

Alice Lisle must have held her breath as she heard Dunne confirm Nelthorp's use of the alias, and even more as he evidently understood, and then shied from, the implications of when he first heard it used. To help an anonymous stranger was one thing; but to help someone using a name she must have realised was false – and, moreover, false for the purpose of explaining a journey to her house – raised extremely awkward questions. Up to this moment she might have been able to say she took both her guests for preachers fleeing religious persecution.

With the name out, however, that defence evaporated so far as Nelthorp was concerned, for she would have realised as soon as she met him that he was not Crofts. And if he was not Crofts, who was he? Why, if a clergyman, should he use another clergyman's name? If not a clergyman, what was he trying to hide? Was it not suspicious that a stranger should choose a name specifically designed to afford a welcome at her, rather than anyone else's, house? Might that not indicate he had dark secrets, particularly when, in Pollexfen's words, 'all the country was full of hurry in pursuit after those wicked rebels . . . forced, like vagabonds, to skulk up and down'?

Might he not, just conceivably, be one of those very rebels? It was this sort of onslaught Alice could expect – and from the bench too, where the name had originated – if she went the least distance towards revealing her reaction to it. But since it was not clear how much Jeffreys knew, she wisely fell back on a defence that avoided the complications of an alias, and was realistically the only one open to her: that she did not know Nelthorp from Adam, or his name, or even that he was coming, until after he had arrived.

The idea for the alias can only have come from Hicks, since he alone knew who Crofts was. Dunne was therefore telling the truth in asserting that Hicks initially ascribed it to Nelthorp. But he was clearly lying when he said he had never heard it used during the journey. That was the one stage at which Nelthorp had had to use it, for, regardless of his rebel status, as an outlaw he could never travel under his own name. East-bound travellers were bound to arouse suspicion; and if a party was stopped and challenged, it was vital that each member should have a convincing, and mutually consistent, explanation of who they were and their destination. By using the description 'two Nonconformist ministers and their servant' visiting a Presbyterian sympathiser in the New Forest, Dunne must have been aware of the position from the outset.

Once at Moyles Court, Nelthorp's pretence was pointless and untenable. Hicks had probably forewarned Alice Lisle about it in his letter: and, no matter how unexpected Nelthorp's arrival, both she and Carpenter would have been extraordinarily naive if their first question to Nelthorp had not been 'Who are you?' One way and another, that conversation 'after we came to the gate, in the court' was something Dunne could not afford to know about.

The same applied to the letter, which was never produced. There were probably two reasons why Hicks had sent it: to introduce Dunne as his envoy; and to spell out what was happening. A week as Dunne's house-guest would have convinced Hicks of what was now obvious to all: Dunne was of limited intelligence, and incapable of remembering or explaining anything that was even marginally complicated. Hicks may have thought it wise to ask

Alice Lisle to warn John Crofts himself to lie low for the time being; and whether she gathered it from the letter or from Dunne, the idea of Hicks's companion masquerading as her former chaplain may have been another reason she burst out laughing in front of Barter. On any view, that letter was highly incriminating, and, if Alice Lisle did not destroy it on the spot after reading it, she would certainly have done so before Colonel Penruddock could find it. But she could not admit to that without risking questions about its contents. The only safe course – and on this she, Dunne and Carpenter were agreed – was to assert the letter had never existed.

Jeffreys' information about the alias can only have come from Nelthorp: and it seems clear that in divulging only half the truth – that he had used the name, but saying nothing about its origin – Nelthorp was acting from the highest motives. From the moment of his arrest, he must have been aware that his only hope of survival lay in turning informer, yet it appears he resolutely refused to do so. The note of his examination in London on 9 August merely states: 'He knows nothing of any correspondents the late D. of Mon. had, but owns he knew of the rising and therefore fledd.' Muddiman's entry for 13 August notes he was one of fourteen rebels examined by the Privy Council that day, and continues: 'Nelthrop [sic] who was taken at the Lady Lisle's House at Moyles Court was brought before them but would confess nothing. Also said he knew he had deserved it and must be hanged and would not bring any others into trouble.' *The Western Martyrology* (1689) says he was 'brought to London and imprisoned in Newgate. He rejected there, with some scorn, some offers made him of saving his own life by taking away other mens . . .'.

After giving evidence, Alice Lisle called a witness, George Creed, to recount what Nelthorp had said at his examination in London. Creed, a Puritan, was an Admiralty clerk and a colleague of Samuel Pepys. For him to have heard Nelthorp's examination, he was probably doing a day's work in the Privy Council office. Presumably his religious sympathy with Alice Lisle prompted him to testify for her. Creed told the court: 'I heard Nelthorp say, that my Lady Lisle did not know of his coming, nor did not know his name, nor had he ever told his name, till he named himself to Colonel Penruddock, when he was taken.'

Nelthorp was hanged as an outlaw on 30 October 1685 outside the Holborn entrance to his own Inn of Court, Gray's, to 'make a more public example' of him, as the court put it. The contemporary record of his execution suggests he was disposed of too swiftly to have been able to read out the 'Last Speech' attributed to him in *The Western Martyrology*. But the relevant passage is nearly identical to Creed's account: 'I was wholly a stranger to her ladyship, and came with Mr Hicks, neither did she (as I verily believe) know who I was, or my name till I was taken.' Nelthorp thus left Alice Lisle free to concede whatever she chose about her knowledge of him, and thus adjust her evidence as best suited her case.

When the moment came, she said she did not know who Nelthorp was 'until after he came to my house'. While less secure than 'until he was taken', this claim was corroborated by Dunne's later allusion to having heard the name 'Crofts or Nelthorp, I am sure one of them', mentioned over supper. No harm was done, because Jeffreys remained as ignorant of the full implications of Crofts's name as Nelthorp intended.

Everything depended on the name and the proclamation. In the absence of the modern apparatus of detection – fingerprints, photographs, DNA tests, documentary proof of identity – an alias was much easier to assume and far more difficult to penetrate than it is today. Failing affirmative proof that Alice Lisle must have known who Nelthorp was before his arrest, a charge of harbouring him would be bound to fail.

Jeffreys therefore simply used the name to cast doubt on Dunne's assertion of Nelthorp's anonymity. Anxious to get more out of him, he tried to treat Dunne slightly more gently than he deserved in the hope of catching him unawares, instead of pushing him along paths that, once he saw where they were leading, he obstinately refused to follow. This was scarcely appreciated by junior counsel for the Crown. They tried to pick up the threads from the stage where Jeffreys had lost both his temper and his train of thought, and they asked Dunne to elaborate on the arrival at the house and the disposal of the horses. But it was too late: he had been over the ground already. His obvious stonewalling prompted another irritated comment from the bench.

Mr Jennings: You say Carpenter met you very civilly, and took
care of your horses; did he make no provision for Hicks and
Nelthorp's horses? What became of them?

Dunne: I cannot tell, my lord.

Mr Rumsay: Did you see their horses afterwards?

Dunne: No, my lord, I did not.

Mr Rumsay: When they alighted from them, were they tied fast to
the gate, or how?

Dunne: They were not tied at all, as I know of.

Mr Jennings: Did you tell Carpenter that their horses were there?

Dunne: I did not tell him any such thing.

LCJ: Thou art a strange, prevaricating, shuffling, snivelling, lying
rascal.

The Crown then turned to its next witness, Barter, but not before
Jeffreys gave Alice Lisle the opportunity to question Dunne, and in
terms that hardly did him credit.

Mr Pollexfen: We will set him by for the present, and call Barter
that is the other fellow.

LCJ: Will the prisoner ask this person any question?

Lisle: No.

LCJ: Perhaps her questions might endanger the coming out of all
the truth, and may be she is well enough pleased to have him
swear as he does; but it carries a very foul face upon my word.

Barter was sworn, Jeffreys warning him that 'his soul was at pawn
for the truth of what he testified'. He recounted his and Dunne's
Saturday visit to Moyles Court, where he saw Dunne deliver a letter
to Carpenter, who took it to Alice Lisle. She then spoke to him in
the kitchen, asking about his background, and whether he could
make bricks. As a husbandman from Wiltshire, he said he could not,
and declined her offer of a plot of land for that purpose. She then
had a private conversation with Dunne when they both laughed,
apparently at his expense. During their return journey from Moyles
Court, Barter pressed Dunne about this. Dunne replied it was
because she asked him whether Barter knew 'anything of the
concern', and he said he did not. This worried Barter, because he felt

it might also implicate him as a traitor; and he decided to go to Colonel Penruddock and tell him what had happened, and of the plan to meet the two other travellers on the Tuesday.

They did not keep the Tuesday appointment. When they did appear, they insisted on taking back routes until they got to Martin, where Dunne was sent to enlist Fane as guide. At this, Barter decided to leave them, but not before Nelthorp had given him ten shillings, and Dunne half a crown. During the journey, Dunne had told him he believed each of his companions was worth around £5,000 a year. Barter then rode over to Compton Chamberlayne to tell Penruddock the party was at Moyles Court.

Any thought of respite that Dunne may have had when Barter came to testify must have been rapidly overtaken by what he had just said. The implications were clear. According to Barter, not merely had Dunne brought a letter, but the party had been careful to travel by back routes the second time. Contrary to Dunne's assertion that Hicks had told him they were men in debt, Barter's account reveals Dunne as corrupt, since he stood to gain a considerable reward if 'the concern' was successful, and that he had joked with Alice Lisle over Barter's apparent ignorance of it and, probably, the Crofts alias. But Barter had drawn his own conclusions about what was going on, and, if only to safeguard himself, he had felt it prudent to keep Penruddock informed.

Dunne must have known that Jeffreys would come back to him on what Barter had said, and he stood his ground as each allegation was put to him. But he was tired, and with the end in sight, his concentration was going. Psychologically, he felt secure and relaxed; indeed, he hardly needed to think at all. This was why the last question, the crucial one, caught him completely off his guard.

THIRTEEN

The Tongue-Tied Liar

Jeffreys' approach was open and direct. Conscious of Dunne's wariness of the dual-purpose probing that had uncovered his knowledge of Hicks's identity and Nelthorp's alias, he fed him simple, easy-to-answer questions designed to restore his confidence. Dunne's answers, a series of stubborn denials, which he knew were safer than admissions, were unimportant: the last question was the one that mattered.

LCJ: Then let my honest man, Mr Dunne, stand forward a little. Come, friend, you have had some time to recollect yourself . . . you talked of carrying a message from Hicks to my lady Lisle: did not you carry a letter?

Dunne: No, my lord, I did not.

LCJ: Did not you show a letter to the bailiff, Carpenter?

Dunne: No, my lord, I did not.

LCJ: What say you, Barter, to that?

Barter: My lord, I did see him produce the letter to the bailiff.

LCJ: Then I will ask you another question: Did you not tell Barter that you should be at Salisbury Plain, with two people, upon the Tuesday?

Dunne: No, my lord, I said between Compton and Fovant.

LCJ: Did not you tell him, that they were brave fellows, and had God knows how many thousand pounds a year a-piece?

Dunne: No, my lord, I did not.

LCJ: Then one thing more: Did you not tell him that you told my lady, when she asked whether he was acquainted with the concern, that he knew nothing of the business?

Dunne: My lord, I did tell him so.

The trap in the question was its slight complexity – how much he had told one person of what he had previously told someone else –

and it entirely occupied Dunne's exhausted mind, momentarily blinding him to the answer's dangers. That, and the thought that he was through, that this really was, as Jeffreys implied, the last hurdle, tripped him into the truth. It was the most devastating answer of the trial and was doubly incriminating, disclosing not merely what he had told Barter and Alice Lisle, but also that he had kept from Barter what he had told her. This holding back increased the probability that his answer was true, and not a point Dunne could have 'forgotten', as his earlier answers implied.

For Jeffreys, the point was a high-risk gamble that had paid off, rather against the odds. He was understandably triumphant.

> LCJ: Did you so? Then you and I must have a little further discourse: Come now, and tell us, what business was that? and tell it us so, that a man may understand and believe that thou dost speak truth.
>
> Dunne: Does your lordship ask what that business was?
>
> LCJ: Yes, it is a plain question; What was that business that my lady asked thee, whether the other man knew; and then you answered her, that he did know nothing of it? (Then he paused a while.)

The hook was in, deep and firm, and Dunne knew it. His echo of Jeffreys' question, as the implications dawned, merely increased the agony. There was no escape this time, as there had been over Fane and Crofts; the line was dragging him from the dark and comfortable depths of his mendacity to the blinding sunlight on the surface, where he would be exposed as a barefaced liar. The rising flood of Jeffreys' anger broke over him for an hour or so as he vainly tried to free himself. Alternately pausing and struggling, he merely devalued the reply he eventually settled on, that 'the business' Barter did not know about was that Hicks was a Nonconformist. Jeffreys pursued the point relentlessly, as much to demonstrate the depths of Dunne's deceit as to underline the threat of damnation for his immortal soul.

> LCJ: Remember, friend, thou art upon thy oath . . . I require from thee a plain answer to a very plain question: What was that

business my lady enquired after, whether the other fellow knew, and thou toldest her, he did not? (Dunne made no answer but stood musing for a while.)

LCJ: Thou didst tell that honest man there, that my lady Lisle asked thee whether he knew anything of the business, and thou saidest no. What was that business?

Dunne: The business that Barter did not know of?

LCJ: Yes, that is the business . . . Oh! how hard the truth is to come out of a lying Presbyterian knave . . . what was that business you and my lady spoke of? (Then he paused for half a quarter of an hour, and at last said:)

Dunne: I cannot give an account of it, my lord . . . (He stood silent for a good while) . . .

With the trial continuing late into the evening, other judges were anxious to know what was happening. Sir William Montagu, Lord Chief Baron of the Exchequer, had joined Jeffreys on the bench in the main court, and now intervened.

L.C. Baron [William Montagu]: Friend, mind what my lord says to you, and consider, how easy a thing it is for a man to speak truth, and give a plain answer to a plain question. You cannot but understand what my lord asks of you; you said even now, that you did tell the other witness, Barter, that my lady asked you, whether he knew any thing of the business; and you told her, he did not. Now my lord would have you tell us, what that business was? (He seemed to turn his head on one side, but returned no answer) . . .

LCJ: I hope, gentlemen of the jury, you take notice of the strange and horrible carriage of this fellow . . . Sirs, Is this that you call the Protestant religion? Shall so glorious a name be applied to so much villainy and hypocrisy? Is this the persuasion you hope to live, and die, and find salvation in? Will any of you all, gentlemen, be contented to die with a lie in your mouth? . . . I charge you once more, as you will answer it at the bar of the great Judge of all the world, that you tell me what that business was you and the prisoner talked about. (Still he would make no answer) . . .

LCJ: Thou wretch! . . . What hopes can there be for so profligate a villain as thou art, that so impudently stands in open defiance of the omnipresence, omniscience, and justice of God, by persisting in so palpable a lie? I therefore require it of you, in his name, to tell me the truth.

Dunne: I cannot tell what to say, my lord.

LCJ: Good God! Was there ever such an impudent rascal! Well, I will try once more, and tell thee what I mean; you said you told that honest man (for truly he seems so to be) that my lady asked you whether he knew of the business, and you told her, he did not: prithee be so free as to tell us what that business was?

Dunne: My lord, pray ask the question over again once more and I will tell you . . .

LCJ: I ask you, with a great desire that thou may'st free thyself from so great a load of falsehood and perjury, tell me what the business was you told the prisoner, the other man Barter did not know?

Dunne: My lord, I told her, he knew nothing of our coming there.

LCJ: Nay, nay, that can never be it, for he came along with thee.

Dunne: He did not know any thing of my coming there until I met him on the way.

LCJ: Prithee mind my question . . . what was the business that thou told'st her, he did not know?

Dunne: She asked me whether I did not know that Hicks was a Nonconformist?

LCJ: Did my lady Lisle ask you that question?

Dunne: Yes, my lord; I told her I did not.

LCJ: But that is not my question: what was that business that he did not know?

Dunne: It was the same thing: whether Mr Hicks was a Non-conformist.

LCJ: That cannot be all; there must be something more in it.

Dunne: Yes, my lord, it is all; I know nothing more . . .

LCJ: Why, dost thou think, that after all this pass that I have been at to get an answer to my question, that thou can'st banter me with such sham stuff as this? Hold the candle to his face, that we may see his brazen face.

Dunne: My lord, I tell you the truth.

LCJ: Did she ask thee whether that man knew any thing of a question she had asked thee, and that was only of being a Nonconformist?

Dunne: Yes, my lord, that was all.

LCJ: That is all nonsense; dost thou imagine that any man hereabouts is so weak as to believe thee?

Dunne: My lord, I am so baulked, I do not know what I say myself; tell me what you would have me to say, for I am cluttered out of my senses.

LCJ: Why prithee, man, there is no body baulks but thee but thy own self, thou art asked questions that are as plain as anything in the world can be . . . but I see all the pains in the world, and all compassion and charity is lost upon thee, and therefore I will say no more to thee.

Religious issues are seldom debated in court today, but Jeffreys' recital of the precepts of the Church of England and of the sanctions for disobedience would not have seemed out of place to his hearers. The Established Church was a pillar in the constitutional edifice of the seventeenth century, and in some ways had a deeper hold on loyalty and conscience than the Crown. After the Restoration, Anglican clergy were men of education and status; their faith, consciously and often conscientiously observed, was much more a part of the fabric of society than it is today.

Furthermore, it was a faith enforceable by law. To deny the truth of the Christian religion was either a blasphemous or a seditious libel. Legislation decreed that Dissenting ministers and their congregations were social as well as religious outcasts. People were often 'presented' by church wardens at Quarter Sessions and fined for not going to church; and public officials could only take office if attendance at communion was certified by the incumbent. More immediately, the country had just been delivered from that 'black and horrid' rebellion, led by a man who had widespread and committed Nonconformist support. In the case of Alice Lisle, Presbyterianism was the bond of fellowship between the defendant and her guests, and it was Hicks's flight from the battlefield that was now so obviously 'the business' of Dunne's guilty secret and the reason for his tongue-tied silence.

For Jeffreys, that rebel faith was as much an affront to the authority of the state as the offence of treason itself. Its present manifestation was proof, if any were needed, of how its followers had abused the toleration shown them in the past, not least by himself. His castigation of Dunne's devotion to Nonconformity, and of his prevarication, was probably a veiled invitation to the jury to identify Alice Lisle's apostasy with her alleged breach of allegiance to the Crown. Had he wished, Jeffreys could have made her religion the basis of a perfectly legitimate inference, that, as a deserter of the Anglican Church, she might be the more disposed to help a Nonconformist rebel, but the argument emerged more crudely than that. Presbyterians, Jeffreys maintained, were necessarily liars. 'How hard is the truth to come out of a lying Presbyterian knave,' he had said in exasperation, a statement he later repeated when Alice Lisle made her defence:

Presbytery has all manner of villainy in it, nothing but Presbytery could lead that fellow Dunne to tell so many lies as he has here told; for shew me a Presbyterian, and I will engage to show a lying knave.

Dunne's performance under the combined impact of Jeffreys' ferocity and Montagu's remonstrance must have seemed more pathetic than courageous, but it certainly helped Alice Lisle in the end. Dunne's slow-moving brain eventually recovered from its terror-struck paralysis, and he began to grope for a refuge. After two unsuccessful scrambles, he settled for Hicks's Nonconformity as 'the business Barter did not know about'. Though the answer had lost some conviction, given the time it had taken to get there, at least it coincided with Alice Lisle's defence.

Jeffreys, much to his annoyance, found he was unable to dislodge Dunne. But Pollexfen decided the time had come to apply pressure from another direction.

Mr Pollexfen: My Lord, because he pretends to ignorance of what Hicks was, I desire to ask Barter one question: Pray, what did he tell you concerning his carriage towards these people?

Barter: My Lord, he told me that he had concealed them in his house ten days before.

Dunne: That I never did in my life.

Barter: I know not whether you did or not but you told me so; and I made answer to him again, my Lord, I wonder how he was able to keep them without being discovered, there being such search; and he answered he did keep them in a chamber all day, and that they walked out at night; for the searches of the houses were usually at night.

Dunne: My Lord, I can bring testimony to the contrary.

LCJ: Well, I will try thee with another question: didst thou tell that man, that it was the best job thou ever hadst in thy life?

Dunne: No, my Lord, I did not.

LCJ: Nor nothing to that purpose?

Dunne: No, my Lord.

LCJ: What say you, Barter, did not he tell you so?

Barter: Yes, my lord, he did; and that he should never lack money again so long as he lived.

LCJ: Then I ask you one question more Barter: did you tell this to col. Penruddock?

Barter: Yes, I did, my lord.

LCJ: Then that will fortify his testimony; therefore swear him, because I would make those concealed wretches (for in my conscience I know there are some such in the bottom of this business) know, that the truth will out one way or other. As for this fellow, I expect it from all you gentlemen of the king's counsel, and others that are concerned, that you take notice and remember what has passed here, and that an information of perjury be preferred against this fellow.

For Dunne, the odds were shortening. The contradictions over the letter; when he first knew Hicks's name and the extent of his wealth; the narrow escape over Nelthorp's alias; the final disaster over 'the business' he thought Barter did not know about – all these showed him as an incompetent liar. Barter had now revealed the extent of Dunne's hospitality to Hicks and Nelthorp before he had set out with them for Moyles Court, which disposed of the 'small black man' who was supposed to have made contact on behalf of Hicks;

he obviously existed only in Dunne's imagination, to protect him from a charge of treason identical to the one Alice Lisle faced, and on which he was supposed to be the principal witness against her. Behind the charge of perjury he now faced there probably rose in his mind the powerful image of the flogging Oates had received only four months earlier for the same offence, on the orders of two of the judges now facing him, Wythens and Jeffreys.

Perhaps prison was preferable. But how long would he remain there? Whether for treason or perjury, the treatment was bound to be painful. As Colonel Penruddock gave his evidence, Dunne began to consider whether telling the truth might help him.

FOURTEEN

Penruddock's Evidence

Colonel Thomas Penruddock was sworn, and recounted Barter's visit, Dunne's failure to appear at the Tuesday morning rendezvous and the subsequent raid on Moyles Court. The most damaging parts of his statement were the way he said Carpenter and Alice Lisle had greeted him.

LCJ: Colonel Penruddock, upon the oath you have taken, did that man, Barter, come to you; and what did he say to you?

Penruddock: My lord, that man, Barter, came to my house in the morning, Monday, and told me, he had been with one Dunne, upon a journey to Mrs Lisle's house, to get entertainment for some people; and that they had appointed to meet him the Tuesday following, between nine and eleven, upon Salisbury Plain, and there if I pleased, I might take them. I ordered him to go according to the appointment, and withal, I sent a servant of my own to watch when they came by; but it happened, I suppose, by their taking another way, that he missed of them: but Barter left word, that in case he did not find them there, we must conclude, that he was gone with them to my lady Lisle's house; and he told me withal, says he, I believe they are rebels, because he that desired me to be their guide, said the same to me. So early the next morning I took some soldiers with me, and beset my lady Lisle's house; it was a pretty while before I could get anybody in the house to hear; at length that man that they say was the bailiff, Carpenter, came out; and I said to him, Friend, you had best be free and ingenuous, and discover who are in your lady's house, for I am sure there were some strangers came hither last night; let me know who they are, and show me what part of the house they are in. He did confess to me there were strangers in the house, and pointed to such part of the house, but pray, says he, do not tell my mistress of it. Accordingly we went in, and immediately we took Mr Hicks and this same Dunne in the malt-house.

LCJ: Was Dunne taken in the malt-house?

Penruddock: Yes, he had covered himself with some sort of stuff there.

LCJ: Well, what did you do then?

Penruddock: My lady afterwards coming to us, I told her, madam, you have done very ill in harbouring rebels, and giving entertainment to the king's enemies. Saith she, I know nothing of them; I am a stranger to it. Pray, said I, madam, be so free and ingenuous with me, and so kind to yourself, as if there be any other person that is concealed in any part of your house, (for I am sure there is somebody else) as to deliver him up, and you shall come to no further trouble. She denied it, and said, I know nothing of them: But we went on, and searched, and at last discovered the other man, Nelthorp, hid in a hole by the chimney.

The next witness, Dowding, said it took about half an hour to rouse an outwardly silent and slumbering household. But there was obviously the deepest concern within. Penruddock's account of how Carpenter at once betrayed Hicks and Dunne while asking Penruddock not to tell Alice Lisle about them indicates the nature of the survival plan, hastily devised in ignorance of Barter's dealings with Penruddock. From the upstairs room where they had eaten and slept, the three were taken to different hiding-places. Nelthorp, the proclaimed traitor and outlaw, and by far the most incriminating guest if discovered, was given the apparently safer refuge of the 'hole by the chimney' in the main house (reputedly an old bread oven, still visible today in the school staffroom).

Hicks, who could plausibly pose as a religious and Nonconformist refugee, was transferred with Dunne, probably via a 'branch-line' underground tunnel, to the malthouse, the large building (since demolished) adjacent to the main house at the back. It could, if necessary, be said they were unknown vagrants who had crept in there during the night; and their discovery might satisfy the hunters' appetite and leave Nelthorp undetected.

Carpenter put this plan into effect immediately. His surrender of Hicks and Dunne was prompted not merely by the vital need to keep the searchers away from Nelthorp, but also by the way Penruddock greeted him. It was 'strangers' he had said he was after, rather than 'rebels', and he wanted to know where they were. By revealing the malthouse occupants in response to that description, Carpenter could be seen to be on the side of the law without incriminating himself. But his request to Penruddock not to tell Alice Lisle about them was clearly a ruse to play down the significance of their presence, and emphasise everyone else's innocence. As Alice Lisle's bailiff, he was responsible for security, and if two tramps had managed to get into one of the outhouses, it was presumably because he had failed to lock up properly the night before. Far from any worries about rebels, or of committing treason by sheltering them, his only apparent concern was to avoid a reprimand from Alice Lisle if she found out about his neglect.

It was a brave effort, and Alice Lisle did her best to go along with it. When she met Penruddock after Hicks's and Dunne's capture, her blanket denial of his challenge, that she had harboured 'rebels', carried a convenient, and probably deliberate, ambiguity. 'I know nothing of them; I am a stranger to it' could mean either 'I never knew they were here at all', which would fit in with Carpenter's assertion that, also unbeknown to him, they had got into the unlocked malthouse: this interpretation might have saved the situation if everyone, including Hicks and Dunne, had told the same tale and Nelthorp had remained undiscovered. Or it could mean 'I know nothing about their being rebels', on the unspoken assumption of what became her defence at the trial – that, though she did know them, or Hicks at least, she sheltered them honestly, believing Hicks was nothing more than a Nonconformist refugee.

Here her defence began to crumble, because, if she did think along these lines, her account was difficult to square with Carpenter's assertion about their getting in undetected: why disclaim all knowledge of two people 'found' in the malthouse whom she had in fact sent for and entertained the night before? Might it not have been more convincing to concede Hicks's presence and his Nonconformist status from the start? But those were minor difficulties compared with the problem of Nelthorp. Penruddock was no fool, and Nelthorp's eventual discovery after Alice Lisle's specific denial of a third person made things immeasurably worse.

The discovery could well have formed the basis of a charge for harbouring him as well as Hicks, for, if he really was a total stranger, why deny his presence? Why try to hide him at all? Why not surrender him as a stranger at the outset, and even more once it was said it was 'rebels' they were after, making the charge the infinitely more serious one of treason? To obstruct an official search in those circumstances was the height of folly. In fact Jeffreys did not pursue these lines of cross-examination with either Alice Lisle or Carpenter, presumably because, having effectively broken Dunne by then, he thought it unnecessary. But the theme was there in his next few questions to Dunne.

LCJ: Dunne, how came you to hide yourself in the malt-house?

Dunne: When I heard the stir and bustle, I went through the chamber where I lay, and came into that room where I was taken.

LCJ: When thou heard'st a stir and bustle, why wert thou afraid of anything?

Dunne: My lord, I was frighted at the noise.

LCJ: Prithee, what need'st thou be afraid, for thou didst not know Hicks, nor Nelthorp; and my lady only asked thee, whether Hicks were a Nonconformist parson: Thou art a very innocent soul, and surely needest no occasion to be afraid. I doubt there was something of that business in the case that we were talking of before, if we could but get out of thee what it was.

Dunne: My lord, I heard a great noise in the house, and I did not know what it meant; and so I went and hid myself.

LCJ: Alack-a-day! That is very strange, that thou should'st hide thyself for a little noise, when thou knewest nothing of the business, nor wert acquainted with anything of the matter at all. But Colonel Penruddock, I would ask you one question more: Did that honest man tell you, that Dunne had told him, that it was the best job that ever he had in his life, and that he should want no money?

Penruddock: I cannot tell that truly, my lord; I do not remember that: but he said, he apprehended them to be rebels, and that Dunne told him as much.

LCJ: What do you say to that, Dunne? It seems you told Barter
    that you apprehended them to be rebels.
Dunne: I apprehend them for rebels, my lord?
LCJ: No, no, you did not apprehend them for rebels, but you hid
    them for rebels. But did you say to Barter, that you took them
    to be rebels?
Dunne: I take them to be rebels!
LCJ: You blockhead, I ask you, did you tell him so?
Dunne: I tell Barter so!
LCJ: Ay, is not that a plain question?
Dunne: I am quite cluttered out of my senses; I do not know what
    I say. (A candle being still held nearer his nose.)

Hiding 'because of the noise' was no more convincing than his
semantic quibble over 'apprehend'. Dunne realised he had run out of
excuses and was at the end of the road. With the candle shining in
his face, his plea of battered non-comprehension was the final
surrender. Before leaving him, Jeffreys drove home the fundamental
contradictions in what he and Alice Lisle were saying: either the
travellers were intruders, or they were invited guests; either there
were reasons for thinking they were rebels, or there were not. They
could not have it both ways. Jeffreys then re-emphasised the
implications of Alice Lisle's denial of Nelthorp's presence, which
drew a defensive protest from the dock.

LCJ: But to tell the truth, would rob thee of none of thy senses, if
    ever thou hadst any; but it should seem that neither thou, nor
    thy mistress the prisoner had any, for she knew nothing of it
    neither, though she had sent for them.
Mr Pollexfen: Pray, Col. Penruddock, did you tell her you came to
    search for rebels?
Penruddock: Yes, Sir, I told her as soon as I saw her; but we had a
    good while beset the house before anybody answered us; at
    length, there were some ladies, or gentlewomen, I imagined
    them to be her daughters, that upon our noise looked out at the
    window; and I told them there were rebels in the house, and I
    required them in the King's name to be delivered to me; but I
    saw not my lady till after I had brought out Hicks and Dunne.

LCJ: What said she to you?

Penruddock: She said, she knew nothing of their being in the house; but I told her there was somebody else besides, and she would do well to deliver him without trouble: but she denying of it, we searched further, and found Nelthorp, as I told you.

LCJ: But she denied it first, it seems?

Lisle: My lord, I hope I shall not be condemned without being heard.

LCJ: No, God forbid, Mrs Lisle; that was a sort of practice in your husband's time; you know very well what I mean: But God be thanked, it is not so now; the King's courts of law never condemn without hearing.

In political debate against an equally matched adversary, such a retort would have been applauded as the knock-out blow Jeffreys intended. But against a defenceless old lady on trial for her life, it was vindictive bullying at its worst. As the better-informed would have understood, the allusion was to John Lisle's trial of Dr John Hewett twenty-seven years earlier.

Even if this point had the slightest relevance to the charge Alice Lisle now faced (and it had none), it was a misleading and unfair comparison. John Lisle's condemnation of Hewett 'unheard' on what amounted to a non-existent defence was unavoidable when Hewett obstinately refused to accept the commission's jurisdiction. Far from not listening, John Lisle had displayed great patience as Hewett aired his long-winded and pedantic challenge to the commission's powers, while warning him of the consequences if he persisted with it. Jeffreys' self-satisfied assertion that such condemnations were a thing of the past, and that the 'king's courts of law' – by implicit contrast with the Protector's usurping courts – never behaved in that way was equally untrue. The automatic consequence of refusing to plead was the same in 1685 as it had always been; the court had no option but to convict and pass sentence. That Jeffreys was aware he had overreached himself seems clear from his summing-up, when he reminded the jury that they should not be influenced by anything Alice Lisle or her husband had done in the past.

Penruddock gave way to Dowding, who repeated Alice Lisle's denial of a third fugitive in the house, which provoked her into a fuller explanation of the point she had just tried to make: not merely were the searchers thieves, and therefore tainted witnesses, but the reason for her lack of cooperation was the havoc they caused during their search.

LCJ: Col. Penruddock, have you any more to say?

Penruddock: No, my lord: But here is one Mr Dowding, that was with me when I searched the house.

LCJ: Swear him. (Which was done.)

Mr Pollexfen: Mr Dowding, pray did you go with Colonel Penruddock to Mrs Lisle's house?

Mr Dowding: Yes, my lord: We came to the house, and beset the house round, some to the back gate and some to the fore gate; we called almost half an hour before we got in; and had found two, and we came to my lady; she said, she knew nothing of anybody being in the house –

Lisle: My lord, this fellow that now speaks against me, broke open my trunk, and stole away a great part of my best linen: and sure, my lord, those persons that rob me, are not fit to be evidences against me, because it behoves them that I be convicted, to prevent their being indicted for felony.

LCJ: Look you, friend, you say you went with Col. Penruddock to search the house, did you find anybody there?

Dowding: Yes, my lord, I found this same Dunne in a little hole in the malt-house.

LCJ: Was he covered, or not?

Dowding: He had taken some stuff or other to cover him.

LCJ: Did you find Hicks there?

Dowding: Yes, my lord, we did find one that said his name was Hicks.

LCJ: Is that the same Hicks that is in Salisbury gaol?

Dowding: Yes, my lord, it is: I saw him yesterday at the George in Salisbury, when he had that discourse with those other gentlemen.

Though apparently superfluous, this last question was designed to cover a crucial gap in the prosecution evidence that anyone less astute than Jeffreys might have overlooked, and that he had glossed over at the beginning of Dunne's evidence.

Today, without Dowding's answer, the entire case against Alice Lisle would have collapsed. That Jeffreys pressed Dowding on the point indicates his awareness of the need for the prosecution to complete their proof – a need no less rigorous then than now. Hicks was not in court, and proof of his treason depended on the three ex-prisoners who could say only they had recognised him the previous day at Salisbury as the man who had earlier tried to dissuade them from their loyalty in the stables at Keynsham. They knew nothing about what had happened after that. Since Dunne had not attended the identification session at Salisbury, he was in no position to say whether the Hicks they recognised was the same 'nameless' individual he had helped. In other words, there was nothing to connect the Keynsham traitor with the guest at Moyles Court. But for Dowding's answer, Alice Lisle might have sheltered an innocent man, and it was for the Crown to prove the contrary. Dowding was the only witness who could identify the man Salisbury as the person arrested in the malthouse.

Before the next two witnesses gave evidence, Dowding mentioned Hicks's admission of the previous day, confirming him as a self-confessed traitor.

Mr Pollexfen: Swear Carpenter and his wife. (Which was done.)
Dowding: My lord, Hicks acknowledged before me that he was at Keynsham, in the duke of Monmouth's army.

FIFTEEN

The Carpenters: Dunne 'comes clean'

William and Rachel Carpenter were long-standing family retainers whose loyalty to the Lisles was not in doubt. This put them in the same category of 'unwilling witnesses' as Dunne: they would say no more to incriminate Alice Lisle than they had to. As bailiff and housekeeper, their duties were to ensure that visitors were properly received and looked after.

Rachel Carpenter said the three travellers had arrived as overnight guests. Though she had not made up any beds, she had got their meal, and Alice Lisle ate with them in the upstairs room where the guests slept. She said Alice Lisle normally dined downstairs.

In contrast to Rachel's mainly noncommittal approach, however, her husband was about to be more positive. He had never seen the letter in question, and denied being offered one by Dunne. To protect Alice Lisle, he recounted the only version of Dunne's first visit consistent with Dunne's assertion that he did not bring any letter with him on his first visit: that Dunne had told her at the outset he was acting for two people, one of whom was Hicks, and the other he did not know until after his arrest. He side-stepped the awkward question of what had been said in the courtyard by denying he was there when the travellers arrived: he met them only after they had separated, Hicks and Nelthorp sleeping in the room where they alone had dined with Alice Lisle. It was not until those two were already in the house that he had been to see about Dunne and his horse. Dunne, he said, had had nothing to drink as far as he knew. Neither of the Carpenters could have realised how completely the man they were trying to support was about to let them down.

Jeffreys was using the same velvet-glove treatment on Carpenter as he had earlier used on Dunne, as a preliminary to springing the awkward question: why had Carpenter tried to misrepresent Hicks and Dunne as vagrant intruders to Colonel Penruddock? In the event, Carpenter was saved from this approach, because Jeffreys was diverted by an interruption; but it left things looking bleaker still for Carpenter. One of the junior counsel announced that Dunne had finally decided to come clean, whatever the consequences. But that was too much to expect from a compulsive, frightened liar. As always, Dunne's first thought was for himself. No sooner had he opened his mouth than the jury were hearing yet again about the spectral messenger between himself and Hicks, and the fact that 'I never entertained these men a night in my house in my life'. True, maybe, but only because he had afforded them daytime shelter.

Panic had taken Dunne beyond simple logic, and every straw was worth clutching at. But he went on to admit rather more about the arrival at Moyles Court. He had seen someone dispose of Hicks's and Nelthorp's horses, and they had gone into the house first while he, and presumably Carpenter, had stabled his own horse. Carpenter had then taken him to join the others at supper with Alice Lisle. Though this supported Carpenter's account up to a point, it left Dunne exposed over what had been said both in the courtyard and during the meal.

Jeffreys was most interested in the supper-time conversation, in particular whether Nelthorp's identity and background had been discussed. Dunne was quickly in difficulties again, and began to regret his burst of courage.

Mr Rumsey: Now, my lord, Dunne says he will tell all, whether it make for him or against him.

LCJ: Let him but tell the truth, and I am satisfied.

Dunne: Sure, my lord I never entertained these men a night in my house in my life; but this Hicks sent that man to me, to go to my lady Lisle's to know whether she would please to entertain him; And when I came, my lady asked me, whether he had been in the army or no? I told her, I could not tell, I did not know that he was. She then asked me, if he had nobody else with him? I told her, I believed there was: This is the very truth of it, my lord. I asked her, might the men be entertained? She said they might. So when we came to my lady Lisle's on the Tuesday night, somebody took the two horses, I cannot tell who, if

I were to die; the two went in; and after I had set up my horse,
I went in along with Carpenter up into the chamber to my lady,
and to this Hicks and Nelthorp; and when I came there, I heard
my lady bid them welcome to her house; and Mr Carpenter, or
the maid, I cannot tell which, brought in the supper, and set it
upon the table.

LCJ: And didst thou eat or drink with them in the room, or not?

Dunne: My lord, I will tell everything that I know; I confess I did
both eat and drink there in the room . . . I did never know these
men were in the army when I carried the message to my lady
Lisle's, nor never did entertain them in my house in my lifetime,
so much as one night . . .

LCJ: What discourse had you that night at the table in the room?
. . . Was there nothing of coming from beyond seas, who came
from thence, and how they came? Come I would have it rather
the effect of thy own ingenuity, than lead thee, by any questions
that I can propound; come, tell us what was the discourse?

Dunne: I do not remember all the discourse.

LCJ: Prithee let me ask thee one question, and answer me it fairly;
Didst thou hear Nelthorp's name named in the room?

Dunne: My lord, I cannot tell whether he were called Nelthorp,
but it was either Crofts or Nelthorp, I am sure one of them . . .

LCJ: I will assure you, Nelthorp told me all the story before I
came out of town.

Dunne: I think, my lord, he was called Nelthorp in the room, and
there was some discourse about him.

LCJ: Ay, there was unquestionably, and I know thou wert by, and
that made me the more concerned to press upon thee the danger
of forswearing thyself.

Dunne: My lady asked Hicks who that gentleman was, and he
said it was Nelthorp, as I remember.

LCJ: Very well, and upon that discourse with Nelthorp, which I
had in town, did I give particular direction, that the outlawry of
Nelthorp should be brought down hither, for he told me
particularly of all the passages and discourses of his being
beyond sea, and coming from beyond sea: I would not mention
any such thing as any piece of evidence to influence this case,
but I could not but tremble to think after what I knew, that

anyone should dare so much to prevaricate with God and man, as to tell such horrid lies in the face of a court.

There seems no doubt, as Jeffreys said, that before leaving London he had heard Nelthorp's account of the rebel expedition from the time he had joined it in Holland. Nelthorp knew he was destined for the gallows, and a confession might possibly save him, even if he was not prepared to incriminate Alice Lisle. It is equally likely, as Dunne was beginning to confirm, that Nelthorp had also recounted his adventures to Alice Lisle; the apparent safety of her house and the conviviality at supper would naturally encourage confidences from all present. But it is scarcely conceivable that Nelthorp had told Jeffreys of his discourse with Alice Lisle: the whole basis of his effort to protect her was to emphasise her ignorance of his background before the arrest. Thus, to the extent that Jeffreys was implying the opposite, he was almost certainly bluffing. His attempt to prompt Dunne into revealing Nelthorp's account of his adventures, by an extremely leading question ('Was there nothing of coming from beyond seas, who came from thence, and how they came?'), discloses the anxiety of someone seeking confirmation of an account he recognises is far more credible and probable than the one he has been given. The pressure began to pay off: Dunne conceded he had heard the name of 'Crofts or Nelthorp, I am sure one of them', mentioned over supper, and 'there was some discourse about him'.

Jeffreys' attitude, more inquisitorial than judicial, is deeply repugnant to the modern legal mind. By usurping the advocate's function, the judge compromises his impartiality and the arena is left without an umpire. Today, even the prosecutor is expected to act with semi-judicial restraint: his task is to present the Crown's case objectively and not to strive for a conviction on equivocal facts. The criminal standard of proof, 'beyond reasonable doubt', reflects the state's recognition that acquitting the guilty is far more tolerable than convicting the innocent, so that, in terms of ultimate justice, a defendant's 'victory' is seldom the Crown's 'defeat'.

In Jeffreys' time, things were otherwise. In most political trials, an acquittal was a disaster for the Crown, and one reason why those charged with treason were allowed neither counsel, a copy of

the indictment nor a list of the witnesses against them. The rules of
evidence, as to the standard and burden of proof, were virtually
unknown, as were today's concepts of relevance and admissibility.
Thus, even though Alice Lisle faced no charge concerning Nelthorp,
his presence in her house as an outlaw and a rebel was more than
enough, in Jeffreys' view, to justify pressing Dunne into
incriminating her on his account as well as Hicks's. Jeffreys did not
shrink from trying to fill the gaps in Dunne's story by alluding to
his own investigations, obliquely suggesting there was a good deal
more to the case against Alice Lisle than the jury were likely to
hear. Somewhere, his lawyer's conscience told him that this was
grossly unfair. His comment that it was 'not a piece of evidence',
and that the jury should not allow it to influence their decision,
shows he knew it was something far better left unsaid in the first
place.

Anxious to bring his oppressive inquisition to an end, Dunne
initiated the next exchange and then, as with his effort to recall
Fane's name, asked for respite. But Jeffreys was unrelenting. He did,
however, withdraw the threat of prosecution for perjury.

Dunne: What does your lordship ask me?

LCJ: Come, I will ask thee a plain question; was there no
    discourse about the battle, and of their being in the army?

Dunne: There was some such discourse, my lord.

LCJ: Ay, prithee now tell us what that discourse was.

Dunne: My lord, I will tell you, when I have recollected it, if you
    will give me time till tomorrow morning.

LCJ: . . . we cannot stay so long, our business must be despatched
    now; but I would have all people consider what a reason there
    is, that they should be pressed to join with me in hearty prayers
    to Almighty God, that this sin of lying and perjury may never be
    laid at thy door. What say'st thou? Prithee tell us what the
    discourse was.

Dunne: My lord, they did talk of fighting, but I cannot exactly tell
    what the discourse was.

LCJ: And thou saidst thou did eat and drink with them in the
    same room?

Dunne: I did so, my lord, I confess it.

LCJ: And it was not a little girl that lighted thee to bed, or conducted thee in?

Dunne: It was not a little girl.

LCJ: Who was it then?

Dunne: It was Mr Carpenter, my lord.

LCJ: And why didst thou tell so many lies then? . . . Prithee be free, and tell us what discourse there was.

Dunne: My lord, they did talk of fighting, but I cannot remember what it was.

LCJ: Did you lie with them?

Dunne: No, my lord, I did not.

LCJ: Well, I see thou wilt answer nothing ingenuously, therefore I will trouble myself no more with thee: go on with your evidence, gentlemen.

Mr Jennings: My lord, we have done, we have no more witnesses.

Dunne's final answer about having spent the night alone was a transparent lie, almost certainly prompted by a deepening sense of shame. It was now obvious he had betrayed Alice Lisle to save himself, for he had elaborated on the supper-time 'discourse about the battle' only after Jeffreys' promise he would not face prosecution for perjury. But this also betrayed the Carpenters, who had gone to such lengths to support his earlier version of a solitary picnic below stairs with nothing to drink.

This final contradiction convinced no one, least of all Jeffreys, who brusquely dismissed him. That was the end of the case for the Crown, and it was now for Alice Lisle to make her defence.

SIXTEEN

Alice Lisle's Defence

At Jeffreys' invitation, Alice Lisle gave her side of the story, though not on oath: procedural rules prevented her and her witness being sworn. That was the least of her difficulties. From the outset she faced abrasive interruptions from the bench, which, whatever sympathy they generated for her with the jury, left her account hard to follow. But it came to this: during the rebellion, which she opposed, she had been in London, and did not return to Moyles Court until about a week before Dunne's arrival on Saturday, 25 July. He had sought shelter for one person only, her old friend John Hicks, whom she knew exclusively as a Presbyterian minister 'that used to preach, and not to fight'. It was because she believed he was a religious refugee, not a rebel, that she told him to come under cover of darkness.

In law, and no doubt she had the benefit of Matthew Browne's advice on this, she understood there could be no question of her being tried for harbouring Hicks until he had first been convicted of treason. She had no idea he was bringing Nelthorp: if that name had been mentioned, she would have remembered his outlawry from the proclamation. She was surprised when Nelthorp arrived, and did not discover who he was until 'later'. Wisely, she avoided mentioning the letter or the 'Crofts' alias used by Nelthorp, though left herself vulnerable when she said 'I never asked his name'. George Creed confirmed Nelthorp's claim that she did not know who he was.

Two passages in Alice Lisle's evidence appear in italics in the first edition of *State Trials*, as shown below, but in ordinary type in all subsequent editions. The most probable explanation is that the reporter recognised their crucial significance for Alice Lisle's defence and, as counsel do today, underlined what she said as he took it down. This tends to confirm not merely that the *State Trials* account is junior counsel's contemporary note, but also that it was first printed, unedited, exactly as it was recorded.

LCJ: Then you that are for the prisoner at the bar, now is your time to make your defence; you hear what is charged upon you, and what a kind of shuffling here has been to stifle the truth . . . What have you to say for yourself?

Mrs Lisle: My lord, that which I have to say to it, is this: I knew of nobody's coming to my house but Mr Hicks, and for him I was informed that he did abscond, by reason of warrants that were out against him for preaching in private meetings, but I never heard that he was in the army, nor that Nelthorp was to come with him; and for that reason it was, that I sent to him to come by night: but for the other man, Nelthorp, I never knew it was Nelthorp, I could die upon it, nor did not know what name he had, till after he came to my house; but as for Mr Hicks, I did not in the least suspect him to have been in the army, being a Presbyterian minister, that used to preach, and not to fight.

LCJ: But I will tell you, there is not one of those lying, snivelling, canting Presbyterian rascals, but one way or other had a hand in the late horrid conspiracy and rebellion . . . show me a Presbyterian, and I will engage to show a lying knave.

Mrs Lisle: My lord, I abhorred both the principles and practices of the late rebellion.

LCJ: I am sure you had great reason for it.

Mrs Lisle: Besides, my lord, I should have been the most ungrateful person living, should I have been disloyal, or acted anything against the present king, considering how much I was obliged to him for my estate.

LCJ: Oh then! Ungrateful! Ungrateful adds to the load which was between man and man, and is the basest crime that any one can be guilty of.

Mrs Lisle: My lord, had I been tried in London I could have had my lady Abergavenny and several other persons of quality, that could have testified how much I was against this rebellion, and with what detestation I spoke against it, during the time of it; for I was at that time at London, and stayed there until after the Duke of Monmouth was beheaded; and if I had certainly known the time of my trial in the country, I could have had the testimony of those persons of honour for me. But, my lord, I am told, and so I thought it would have been; that I should not have been tried as a traitor for harbouring him, till he was convict for a traitor. My lord, I would take my death of it, that I never knew of Nelthorp's coming nor anything of his being Nelthorp; I never asked his name, and if he had told it me, I had then remembered the proclamation. I do assure you, my lord, for my own part, I did abhor those that were in that horrid plot and conspiracy against the king's life; I know my duty to my king better, and have always exercised it; I defy anybody in the world that ever knew the contrary, to come to give testimony.

Accepting Penruddock's account of the sequence of the arrests, Alice Lisle continued with her reasons for denying Nelthorp's presence after the other two had been arrested. Shocked by the aggressive search, and particularly by Dowding's efforts ('that white headed man . . . was one of those that rifled and plundered my house, and tore open my trunk'), she had hoped to limit the havoc the soldiers were causing by trying to persuade them there was no one there instead of surrendering the hidden man.

This was dangerous ground. If Nelthorp really was the stranger she believed, and she had never even asked his name, why not give him up at the outset and avert the search? She was clearly conscious of the danger, because, despite Jeffreys' observation that she faced no charge concerning Nelthorp, she insisted on her ignorance of his identity six times before the jury retired. In the result, she 'protested too much', lending silent emphasis to the fact she wanted to conceal.

Her point about the deterrent impact of the risk was convincing: 'It cannot be imagined, that I would venture the hazard of my own life, and the ruin both of myself and my children, to conceal one that I never knew in my life, as I did not know Mr Nelthorp, but had heard of him in the proclamation.' She explained that her social commitments would have limited the guests' stay to a week; and, conscious of her murdered husband's political shadow over the case – as one of Charles I's 'regicides', and the man who had joined in condemning Penruddock's father, facts no 'quality' jury could fail to know about – she underlined her own strongly royalist loyalties.

'I went not out of my chamber all the day, in which that king was beheaded, and I believe I shed more tears for him, than any woman then living did.' She pointed to her son's upbringing and recent patriotic service against Monmouth: 'He was in arms on the king's side in this business: it was I that bred him up to fight for the king.'

LCJ: Have you any more to say?

Mrs Lisle: As to what they say of my denying Nelthorp to be in my house, *I was in great consternation and fear of the soldiers, who were very rude and violent, and could not be restrained by their officers from robbery, and plundering my house.* And I beseech your lordship to make that construction of it; and I humbly beg of your lordship not to harbour an ill opinion of me, because of those false reports that go about of me, relating to my carriage towards the old king, that I was any ways consenting to the death of king Charles I, for, my lord, that is as false as God is true; my lord, I went not out of my chamber all the day, in which that king was beheaded, and I believe I shed more tears for him, than any woman then living did; and this the late countess of Monmouth, and my lady Marlborough, and my lord chancellor Hyde, if they were alive, and twenty persons of the most eminent quality could bear witness for me. And I do repeat it, my lord, as I hope to attain salvation, I never did know Nelthorp, nor never did see him before in my life, nor did I know of anybody coming, but Mr Hicks, and him I did know to be a Nonconformist minister; and there being as is well known, warrants out to apprehend nonconformist ministers,[1] I was willing to give him shelter from these warrants. I was come down but that week into the country, when this man came to me from Mr Hicks, to know if he might be received at my house; and I told him, if Mr Hicks pleased, he might come upon Tuesday in the evening, and should be welcome; but withal I told him, I must go away the Monday following from that place, but while I stayed I would entertain him. And I beseech your lordship to believe, I had no intention to harbour him but as a Nonconformist, and that I knew was no treason. It cannot be imagined that I would venture the hazard of my own life, and the ruin both of myself and children, to conceal one that I never knew in my life, as I did not know Mr Nelthorp, but had heard of him in the proclamation. And for that whiteheaded man that speaks of my denying them, as I said before, he was one of them that rifled and plundered my house, and tore open my trunk; and if I should not be convicted, he and the rest of them may be called to an account for what they did, for they ought not to have meddled with my goods: Besides, my lord, I have a witness that can testify what Mr Nelthorp said, when he was examined before –

LCJ: Look you, Mrs Lisle, that will signify little; but if you have any witnesses, call them, we will hear what they say: Who is that man you speak of?

Mrs Lisle: George Creed his name is; there he is.

LCJ: Well, what do you know?

Creed: I heard Nelthorp say, that my lady Lisle did not know of his coming, nor did not know his name, nor had he ever told his name, till he named himself to Colonel Penruddock, when he was taken.

LCJ: Well, this is nothing; she is not indicted for harbouring Nelthorp, but Hicks: Have you any more witnesses?

Mrs Lisle: No, my lord.

LCJ: Have you any more to say for yourself?

Mrs Lisle: My lord, I came but five days before this into the country –

LCJ: Nay, I cannot tell when you came into the country, nor I do not care; it seems you came time enough to harbour rebels.

Mrs Lisle: I stayed in London till all the rebellion was past and over; and I never uttered a good word for the rebels, nor ever harboured so much as a good wish for them in my mind: I know the king is my sovereign, and I know my duty to him; and if I would have ventured my life for anything, it should have been to serve him. I know it is his due, and I owed all I had in the world to him: But though I could not fight for him myself, my son did; he was actually in arms on the king's side in this business; I instructed him always in loyalty, and sent him thither; it was I that bred him up to fight for the king.

LCJ: Well, have you done?

Mrs Lisle: Yes, my lord.

LCJ: Have you a mind to say any thing more?

Mrs Lisle: No, my lord.

LCJ: Then command silence.

But she had not quite finished. No doubt guided by Browne, she raised the point of venue, challenging the court's jurisdiction in Hampshire over an act of treason by Hicks in Somerset. As a good lawyer, Browne may have recalled the decision in Edward Noseworthy's case the previous November. Charged with seditious libel for words allegedly spoken in Wiltshire ('I hope to live to see the judges hanged that tried Fitzharris'), Noseworthy was acquitted when the evidence showed they had been spoken in Dorset. But the bench was unreceptive. Regardless of wherever Hicks might have broken the law, the offence Alice Lisle had 'committed' – Jeffreys was in no mood to concede her innocence – was in Hampshire. She accordingly left the point, and contented herself with repeating the main plank of her defence before he started his summing-up.

Lisle: My Lord, may I speak one word more? My lord, I beseech you afford me your patience and your advice; Keynsham, where Mr Hicks is said to be in arms, does not lie in this county.

LCJ: That is nothing: But the treason you committed was in this county.

Mrs Lisle: But I assure you lordship I never knew he was in the army; and for any talk or discourse in private, about his or Nelthorp's being there, I never heard any; indeed one of them asked me, whether the duke of Monmouth was beheaded? And I told them, yes, for so he was before I came out of town: And that is all the discourse that I can remember, wherein he is concerned.

LCJ: Well, have you any more to say now?

Mrs Lisle: No, my lord.

Alice Lisle's argument was not as superficial as Jeffreys' curt rejection might have implied. It raised two linked, but distinct, issues: the Hampshire court's jurisdiction over an offence in Somerset; and, if that was questionable, the propriety of proceedings in Hampshire that depended on conclusive proof and recognition of the Somerset offence. Jeffreys answered only the second question on the assumption that there was no doubt about the first. But that was the point Alice Lisle was now challenging. If she was right, and Hicks could only be tried in Somerset, it immeasurably strengthened her other argument, that she could not be tried at all for harbouring until Hicks had first been convicted of treason. For practical purposes, however, he had been tried and convicted in Hampshire, but behind his back, in the wrong county, and on evidence he had had no chance to contradict. If he had a defence, no one knew what it was, nor had any jury been asked to assess it. The argument was not merely legalistic: it went to the root of a man's right to a fair trial.

Probably because it was getting late and he wanted to finish, Jeffreys gave her no opportunity to develop the point so that he could demolish it head on, as he should have done. But there was perhaps another, rather less creditable, reason for his reluctance. The question of venue had already been decided against Alice Lisle in the case of Lord Maguire in 1645. As ringleader of a rebellion in Dublin, where he was caught, Maguire claimed that the appropriate mode of trial was by his fellow peers in Dublin, since he was a member of the peerage. After a lengthy argument by William Prynn, it was held that 'he may and shall be tried here by an ordinary jury of Middlesex and outed of his peerage'. If a peer could be taken from Dublin to London to face trial by jury, what objection could there be to a commoner captured in England being dealt with in whatever county was most convenient? Thus there was no valid legal reason for Hicks's absence from the dock at Winchester alongside Alice Lisle. On the other hand, there was the very practical reason that his evidence might easily tip the scales in her favour on the question of what she knew about him. If the jury ever got the idea that Hicks was deliberately kept away to help the prosecution, they might redress the balance by acquitting her. From the Crown's perspective, the point was better left where it was, and particularly when the main point, the propriety of prosecuting Alice Lisle before Hicks had been convicted, remained unaffected. It was an issue that the jury would scrutinise with care.

SEVENTEEN

Jeffreys' Summing-up: Part 1

Jeffreys began his summing-up in terms familiar to the modern
practitioner. He reminded the jury of their task and their oath:
they had to decide according to 'the evidence that has here been
given forth', and make their assessment independently of any
opinions or arguments put forward by either side or by the bench.
Jeffreys' own function was simply to remind them of what had been
said, in accordance with his judicial oath.

LCJ: Then, gentlemen of the jury: This is a case . . . of very great
weight and moment; wherein the interest of the public, and the
life of a person of quality and fortune are put into your hands.
And the great business which has detained both us and you so
long, has been an endeavour (if it were possible) to find out the
truth: which indeed is the business of all enquiries of this
nature: we sit not here, nor are you there, upon any other
errand; nor is anything desired by the court, or required of you,
but that the truth may be made manifest. 'Tis that you are
bound to . . . for your oath is, "That you shall well and truly
try, and true deliverance make, between our sovereign lord the
king and the prisoner at the bar, according to your evidence, as
you shall answer it to God". . . . Gentlemen . . . you being all
persons of quality and reputation in your country . . . it is to be
hoped, that not anything can move you, either to compassion
of the prisoner on the one hand, or her allegations and
protestations of innocence; nor, on the other hand, to be
influenced by anything that comes from the court, or is
insinuated by the learned counsel . . . but that you will entirely
consider what evidence has been given to you, and being guided
by that evidence alone, you that are judges of the fact, will let us
know the truth of that fact, by a sincere and upright verdict.

And inasmuch, gentlemen, as the evidence has been long in giving (though the substantial part of it, perhaps, be in a narrow compass) I will repeat it to you, as near as I can, with all faithfulness and integrity, as I shall answer it to the Great Judge of heaven and earth . . . without any aggravation or alteration on the one side, and without any omission on the other: and I shall do it, purely to help your memories who are to determine the fact . . . And I would repeat it once more, that you are not to be led by any insinuations of the prisoner, nor by any allegations from the learned counsel, whose business it is to open the fact; but that fact so opened, is no further to guide you in your enquiry than as it is proved.

Thus far, Jeffreys' address was beyond reproach and could serve as a model for any Crown Court judge today. The same cannot be said of what followed. This fell into two parts: a highly partisan outline of the rebellion's historical and religious context, and then a review of the evidence, which fell well short of being either balanced or fair.

As with his earlier tirade against Dunne, Jeffreys highlighted the power of the Almighty, the truth of the Christian religion and the authority of the Established Church, all overwhelmingly vindicated by the rebels' defeat. Divine intervention had delivered the kingdom from 'the late horrid and detestable rebellion', and not for the first time. Jeffreys recalled the 'state of confusion and misery' under Cromwell, which ended only when 'God of his infinite mercy brought our blessed sovereign (now in heaven)' back to the throne in 1660.

Thereafter, Restoration England under Charles II had been Utopia. 'Our lives, liberties and properties inviolably were secured; every man safe under the shadow of his own vine, and eat the fruit of his own labour; and while our neighbours suffered the calamities of war, we were surrounded with the blessings of peace.'

When Charles was succeeded by his bountiful brother, James II, at the beginning of the year, this idyllic state of affairs would doubtless have continued but for the efforts of a 'corrupted and bigoted' faction who rejected their monarch's fatherly hand despite his declared support for the Anglican Church. This they had done 'in the name of religion', the ultimate sacrilege: 'These men will hardly be brought to believe that rebellion is the sin of witchcraft, though the scriptures have directly given it that character.'

Worse, this faction 'call themselves ministers of the gospel . . . and cry out they are fighting the Lord's battle, when they are attempting to kill the Lord's anointed'. From this thinly veiled allusion, Jeffreys came into the open about who he was getting at: 'Those hypocrites, the Nonconformist parsons'. And the one he had particularly in mind was Hicks, 'that wretch, that had nothing but the name of religion; for his soul is blacker in the eyes of God, and the thoughts of all honest men, than ever his coat was'.

Such doctrinal polemics seem more appropriate to the Victorian pulpit than the bench, and one can scarcely imagine anything comparable in court or church today. But the seventeenth-century alignment of judicial and religious authority was very much closer. The criminal penalties handed down by the judges clearly reflected Old Testament ideas of retribution; the court of Heaven, as distinct from paradise, was in every sense a judgment-seat presided over by the Almighty; and the penalties for poor performance in getting there were hardly less painful than those imposed by the secular authorities. While parts of Jeffreys' address may have been embroidered, it echoes the sermons preached and published at the time, particularly those heard on 26 July, that Sunday 'appointed to be a Day of Thanksgiving for Deliverance from the Rebellion', when Dunne was finding his way home from Moyles Court.

Jeffreys' depiction of Nonconformity as a species of treason pointed to its rejection of Anglican authority as well as the hypocrisy of its followers. His purpose was to encourage the jury to treat Hicks's and Alice Lisle's faith as an additional reason for convicting the prisoner, and sideline any defence based on her belief that Hicks was a preacher rather than a rebel.

Gentlemen, before I come to the particular evidence of this fact, I must crave leave to say something of a matter in general that is very well known . . . we are all of us here unspeakably obliged to bless the great God of heaven . . . for his infinite goodness in preserving and protecting us from the imminent ruin which the late horrid and detestable rebellion would (had it succeeded) have inevitably brought upon us . . .

We are by no means to forget his mercy towards our late
sovereign of blessed memory, and with him towards us, when he
brought him out of exile and bondage, and us out of that state of
confusion and misery, which our country had for many years
groaned under: when all religion as well as sovereignty, and all
obedience, duty and deference to superiors were quite lost, God of
his infinite mercy . . . brought our blessed sovereign (now in
heaven), and his gracious majesty that now reigns . . . after a long
and tedious rebellion, into a quiet and peaceable possession of
their undoubted rights and inheritances, and with him restored to
us our religion, the best of religions, the true Protestant reformed
religion . . .

Besides, gentlemen, we cannot be sufficiently thankful to our
God for the mercies we enjoyed under that blessed king . . . we
safely and uninterruptedly enjoyed our religion, the greatest
blessing on this side [of] immortality; our lives, liberties, and
properties inviolably were secured; every man safe under the
shadow of his own vine, and eat the fruit of his own labour; and
while our neighbours suffered the calamities of war, we were
surrounded with all the blessings of peace and slept securely under
the government of a gracious and merciful king: every one of us
had even what our own hearts could desire; and if we wanted
anything, it could be only thankful and dutiful hearts to our God
and our prince, during whose life we continued in a happy state
and condition.

But it having pleased God . . . to take that blessed prince to
himself; what thanks ought we to pay him for his gracious
goodness, in leaving so great and so glorious a successor as his
royal brother, our present sovereign . . . whom I pray Almighty
God may long live and happily reign among us. This gracious
prince, as soon as ever he came to the possession of his undoubted
right and inheritance . . . what does he? Even before he was asked,
in the very first minutes of his reign, he begins with bounty to his
subjects, and declares his resolution to preserve them safe in their
dearest and most precious enjoyments, in their religion . . . (and)
in their laws, liberties, rights and properties . . .

But alas! . . . we cannot but remember, that . . . faction and
sedition, hypocrisy and malice had besotted and bewitched a

great part of his subjects, and corrupted, blinded, and bigoted them to such an height of impiety, that a rebellion must begin his reign . . .

Blessed God! What is the way that this devil of sedition comes to bewitch people to such a height, when Almighty God had so lately delivered us from the misery and confusion of a civil war? . . . These men . . . will hardly be brought to believe that rebellion is the sin of witchcraft, though the scriptures have directly given it that character . . .

Nay, is it not yet more strange and horrid, that some men, who call themselves ministers of the gospel, shall come to be bell-wethers of rebellion, and cry out they are fighting the Lord's battle, when they are attempting to kill the Lord's anointed? . . .

When we consider, gentlemen, the ring-leader of this late rebellion . . . the arch-rebel and traitor Monmouth I mean, should arrive to such an height of impudence and villainy, as to bless God that he could with satisfaction reflect upon two years life very regularly spent; but how? In manifest adultery and uncleanness; nor can it be spoke or thought of without inexpressible horror.

Alack! gentlemen, when we find religion made use of as a subterfuge and cloak for such impious practices, it gives too much occasion for our enemies to think us Atheists. The very Turks will hate us, and Pagans detest us, as the most irreligious, profane people in the world . . .

Gentlemen, I do not speak this for the sake of speaking, but I would fain deliver my own soul and yours from having any hand in such horrible impieties, and that, by testifying our abhorrence of them by publicly declaring ourselves to be enemies to those hypocrites, the Nonconformist parsons . . .

Consider, gentlemen, this is that which has brought this poor unfortunate gentlewoman, the prisoner at the bar, into this deplorable condition: What could prevail upon her to run such a hazard as this, but only her affection and deluded zeal for that wretch, that had nothing but the name of religion; for his soul is blacker in the eyes of God, and the thoughts of all honest men, than ever his coat was? You see by the proofs what an impudent unsanctified villain he was; for when these gentlemen that have given evidence, were in the custody and under the power of the rebels, he must tempt and provoke them to leave off and forsake their duty to their natural lord and lawful sovereign the king . . .

This review, spanning Jeffreys' lifetime, was a highly personal perspective. In retrospect, through the eyes of an Anglican royalist, the prosperity Jeffreys had achieved after the Restoration stood in glowing contrast to the austerity of his adolescence, when the country had 'groaned' under the Commonwealth. The ascetic hand of Puritanism had in fact descended well before Cromwell's victory: the theatres were closed in 1642; and in 1644, the year of Jeffreys' birth, it became illegal even to celebrate Christmas, though many continued to do so secretly. The compulsory Sunday observance laws, forbidding most sports and recreations, merely deepened the gloom.

Born in Shropshire during the Civil War, Jeffreys may also have remembered the ravaging impact of those years on his father's finances. He was nevertheless educated during the Protectorate under the staunchly royalist headmasters of Shrewsbury, St Paul's and Westminster, the last of whom, Dr Busby, remained there for fifty-seven years, and was able to encourage his pupils' abilities despite the energetic floggings he gave them.

Jeffreys went up to Trinity College, Cambridge, in 1662, when most ministers who rejected Anglican principles had been ejected from their livings and thus excluded from the dawn of the Restoration. Jeffreys preferred to overlook such ministers in his portrayal of the blessings of post-1660 society. The Clarendon Code drove them underground to the shelter of sympathetic patrons such as Alice Lisle and Frances Fiennes, sometimes to penury and starvation, where they remained, apart from the intervals of the 1672 and 1687 Indulgences, until the Toleration Act of 1689. While enforcement tended to be intermittent and the penalties variable (Nonconformists never suffered the ferocious persecution of the Catholics, or the Huguenots in France), the tables were effectively turned on what had been the position under the Commonwealth. Not for Dissenters the safe and comforting 'shadow of the vine', or the safety of life, liberty and property: those were the privileges of loyal, Anglican subjects prepared to conform and not make trouble.

This was not the only omission from Jeffreys' otherwise tranquil landscape. Though there had been no invasion as such, Dutch warships had sailed up the Medway in 1667 and burned part of the English fleet, causing many Londoners to evacuate; and Charles had joined forces with France in the campaign against the Dutch between 1672 and 1674. In the summer of 1678, Titus Oates had concocted his mainly imaginary Popish Plot, which, after the unsolved murder that October of the Protestant magistrate, Sir Edmund Berry Godfrey, threw the nation into panic and sent many innocent Catholics to the gallows. Oates's fabrications had recently caught up with him: Jeffreys had presided over his trial for perjury only four months earlier, in May 1685, and with Wythens had imposed the fearsome penalty of a double flogging through London.

The Popish Plot had preceded the much less fanciful Insurrection and Rye House plots instigated by the Whigs in 1682 and 1683 to assassinate Charles II and bring down the government, in which both Monmouth and Nelthorp had been deeply involved. Jeffreys had acted first as prosecutor and then, in September 1683, as Lord Chief Justice, in the treason and sedition trials that followed. He knew the reality of the Whig threat to the nation's stability, which it had been the main purpose of his appointment to counter; it could never be said that the people had 'slept securely' at that stage of the reign. Conscious, perhaps, that his audience might feel insulted by such a flagrant rewriting of history, Jeffreys referred to the plots simply to emphasise the religious respectability the conspirators had sought.

Monmouth's rebellion, as Jeffreys would have it, was an unprompted eruption of Nonconformist zealots, who merely bit the hand of toleration offered by James II, and rejected the Anglican comfort they could not recognise. Yet they paraded under the spurious banner of Protestantism, led by a man whose illegitimacy and adultery were enough to condemn him quite apart from his political aspirations: 'I dare boldly affirm, that the meanest subject within the kingdom that is legitimate has a better title to the Crown, than he had; . . . and that prince of theirs must have the title of a Protestant prince'.

The truth was that, regardless of his origins or philandering, Monmouth, like most revolutionaries, wanted power. His Protestant banner was a more or less respectable challenge to his uncle's Catholicism, and while that may have been one reason why he gathered a sizeable Nonconformist following, a much more powerful draw was his personality. He was young, handsome, adventurous and, at the beginning at least, successful. Humble country-folk with little to lose joined him for the excitement; but with neither a decisive military victory nor a general's determination, the campaign lost momentum. The powerful Whig landowners, with much to lose, remained sceptical spectators, and the rebellion ended as it had begun, a grassroots rising.

Jeffreys' diatribe misrepresenting the politics of the rebellion was designed not merely to obtain a verdict on religious grounds: it was also a sycophantic attempt to ingratiate himself with the king. He knew he was on the verge of the appointment he coveted most, the Lord Chancellorship, and was publicly proclaiming his own allegiance. Though he was undoubtedly aware of James II's Catholicism, the arguments over the status of Catholics had not yet developed, and were irrelevant to the rebellion. Jeffreys therefore avoided all reference to these points, confining the debate to the Anglican–Nonconformist conflict. There was no reason yet to doubt the monarch's support for the Church of England, as declared at his first Privy Council in February. Loyalty to that faith was as much a citizen's obligation as loyalty to the Crown, and Jeffreys put himself forward as the prime exponent of both.

EIGHTEEN

Jeffreys' Summing-up: Part 2

Jeffreys turned to the charge before the jury. The first point was whether Hicks had been proved a traitor: 'But now, gentlemen . . . it is very notorious this fellow Hicks was actually in this rebellion; you have it sworn by three several persons that saw him . . . they tell you, when they were in prison he would have corrupted them from their duty; and yesterday they saw him . . . and he could not deny but he was there.'

Hicks faced two accusations. First, according to Monmouth's ex-prisoners, of having been 'actually in this rebellion'; and second, of having tried 'to corrupt them from their duty'. Each charge was partially confirmed by Hicks's admission, at the confrontation the previous day in Salisbury, of having at least seen the captives at Keynsham, and by his confession to Dowding of having joined the rebel army.

What Jeffreys did not mention was the reasons for Hicks's conspicuous absence from court, and that any defences remained untested. Even less was he disposed to point out that there was no suggestion that Alice Lisle knew anything about Hicks's 'corrupting advocacy' in the stables at Keynsham. The prosecution case was simply that the conversation at the Moyles Court supper had ranged over 'the battle, their being in the army and the fighting', cast in generalised terms that the jury were to find deeply unsatisfactory. Jeffreys would have simplified their task had he explained the two species of Hicks's treason, and had then analysed how much Alice Lisle knew, and the room for her belief that he was only a persecuted priest. In fact, he never mentioned this defence, and made what amounted to a closing speech for the Crown, leaving no doubt about what he thought the verdict should be.

After telling the jury the law was for him, and the facts for them, Jeffreys embarked on his main theme: Dunne's prevarication over his journeys to Moyles Court, and what had happened there, pointed as positively to Alice Lisle's guilt as the admissions that had been wrung from him.

> This person, Mrs Lisle, the prisoner at the bar, she is accused for receiving and harbouring this person; And, gentlemen, I must tell you for law, of which we are judges, and not you, That if any person be in actual rebellion against the king, and another person (who really and actually was not in rebellion) does receive, harbour, comfort and conceal him that was such, a receiver is as much a traitor as he who . . . bore arms: We are bound by our oaths and consciences, to deliver and declare what is law; and you are bound . . . to deliver and declare to us, by your verdict, the truth of the fact.
>
> Gentlemen, that he was there in rebellion, is . . . unquestionably proved: That there are sufficient testimonies to satisfy you that this woman did receive and harbour him, is that which is left to your consideration . . . truly I am sorry to have occasion for repeating the circumstances of the proof; I mean . . . what time has been spent in endeavouring to find out the truth in a fellow, that in defiance of . . . threats and persuasion, would prevaricate and shuffle to conceal that truth . . . But out of true Christian charity, as I told him, so I tell you, I do heartily pray, and all good Christians I hope will join with me in it, to the God of infinite mercy that he would have mercy upon his soul, upon which he hath contracted so great a guilt by the impudence of his behaviour . . .

Despite the tangle of Dunne's lies, Jeffreys believed the truth had finally surfaced. He was prepared to accept that Nelthorp's identity had not begun to emerge before supper had been served.

> Gentlemen, I . . . must take notice of his prevarications . . . in short, to come to the truth. First, he says, he came upon an errand from a man, he knows not whom, to my Lady Lisle's house; and thither he is brought by one Barter; and when he comes there, he tells her, he comes in the name of one Hicks, who desired to be entertained there. Then she asks . . . whether Hicks had been in

the army; and he told her he did not know; and he swears now he did not: But at last it came out, that it was to entertain Hicks and another person; but it should seem that other person was not named; and Barter tells you that Hicks and another person (who afterwards proved to be Nelthorp) are promised to be entertained, and ordered to come in the evening. But not to go backward and forward, as he has done in his evidence, denying what he afterwards acknowledged, that he saw any body besides a little girl: that he pulled down the hay out of the rack for his horse; that he eat any thing but cake and cheese that he had brought with him from home; that he was ever made to drink, or to eat or drink in the house, or ever meddled or made with any body in the house:[1] At last we are told that Carpenter met with him; and came out with a lanthorn and candle, took care of his horse, carried him into the room where Hicks and Nelthorp were, and the prisoner at the bar, Mrs Lisle; there they all supped together; there they fell into discourse; there Nelthorp's name was named, and they talked of being in the army, and of the fight: and so it is all come out, and makes a full and positive evidence.

Quite apart from Dunne's incompetent performance, Jeffreys believed that the evidence Alice Lisle had not challenged was more than enough to convict her. With rebels seeking refuge where they could, to arrange for strangers to come after dark, to entertain them and to feed them in near-total seclusion even within her own house, raised questions that required cogent explanations if her innocence was to be accepted. But this part of Jeffreys' address totally ignored the main plank of her defence, the claim that she thought Hicks was a religious refugee rather than a rebel. Had he wished, Jeffreys could have dealt with this defence, and its inherent weaknesses, by exposing the contradictions in the way she and Carpenter had greeted Penruddock. He preferred, however, to disregard it: it was late at night, and he may have felt it would be too much for a tired jury to grapple with. Maybe there was a risk they might even accept her claim.

But then . . . you are to consider . . . this was after the rebellion was all over; for it seems during the rebellion she was in London, and it was notoriously known that the King's forces were in pursuit of the rebels . . . and this would . . . convince any considerate person that she was to conceal those she ought not to conceal; because she directed the particular time wherein they should come, and that was at night; and no prudent person would receive strangers in the night, and give such directions in such a season without some extraordinary ground for it. When they came there, she provided a supper for them; and you see what care is taken that the woman only is permitted to bring the supper to the door, and the husband must set it on the table; nobody is permitted to attend there but he. Works of darkness always desire to be in the dark: works of rebellion and such like are never done in the light.

Jeffreys believed the key to what had really happened was Barter. His visit to Moyles Court, Alice Lisle's attempt to befriend him, and Dunne's change of tune over the money he expected to make, gave a clear insight into what was going on, and Barter had been fearful for his own safety unless he informed the authorities of what he had seen and heard.

But then comes that honest fellow Barter (. . . he ought to be remembered with a great remark for his honesty), he tells you, he conducted him to the house, and what discourse passed there in his hearing. The prisoner asked him what countryman he was, and whether he was a brickmaker, and promised him so many acres of land in Carolina.[2] The fellow . . . could not eat or sleep quietly, as men that have honest minds are uneasy under such things; falsehood, and treason, and hypocrisy are a heavy load; and, blessed be God, things were by this means discovered: for he goes and tells Colonel Penruddock; and withal, Dunne swears to Barter it was the bravest job that he ever had in his life; whereas in the beginning of his story, he would have told you a strange story of a black beard and I do not know what, and that he got not one groat by it: that he gave the man half a crown out of his own pocket, and was so industrious, as when he knew the way no farther, that he would hire one himself to show him the way, and all for nothing, but only for the kindness he had for a black beard.

Jeffreys then suggested that Alice Lisle was as much a hypocrite as a traitor. Her religious observance, her 'grief' at Charles I's execution and her 'gratitude' for the benevolence Charles II and his brother James had shown by restoring her property were, as her willingness to harbour rebels plainly demonstrated, a transparent façade. Worse, she was the widow of a well-known regicide, whose condemnation of 'that blessed martyr' was the ultimate treason.

Later commentators who criticise Jeffreys for this insinuating allusion to John Lisle are fully justified, given his immediate acknowledgement of its irrelevance on the issue of Alice's guilt. They do, however, overlook the judicial dilemma in dealing with those who have achieved notoriety. Must the judge ignore their background entirely, in the hope that the jury, through ignorance or fair-mindedness, will do likewise? Or should he deal with it head-on, assuming that better-informed jurors will act more conscientiously than those who know only part of the truth? There is no easy answer; and in the seventeenth century, it is doubtful whether Jeffreys went further than lawyers or laymen considered tolerable. He probably also felt the need to deal with the point in view of his complacent comment, at the end of Penruddock's evidence, about John Lisle's handling of Hewett's trial.

At all events, Jeffreys was open about the approach he had received the previous evening from a 'Mr Tipping', one of Alice Lisle's nephews, who had come from her sister's family home at Wheatfield, Oxfordshire, for the trial. Tipping was concerned that Alice Lisle should be judged on the facts rather than on gossip about her past loyalties. In publicly endorsing this view, Jeffreys clearly felt it was better to mention Tipping's approach than to conceal it, if only to forestall later rumours about clandestine conversations.

Besides, gentlemen, I am sorry to remember something that dropped even from the gentlewoman herself; she pretends to religion and loyalty very much, how greatly she wept at the death of king Charles the Martyr, and owns her great obligations to the late King and his royal brother; that she had not had a being, nor anything to maintain it for twenty years last past but from their bounty, and yet no sooner is one in the grave, but she forgets all gratitude, and entertains . . . rebels against his royal successor.

I will not say what hand her husband had in the death of that blessed martyr, she has enough to answer for . . . and I must confess it ought not one way or other to make any ingredient into this case what she was in former times: and I told a relation of hers, Mr Tipping by name, that came to me last night, to desire that she might not lie under some imputations that were gone abroad of her, that she rejoiced at the death of king Charles I, nor that any false report of that nature might influence the court or jury against her, that it should not: be the thing true or false, it is of no weight one way or other in the trial of this case, nor is she to be accountable for it.

Jeffreys now touched, albeit too briefly, on a point of 'very great moment' and relevance to Alice Lisle's guilt: her denial to Penruddock that there was anyone in the house, when she had actually entertained two men who 'had discoursed . . . about being in the army'. He was unable to resist a further irrelevant allusion to John Lisle's judicial record, this time to his membership of the tribunal that had sent John Penruddock to the scaffold. Instead of mentioning that, and the 'truth' allegedly told by the nefarious Nelthorp, Jeffreys should have elaborated on the implications of Alice Lisle's lie, and how far it went towards destroying her defence. As it was, after a further, and barely coherent, tirade against Hicks and Nelthorp, he contented himself with the comment that, if the witnesses and the recalcitrant Dunne were to be believed, the proof was 'as evident as the sun at noon day'.

But I must remember you of one particular . . . of very great moment in this case; that after all these private messages and directions given to come by night, and the kind reception they met with when they came, and after all this care to lodge them and feed them, when colonel Penruddock, after the discovery made by Barter, came to search her house, then she had nobody in it truly, which is an aggravation of the offence testified by colonel Penruddock himself, whose father likewise was a martyr, and died for his fidelity to the crown; and who was the judge of that father, we all very well know. God Almighty is a just God, and it may be worth considering (especially by her) how God has been pleased to make use of him as the instrument in this business; and she would likewise do well to consider the finger of God in working upon the heart of that man Barter, who was employed in all this affair, and that all the truth has been told by Nelthorp, that blackest of villains Nelthorp, that would have murdered the late king and his royal brother; that he was one of those barbarous, malicious assassinates in that black conspiracy, and outlawed, should be harboured, by one that pretends a love for the royal family, and entertained and discoursed with at night about being in the army; yet that he and that other villain Hicks, who pretends to religion and to be a preacher of the gospel, but is found in rebellion and in the company of traitors, should be denied the next morning . . .

And I must needs say, if all these witnesses that have freely discovered their knowledge, joined to that truth which is at length drawn from Dunne, be worthy of any credit, it is as plain a proof as can be given, and as evident as the sun at noon day.

Jeffreys concluded by telling the jury to decide the facts and deliver their verdict 'according to conscience and truth'. Alice Lisle's age and sex were irrelevant, and the jury were to have 'no such thing as a friend in the administration of justice'.

Gentlemen, upon your consciences be it: the preservation of the government, the life of the king, the safety and honour of our religion, and the discharge of our consciences as loyal men, good Christians, and faithful subjects, are at stake; neither her age nor her sex are to move you, who have nothing else to consider but the evidence of the fact you are to try. I charge you, therefore, as you will answer it at the bar of the last judgement, where you and we must all appear, deliver your verdict according to conscience and truth. With that great God, the impartial judge, there is no such thing as respect of persons; and in our discharge of our duty in courts of justice, he has enjoined us . . . that we must have no such thing as a friend in the administration of justice, all our friendship must be to truth, and our care to preserve that inviolate.

But any hopes he may have had for a swift conviction went unfulfilled. No sooner had he finished speaking than he had to deal with an interruption from Alice Lisle about his references to Nelthorp, which was followed by a request from the jury for legal guidance.

> Lisle: My lord, if your lordship please –
> LCJ: Mistress, you have had your turn, you cannot now be heard any more after the jury is charged.
> Lisle: My lord, I did not know Nelthorp, I declare it, before he was taken.
> LCJ: You are not indicted for Nelthorp, but we are not to enter into dialogues now, the jury must consider of it.
> Jury-man: Pray my lord, some of us desire to know of your lordship, in point of law, whether it be the same thing, and equally treason, in receiving him before he was convicted of treason, as if it had been after.
> LCJ: It is all the same, that certainly can be no doubt: for, if in case this Hicks had been wounded in the rebels army, and had come to her house and had there been entertained, but had died there of his wounds, and so could never have been convicted, she had been nevertheless a traitor.

This final protest by Alice Lisle over Nelthorp was probably generated as much by the prejudice she felt Jeffreys' final references to him would create as by her desire to offset the implicit implications of the Crofts alias. The jury's concern echoed the point she had made earlier – the legal requirement that the principal traitor, Hicks, should be convicted, and in the county where his offence had been committed, before any question of her guilt could arise. Though Jeffreys rejected both arguments, four years later Parliament decided she had been right, treating it as one ground for reversing her conviction and attainder.

In Halsbury's *Laws of England* Alice's argument over the need for the principal traitor to be convicted first is asserted as a correct statement of the law today. Where that traitor is still alive, it is clearly more convincing to have him dealt with before, or at the same time as, his harbourer. This avoids the unfairness of a conviction in his absence and on evidence he has no chance to contradict, which is what happened to Hicks at Alice Lisle's trial. Jeffreys' point, that the death of the principal traitor before trial leaves the authorities with no alternative to trying his harbourer despite the absence of a prior conviction, is convincing only where the death has actually occurred. In this case, it had not. Jeffreys used the argument simply to coerce the jury. This seems to have been appreciated even then, because there were at least two instances later in the assize of rebels being brought to trial well before those who had given them shelter were tried.[3]

The jury retired again. The looming prospect of an acquittal made Jeffreys visibly worried and impatient. The next question from the jury reinforced both his misgivings and his determination to secure the verdict he wanted.

Then the jury withdrew, and staying out a while, the lord Jeffreys expressed a great deal of impatience, and said, he wondered that in so plain a case they would go from the bar, and would have sent for them with an intimation, that if they did not come quickly, he would adjourn, and let them lie by it all night; but after about half an hour's stay the Jury returned, and the Foreman addressed himself to the court thus:

Foreman: My lord, we have one thing to beg of your lordship some directions in, before we can give our verdict in this case; We have some doubt upon us, whether there be sufficient proof that she knew Hicks to have been in the army.

LCJ: There is as full proof as proof can be; but you are judges of the proof, for my part I thought there was no difficulty in it.

Foreman: My lord, we are in some doubt of it.

LCJ: I cannot help your doubts: was there not proved a discourse of the battle and of the army at supper-time?

Foreman: But, my lord, we are not satisfied that she had notice that Hicks was in the army.

LCJ: I cannot tell what would satisfy you; Did she not enquire of Dunne, whether Hicks had been in the army? And when he told her he did not know, she did not say she would refuse him if he had been there, but ordered him to come by night, by which it is evident she suspected it; and when he and Nelthorp came, discoursed with them about the battle and the army. Come, come, gentlemen, it is a plain proof.

Foreman: My lord, we do not remember that it was proved that she did ask any such question when they were there.

LCJ: Sure you do not remember anything that has passed? Did not Dunne tell you there was such discourse, and she was by and Nelthorp's name was named? But if there were no such proof the circumstances and management of the thing is as full a proof as can be; I wonder what it is you doubt of?

Mrs Lisle: My lord, I hope . . .

LCJ: You must not speak now.

The jury laid their heads together for near a quarter of an hour, and at length agreed; and being called over, delivered in this verdict by the Foreman.

Clerk of Arraigns: Alice Lisle, Hold up thy hand. Gentlemen of the jury, look upon the prisoner, how say ye? Is she guilty of the treason whereof she stands indicted, or not guilty?

Foreman: Guilty.

The news reached London after the weekend. Muddiman's record of the Winchester assize, dated 1 September, is almost laconic in its misleading assertion that she was convicted on overwhelming evidence. As the official version, this was in line with the authorities' expectations, rather than any reference to the pressure Jeffreys had exerted to get the desired result. Muddiman's note said nothing of the cliff-hanging suspense of the moment the jury announced their decision:

At the Gaol Delivery at Winchester many were convicted for several sorts of crimes. On the 27 Mrs Lisle was brought upon her Trial about 5 in the afternoon. The evidence was full against her that she aided and maintained one knowing him to be a Rebell, actually in arms. This Trial lasted long so that it was about 11 that night when the jury brought her in Guilty of High Treason.

The Clerk of Arraigns concluded the case for the night with the formal question to initiate forfeiture procedures. Jeffreys, however, was still angry at what he saw as the jury's determined refusal to face facts. His parting shot made it obvious what he thought.

Clerk of Arraigns: What goods or chattels, lands or tenements had she?

Foreman: None that we know of.

Clerk of Arraigns: Look to her, jailor, she is found guilty of high treason; and prepare yourself to die.

Then the verdict was recorded.

LCJ: Gentlemen, I did not think I should have had any occasion to speak after your verdict, but finding some hesitancy and doubt among you, I cannot but say, I wonder it should come about; for I think in my conscience, the evidence was as full and plain as could be, and if I had been among you, and she had been my own mother, I should have found her guilty.

Then the court adjourned until the next morning.

NINETEEN

Sentencing and Execution

The court reassembled the following morning for those convicted of capital offences to be sentenced. There were ten in all: Alice Lisle the traitor; Hayes the house-breaker, four burglars, a rapist and two coin-clippers; and the highwayman Bateley.

Muddiman's entry is short and to the point: 'On the 28 the Lord Jeffreys . . . went into Court and passed sentence upon her and the rest of the Malefactors after, her to be burned.' His note of 3 September states: 'Of those who were sentenced at Winchester, 5 were reprieved, 1 for a rape, 4 for burglary and 1 ordered to be hanged at Portsmouth.'

Muddiman's only omission was Hayes, the daytime house-breaker (as opposed to nocturnal burglar), whom the Gaol Book also records as having been reprieved. Clearly the rapist survived, the only one dealt with during the assize. It was almost certainly Bateley who went to the gallows at Portsmouth, probably to make an example of him where he was known. The four executed were therefore Bateley, the two coin-clippers and Alice Lisle.

Jeffreys went on to elaborate at far greater length than Muddiman, emphasising the excellence of the trial procedure and the fairness of Alice Lisle's conviction. He singled her out for censure, as much for her crime as for her adherence to her faith. He also hinted that more had emerged even since the previous evening about the arrangements made for her guests' arrival at Moyles Court, further proof, he claimed, of her perjury.

The report continues:

Friday, 28 August 1685
This day Alice Lisle was brought to the bar, and being asked what she had to say for herself, why judgment of death should not pass upon her, being convicted of high treason; but offering nothing,

she was, with the rest of the prisoners that were to receive the sentence of death, condemned by the lord Jeffreys, who passed sentence thus:

LCJ: Alice Lisle and you the several prisoners now at the bar, you have been severally indicted, arraigned, and now stand severally convicted of crimes that . . . are to be punished with death; you stand convicted by your equals, by a jury of your country, against whom you might have had, and were allowed to make (and one of you did make) what challenges you could: but upon full evidence, by that Jury of your own countrymen you have been found guilty of those crimes for which you are to die; . . .

Particularly, I cannot but lament the deplorable condition of you, Mrs Lisle, a gentlewoman of quality and of fortune, so far stricken in years, therefore ought to have had more discretion; one, who all your lifetime have been a great pretender to, and professor of, religion, and of that religion which bears a very good name, the Protestant religion: but that name has been perverted to very ill purposes by some people, who have had nothing but the name to protect themselves under.

There is no religion whatsoever (except that hypocritical profession of theirs which deserves not the name of religion, I mean the canting, whining, Presbyterian, fanatical profession) that gives the least countenance to rebellion or faction; and I cannot but lament to find you involved in that herd . . .

You would do well to bethink yourself with all seriousness and remorse, of your own false asseverations and protestations, that you upon your salvation should pretend ignorance in the business, when since that time, even since the last night, there has been but too much discovered how far you were concerned; no, it is not unknown who were sent for upon the Monday night, in order to have that rebellious, seditious fellow to preach to them, what directions were given to come through the orchard the back and private way, what orders were given for provision, and how the horses were appointed to be disposed of. I only speak this, that you should bethink yourself in this short time that you have left here upon earth, to get these sins of yours duly repented of, and truly pardoned; and not only so, but consider you have it now in your power to make some recompense to the public justice of the nation, by discovering the truth in this matter, and all religion enjoins you to do what you can: for without the infinite mercy of the great God you are in a deplorable condition, and without true contrition and repentance . . . you can never hope for the mercy of that God to be extended to you.

Sirs; It is not my province to advise you in your preparation for that eternity you are all suddenly to enter into: but out of pure charity, and hearty compassion to you, and the miserable condition you have brought yourselves into, and out of a tender regard to your precious immortal souls, I cannot but assure you of my own, and recommend you to the earnest and fervent prayers of all good Christians, to the God of infinite mercy, that he would be merciful unto you all . . .

There remains no more for me to do, I say, but to pronounce the sentence of the law, which is this; and the Court does award:

That you, Mrs Lisle, be conveyed from hence to the place from whence you came, and from thence you are to be drawn on a hurdle to the place of execution, where your body is to be burnt alive till you be dead. And the Lord have mercy upon your Soul.

The rest of the Prisoners had the usual judgment as in Cases of Felony.

The Gaol Book entry concerning Alice Lisle records, to the left of her name, that the charge was 'H: Treason' and, to the right, that this consisted of 'Treason in receiving ayding assisting & comforting Johannem Hicks being a Rebell against the king'. Immediately above her name is the note that she pleaded not guilty ('po: se'); that she was found guilty ('cul'); and that the jury decided she had no goods ('ca null.'). In the left-hand margin is the large asterisk indicating her death sentence, next to which appears the Latin record of how this was to be carried out: 'Trahetur ad furcam & igne concrementur quo usque mortua sit', which means 'Let her be dragged to the stake and let her be consumed by fire until she be dead'.

Jeffreys' address shows he was more concerned to satisfy his own curiosity about Alice Lisle than to save souls. By bluff and blackmail (his contact with the 'overnight informants', which may or may not have been true); the moral obligation on Alice Lisle to 'make some recompense . . . by discovering the truth in this matter'; and, as the report goes on to state, his next and rather pointed suggestion that she spend a useful hour or two with 'pen, ink and paper . . . you understand what I mean' – he tried to coerce a confession out of her. It was Friday, and the assize at Salisbury, some 20 miles away, was due to start that morning. Yet he was prepared to delay his departure in the hope that he could make Alice Lisle come clean by offering to delay her execution. One passage towards the end of her last speech suggests she did write something, to the effect that she and Nelthorp had conversed at rather greater length than she had been prepared to concede during the trial. According to the report, it was the intervention of the clergy, rather than anything she wrote, that procured a respite for her.

LCJ: Look you, Mrs Lisle, when I left his majesty, he was pleased to remit the time of all executions to me: that wherever I found any obstinacy or impenitence, I might order the executions with what speed I should think best: therefore, Mr Sheriff, take notice, you are to prepare for the execution of this gentlewoman this afternoon. But withal, I give you, the prisoner, this intimation: we that are the judges, shall stay in town an hour of two; you shall have pen, ink, and paper, brought you, and if in the meantime you employ that pen, ink and paper and this hour or two well, (you understand what I mean) it may be you may hear further from us, in a deferring the execution.

Then the prisoner was taken away. But afterwards, upon the intercession of some divines of the church of Winchester, she was respited till Wednesday the 2nd of September.

For Alice Lisle, the priority was to seek a complete reprieve, a task immediately undertaken by two of her better-connected friends, Mary St John and Elizabeth Abergavenny, distantly related to each other. Mary St John, a daughter of Sir Charles Rich, had married into a collateral branch of the influential Warwick family. Elizabeth Abergavenny was a baroness dowager who lived at Sherborne Castle in Oxfordshire. She was the widow of another member of the Warwick line, John Neville, and the person Alice Lisle had wanted to call as a second witness at her trial. They put their names to a letter underlining her long-standing loyalty to the Crown, and the unfounded rumours that she had opposed it in time of war. It reached the king at Windsor on Sunday, 30 August, but was rejected out of hand.

Alice Lisle must have expected this, because it was followed almost at once with her own petition for the execution to be altered from burning to beheading, and for it to be delayed until the following Sunday, 6 September. While the monarch was amenable to the sentence being altered, provided there were precedents, he maintained his point-blank refusal that it should be delayed.

On Sunday the 30th of August, the following letter was sent to the right honourable the earl of Clarendon, Lord Privy Seal, at Windsor; [which the earl did then read to the king] who answered, That he would do nothing in it, having left all to the lord chief justice.

My Lord,

Understanding that Mrs Lisle is condemned, and that many false things are reported of her, that may hinder the king from showing her mercy; particularly, that she was an enemy to the king's friends in the time of the late wars: As to that, we can assure your lordship, that she was a favourer of them in their greatest extremities; and particularly of us, and of some others that are since dead: And for these late years we have often been in her company, and never heard her say anything but what became a loyal subject. This we desire your lordship would be pleased to present to the king, and to intercede for her reprieve; which will be a great obligation to your lordships humble servants,

M. St John

E. Abergavenny

On Monday the 31st of August the following Petition was presented to the King:

> To the King's most excellent Majesty; The humble petition of Alicia Lisle.
> Humbly Sheweth;
> That your Petitioner lieth under a sentence of death, for harbouring one John Hicks, and is sentenced to be burnt on Wednesday next. – That she is the daughter of Sir White Beconsaw, descended of an ancient and honourable family, and related to several of the best families of the nobility of this kingdom. – Wherefore your Petitioner humbly begs your Majesty, that execution may be altered from burning to beheading, and may be respited for four days. . . .

To which his majesty answered: 'That he would not reprieve her one day; but for altering the Sentence he would do it, if there were any Precedents for it.'

Thereupon the following Precedents, for the altering of the Sentence, were offered to the king.

That execution may vary from the judgment, see the Register, fol. 165 in Felony, where the judgment is always suspendatur per collum; yet the party may be beheaded, which is no part of the Sentence [Parl.8.E.3.]. So was the duke of Somerset in the time of Edw. 6 for felony: So was the lord Audley, 7 Car 1. for felony (Rape.) Queen Catherine Howard for treason, Hen. 8. and Jane Gray primo Mariae. The countess of Salisbury, being attainted for treason, Anno 1541, was beheaded 32 Hen. 8. See 3 Co. Inst. p. 211, 212.'

Of the cases cited, Edward, Duke of Somerset, had been tried by the House of Lords on 1 December 1551, accused of plotting to murder a Privy Councillor, the Duke of Northumberland, and to overthrow the king, Edward VI. Though acquitted of treason, he was convicted of felony for his preliminary conspiracy to kidnap Northumberland (who was himself subsequently executed for trying to put his daughter-in-law, Lady Jane Grey, on the throne). The sentence that Somerset should hang was altered to beheading, and was carried out on 22 January 1552.

Lord Mervin Audley, who lived at Fonthill Gifford, in Wiltshire, was charged on 25 April 1631 with rape and sodomy. According to his household's evidence to the Lords, he presided over a regime of rampant debauchery and voyeurism that was decadent even by seventeenth-century standards. It was claimed that, within days of their marriage, he encouraged his second wife, Lady Anne Audley, to have intercourse with his son-in-law; he had held her down while she was raped by a servant, Giles Brodway, on whom he had then pressed his own favours; he was in the habit of parading the entire male staff naked in their bedroom 'to shew her their Nudities, recommending the largest to her'; he had made his servant, Henry Skipwith, repeatedly rape his 12-year-old daughter-in-law, the girl herself adding that this had happened in front of an audience of servants; and that he and a few privileged staff used to watch each other performing with Blandina, the resident prostitute. Views differed as to how long she was there: Lawrence Fitzpatrick, another servant, said she stayed six months, but Audley claimed he dismissed her after only a fortnight because 'she bestowed an ill disease on the house'.

Blandina apart, Audley maintained that the accusations were all lies, and a plot by his wife and his son, who had just come of age, to get their hands on the family estates. The Lords did not believe him, and they were right, because the 'plot' explanation was only part of the truth. What he avoided mentioning was that he was making large parts of his inheritance over to his homosexual retinue. He was convicted and 'judgment was afterwards passed . . . that he should be hanged: However, he obtained the Favour of being beheaded.' Two witnesses against him, Brodway and Fitzpatrick, also his sexual partner, were hanged, which Salmon, who edited the report, describes as 'a little hard'.

Though sceptical of Lady Audley's claim to having endured her husband's behaviour uncomplainingly for so long, Salmon considered her reason for accusing him was self-preservation rather than avarice. If she could tolerate sexual diversity, she was not prepared for penury and starvation. In her view, a prosecution was the only way of preserving the family assets.

Catherine Howard and Margaret Pole, Countess of Salisbury, were two of the more distinguished victims of Henry VIII's blood-spattered reign, when the axe was as much an instrument of policy as diplomacy or divorce. A member of the Duke of Norfolk's family, Catherine Howard became Henry's fifth wife on 28 July 1540, the day his Lord Chamberlain, Thomas Cromwell, was executed for treason, and three weeks after he had divorced Anne of Cleves, to whom Catherine had been lady-in-waiting. Uncrowned, because of her apparent inability to conceive, Catherine was aged about 22 when she went to the scaffold in February 1542. It was her wayward affections that took her there. Her first affair with her music teacher, Henry Manox, was less significant than later ones with two cousins, Francis Dereham and Thomas Culpeper, which she made the mistake of continuing after marrying the king.

Her relationship with Dereham had begun in 1538 and developed to the point where, though never formally married, they regarded themselves as husband and wife. Their parting in 1539, when Catherine first joined the royal circle and he went to Ireland to make a living from high seas piracy, was only temporary. Pressed by her grandmother, Catherine appointed Dereham her 'private secretary and usher of the chamber' in August 1541, but the appointment went to his head. Boastful and arrogant, he was anything but discreet about the advantages he enjoyed, and the affection he believed Catherine felt for him.

Culpeper was at court before Catherine arrived, and took Dereham's place in her affections shortly after her own introduction there. Though sensible enough to discard him immediately before and after marrying the monarch, by the spring of 1541, barely eight months after the wedding, she was writing Culpeper love letters and sending him presents. This was only the start. Her lady-in-waiting, Lady Jane Rochford, arranged dangerous nocturnal assignations for the couple, with Culpeper in the role of an accomplished cat-burglar. He and Catherine met in London, and then at Lincoln, Hatfield, Pontefract and York during the king's tour of the north in the second half of 1541.

The cuckolded husband was the last to know. On 2 November 1541, the day after Henry had thanked the Almighty for a wife he considered the 'jewel of womanhood', a fearful Thomas Cranmer, Archbishop of Canterbury, handed him a letter outlining Catherine's amorous adventures. After a week's stunned incredulity, Henry ordered a thorough investigation. Manox and Dereham confessed first, followed by Catherine herself and then Culpeper. Dereham and Culpeper were executed at Tyburn on 10 December, and Jane Rochford was beheaded immediately after Catherine on Tower Green on 13 February 1542. Manox alone survived. Officially, those who died were punished for treason, based on Catherine's presumed adultery and the others' complicity. Whether Catherine's pre-marital affairs were reprehensible, and whether there was legal proof that she actually committed adultery after marriage, were niceties of marginal significance when it came to assuaging the king's wrath and extricating him from matrimonial embarrassment.

Margaret Pole, the widow of one of Henry VII's wealthier courtiers, was dubbed 'the most saintly woman in England' by Henry VIII on his accession in 1509. She benefited from his recognition of the gross injustice to her brother, the Earl of Warwick, a political prisoner from the age of 9 until executed on a trumped-up charge of treason in 1499, to secure Henry VII's claim to the throne as head of the house of Lancaster. In reality, Warwick's only offence was to have been the son of the Yorkist Duke of Clarence, himself executed by drowning in a butt of malmsey wine in 1478 after spending most of his life trying to usurp his brother, Edward IV. The family lands in Wiltshire, Hampshire and Essex, though burdened with debts, were restored to Margaret, and in 1513 she was created Countess of Salisbury. She was governess to Princess Mary, her god-daughter and Edward VI's eventual successor as queen, to whom she was deeply protective after Henry divorced Mary's mother, Catherine of Aragon, to marry Anne Boleyn.

Margaret Pole's undoing was her opposition to this union and the unswerving loyalty to the pope of her son Reginald, a cardinal. Though she publicly disowned Reginald and his beliefs, Henry was determined to destroy her. She was arrested in the autumn of 1538, examined and imprisoned in the Tower. The following May, Parliament condemned her to death by an act of attainder on the basis of accusations she never had a chance to answer. While there was a possibility of her release in 1540, it was the Yorkshire rebellion of 1541 that finally decided Parliament that potential subversives could not be tolerated, and she was beheaded at East Smithfield on 27 May 1541.

Lady Jane Grey, the 'nine-day queen', was aged 16 when she was beheaded on Tower Hill on 12 February 1554. Beautiful, cultured and intelligent, she was caught up in the rivalry over the succession to her dying cousin, Edward VI. Her corrupt father-in-law, the Duke of Northumberland, inveigled Edward into naming her as his successor over the heads of Henry VIII's daughters, Mary and Elizabeth. But the popular support he expected for her failed to materialise; he was executed and she followed him to the scaffold six months later.

Reassured, no doubt, by this colourful catalogue of condemnation that the scaffold could be lawfully substituted for the stake, regardless of sex, James signed the document that made Alice Lisle the first victim of the Bloody Assize and the last woman in Britain to be beheaded.

Whereupon his majesty was pleased to sign the following Warrant:

J.R.
Whereas we are informed that Alicia Lisle has received Sentence of death for high treason at the sessions of Oyer and Terminer, and gaol delivery, held at our city of Winchester, for harbouring of John Hicks a rebel, and that the sentence is to be executed upon her the second of September next, by burning her alive: And whereas the said Alicia Lisle has humbly petitioned us to alter the manner of the said execution, by causing her head to be severed from her body: We, being graciously pleased to condescend to her request, have thought fit hereby to signify our will and pleasure accordingly. And our further will and pleasure is, that you deliver the head and body to her relations to be privately and decently interred: And for so doing this shall be your warrant. – Given at our court at Windsor, the 31st day of August 1685, in the first year of our reign.
　　　Sunderland.
To our trusty and well-beloved the High-Sheriff of our county of Hants, and to all others whom it may concern.

Which warrant being delivered to the Sheriff, she was, on Wednesday the second of September, in the afternoon, brought to execution; which was performed upon a scaffold erected in the market-place of the city of Winchester, where she behaved herself with a great deal of Christian resolution. She then delivered a paper to the sheriff, a copy of which follows; and after some little time was executed, having her head sever'd from her body.

A stone plaque in the wall of Winchester city museum indicates the site of Alice Lisle's execution, in the roadway of what was then the marketplace and is now The Square. She went to the scaffold three weeks before her sixty-eighth birthday, wearing the obligatory 'red-quilted petticoat' that her daughter, Anne Harfell, mentioned in her will as a family heirloom. The only surviving contemporary account of the event is that which reached London a day or two later, as minuted by Muddiman:

On the 2nd . . . about 4 in the afternoon Mrs Lisle was beheaded at Winchester. They give not anything of her remarks on the scaffold but that she was old and dozy and died without much concern.

He concluded with the government's reaction – one of deep satisfaction. It was what they had been waiting to hear, for not merely was this the first trial of an important assize, but it involved a lady of rank and distinction. The deterrent impact of making an example of her would be that much more telling: 'This may be a fair caution to all ill-minded persons from harbouring any of the Protestant Rebell-Bandits who are said sometime to be still skulking abroad or rather Moss-Troopers as being found out of the Whiggs.'

The official announcement appeared in the *London Gazette* of 7 September:

Winchester, September 3. Alicia Lisle being convicted of High Treason at the Sessions of Oyer and Terminer and Gaol Delivery held here for harbouring John Hicks, a Rebell, received sentence of Death accordingly: and yesterday she was executed.

Strangely, there is no contemporary record in Winchester itself of the event, apart possibly from a note in the city's 'Payments out of

Coffer' ledger for 9 October 1685. This authorised an official fee of ten shillings 'for tilling the bell' to Mr Wallace. The Reverend Stamford Wallace was the rector of St Thomas's in Southgate Street (the present church building eventually became the Hampshire Record Office and is now a charity centre), and, since there was no occasion apart from Alice Lisle's execution for tolling a bell at about that time, it seems probable the city was paying him for having marked her passing.

The source of Alice Lisle's last speech, which the report describes as the 'paper she delivered to the sheriff', is not identified.[1] There have been suggestions that it is propaganda from an unknown hand. However, its drafting tends to confirm its authenticity:

Gentlemen, Friends and Neighbours,

It may be expected that I should say something at my death, my birth and education being near this place. My parents instructed me in the fear of God, and I now die of the reformed religion, always being instructed in that belief, that if Popery should return this nation, it would be a great judgment. I die in the expectation of pardon of my sins and acceptation with the Father, by the imputed righteousness of Jesus Christ, he being the end of the law for righteousness to everyone that believes. I thank God through Jesus Christ, I depart under the Blood of Sprinkling which speaketh better things than the Blood of Abel, God having made this chastisement an ordinance to my soul.

I did as little expect to come to this place on this occasion as any person in this nation; therefore let us learn not to be high-minded, but fear the Lord: The Lord is a Sovereign and will take what way he sees best to glorify himself by his poor creatures; therefore, do humbly desire to submit to his will, praying him, that in patience I may possess my soul.

My crime was entertaining a nonconformist minister, who is since sworn to have been in the late duke of Monmouth's army. I am told, if I had not denied them, it would not have affected me. I have no excuse but surprise and fear; which I believe my jury must make use of to excuse their verdict to the world.

I have been told, the court ought to be counsel for the prisoner, instead of which, there was evidence given from thence; which, though it were but hearsay, might possibly affect my jury. My defence was such as might be expected from a weak woman: but such as it was, I did not hear it repeated again to the jury. But I forgive all persons that have done me wrong, and I desire that God will do so likewise.

I forgive colonel Penruddock, though he told me, he could have taken those men before they came to my house.

As to what may be objected, that I gave it under my hand that I had discoursed with Nelthorp, that could be no evidence to the court or jury, it being after my conviction and sentence.

I acknowledge his majesty's favour in altering my sentence; and I pray God to preserve him, that he may long reign in peace, and the true religion flourish under him.

Two things I have omitted to say, which is, that I forgive him that desired to be taken from the Grand Jury to the petty jury, that he might be the more nearly concerned in my death.

Also, I return humble thanks to Almighty God, and the reverend clergy that assisted me in my imprisonment.

Sept. 2, 1685   ALICE LISLE

The argument that 'if I had not denied them [the presence of the three travellers at her house when she first greeted Penruddock, and Nelthorp's presence once Hicks and Dunne had been discovered], it would not have affected me', precisely reflects the indulgence Penruddock told the court he offered her to surrender the third fugitive; and the speech repeats the substance of her defence, that her denial of the third fugitive was simply because she was surprised and afraid. Only someone who had been present at the trial would have known enough to make those points; and, while others may have helped her draft it, it at least purports to bear her signature.

PART THREE

TWENTY

Was Justice Done?

Whatever else Alice Lisle may have felt about her trial, she could hardly have complained that justice – if that is what she received – was slow: she was executed on Wednesday, 2 September, exactly five weeks after her arrest on Wednesday, 29 July.

Did she receive justice? By present-day standards, and probably by those of the time, she certainly did not. For a judge to keep a material witness from court, conduct a prosecution from the bench, and coerce a doubting jury into a guilty verdict, could hardly be more offensive to basic concepts of fair play. For all its brilliance as cross-examination, and brilliant it undoubtedly was, Jeffreys' conduct of her trial was as much a disgrace to his position as Lord Chief Justice as it was to the system over which he presided. As a *Country Life* writer put it in December 1909: 'Among Judge Jeffreys' iniquities, none stains him more deeply with the mark of blood, none makes the task of the would-be rehabilitator of his character more impossible, than the judicial murder of Dame Alice Lisle of Moyles Court.'[1]

There is another reason why Alice Lisle received less than her due. It is extremely doubtful whether the prosecution ever produced a second witness to her knowledge of Hicks's rebel status. The need for this level of proof in treason cases was laid down by a statute in Edward VI's reign during the previous century, and it remained the law until the Treason Act of 1945. That the Crown was aware of this requirement is clear from its three witnesses who recounted Hicks's disloyal talk in the stables at Keynsham. But that proved nothing against Alice Lisle. Even if the jury believed Dunne's account of the supper-table discussion, the Carpenters, who had served the meal, had added nothing.

The only second witness to Alice Lisle's possible awareness of what was afoot was Barter, when he described how she and Dunne had apparently joked at his expense. Even then, there was still only Dunne's claim as to what the joke was about, so that Barter's repetition of what Dunne had told him was in no sense additional testimony of an act of treason. At the time, when the only safeguard for the accused was the two-witness rule, Jeffreys should have told the jury to disregard Barter's evidence of Dunne's account.

Alice Lisle's instruction to the travellers to 'come after dark', which Jeffreys regarded as so significant, was, since it was given before she met them, arguably as consistent with her belief that they were religious refugees as with any thought that they might have been rebels. Equally, as recounted by Dunne, the discussion of what had happened at Sedgemoor was generalised and imprecise. From the little he said, the talk could merely have been about the battle as a newsworthy event, rather than revealing that Hicks and Nelthorp had fought for Monmouth.

Salmon believed she was illegally treated in being put on trial before Hicks. But he had no doubt about her guilt, sharing Jeffreys' view of the travellers' night-time arrival at Moyles Court and the discussion of the battle. In his *Critical Review of State Trials* (1738), he said:

[The jury] desired to be satisfied in two Points. 1. Whether it was Treason to receive a Rebel before he was convicted: To which the Court answered, It was. 2. They doubted whether she knew Hicks was in the Army: To which the Chief Justice answered, The Prisoner's ordering them to come in the Night, was a strong Presumption of it; but the talking of the battle at Supper, left them no Room to doubt of it. Whereupon the Jury, without withdrawing again, gave their Verdict, that she was guilty. And perhaps the only Thing that deserves Censure in this Trial was, the convicting her of High-Treason, for harbouring Hicks before he was convicted of Treason. There is no Doubt to be made that it is High-Treason knowingly to harbour a Traitor before he is convicted: But the Act for reversing the Attainder seems to intimate, that a Person cannot be tried for receiving or harbouring a Traitor till that Traitor is convicted; and in this I am apt to think Mrs Lisle had Injustice done her. I do not doubt her Guilt; but yet I think she was not legally convicted.

Alice Lisle's guilt of knowingly harbouring two rebels, one of them also an outlaw, could have been demonstrated far more convincingly had the Crown been more alert. It had already proved potentially incriminating facts: the guests' night-time arrival; the disposal of the horses; Dunne's reluctance to recount what had been said either on arrival at the house or over supper; and the conflicts between Dunne's claim that Alice Lisle knew from the outset that two guests were coming, rather than the single guest she said she expected; and between Barter's assertion that Dunne had a letter that he handed to Carpenter to give to Alice Lisle, and her own, Dunne's and Carpenter's denial that any letter ever existed.

With those points established, the Crown should have followed through the logic of Penruddock's account of how Carpenter and Alice Lisle greeted him at Moyles Court on the morning of 29 July. Carpenter had implied that the pair hiding in the outhouse were nocturnal vagrants who had slipped in unobserved. His plea to Penruddock not to tell Alice Lisle about them suggested his sole concern was to avoid a dressing-down from her if she found out about his failure to lock up properly. Whether rebels or religious fugitives – and how could he know if he had not even realised they were there? – neither he nor Alice Lisle could conceivably be held responsible for unwittingly housing trespassing tramps. The last thing that crossed his mind, he implied, was the possibility that they might be rebels. Alice Lisle initially played along with this deception when she first spoke to Penruddock.

That, however, raised the following difficulties for her defence. Carpenter's claim was untrue. It was also in direct conflict with Alice's main assertion, that she fed and sheltered Hicks genuinely believing him to be a religious refugee. Why adopt the drastic expedient of surrendering him as a 'stranger', and so risk destroying that main defence, if not for the purpose of keeping Nelthorp undiscovered? And why was it so crucial to keep Nelthorp undiscovered, if not for the reason, contrary to what she claimed, that, far from being ignorant of his identity or believing him to be a pseudonymous priest, she knew who he was; and that to shelter him as an outlaw was as much an act of treason as if he were also a rebel?

The inference was obvious: Nelthorp was given the apparently safer refuge inside the house, proportionate to his doubly dangerous status as outlaw and rebel. Unlike Hicks and Dunne, he could not have gained access to an indoor hiding-place unwanted and unobserved. The purpose was equally apparent: if the surrender of Hicks and Dunne, as intruders, had left the hunters satisfied, Nelthorp would have escaped and Alice Lisle would have avoided prosecution. In short, it was a high-risk gamble that depended on Penruddock's gullibility. But it failed: Penruddock was not taken in, and Nelthorp's discovery 'in the hole by the chimney' effectively destroyed her defence. Had she settled for slightly lower stakes, either by putting Nelthorp in the malthouse with the others, or by surrendering him in response to Penruddock's offer of immunity after the arrest of the other two, she might not have been charged at all, or at least would have stood a far better chance of acquittal.

The Crown did not develop these arguments, probably because the trial lasted so long into the evening and concentration was fading. But the final difficulty in the path of Alice Lisle's defence, and the second point on which further research by the Crown could have secured its case, was Nelthorp's alias. As we now know, his reason for adopting Crofts's name was known only to him, Hicks, Dunne and Alice Lisle. To have given any indication that she knew this supposedly 'anonymous' guest was parading as one of her former chaplains would have exposed her to extremely damaging cross-examination: for example, why she imagined he might have been doing that, particularly when southern England was supposed to be on the look-out for fugitive rebels. She had admitted remembering the proclamation that declared Nelthorp – the very man he turned out to be – an outlaw. Proof that she had a fairly clear idea of what was going on, and was prepared to surrender the less dangerous guests to protect Nelthorp, would have justified charging her with harbouring him as both an outlaw and a rebel. On that basis, the Crown would have stood a far better chance of obtaining a convincing conviction for having knowingly sheltered both of her fugitive guests.

Nelthorp himself maintained the deception about her ignorance of his identity to the end. In the course of his last speech, written in Newgate gaol on 29 October 1685, the night before he was executed, he said:

> I most humbly ask Pardon of the Lady Lisle's Family and Relations, for that being succoured there one night with Mr Hicks, brought that worthy Lady to suffer death: I was wholly a Stranger to her Ladyship, and came with Mr Hicks; neither did she (as I verily believe) know who I was, or my Name, 'till I was taken.[2]

The truly innocent – those who have done nothing wrong, as opposed to those who try to extricate themselves through legal loopholes – tend to proclaim their sense of injustice, and their supporters are seriously handicapped if they do not. In Alice Lisle's case, this gap is conspicuous and striking. Her last speech raises what were essentially subsidiary issues: that she was told she would not have been charged had she surrendered all the fugitives; the reason she did not was her 'surprise and fear'; that the bench, far from safeguarding her interests, gave evidence against her and did not put her defence to the jury; and that Penruddock told her he could have captured the fugitives before they reached Moyles Court.

More significant is the allusion in her speech to what she claimed she had written in response to Jeffreys' offer to delay her execution. She said: 'As to what may be objected in reference to my conviction, that I gave it under my hand, that I had discoursed with Nelthorp; that could be no evidence against me, being after my conviction and sentence.' This seems to concede that her paper may have disclosed more about Nelthorp than she had been prepared to tell the jury, because she recognised it was incriminating. It contrasts vividly with her persistent repetition during the trial, consistent with his account, that she 'did not know it was Nelthorp until after he was taken'. Nowhere in her speech is there any outright rejection of the charge against her, asserting: 'I am innocent because I had no idea Hicks was a rebel.'

Alice Lisle was no innocent martyr. A heroine she may have been, but there can be no doubt about her guilt on the charge she faced. The tragedy, for both her and the law, was that she was unfairly and unlawfully convicted.

*   *   *

Alice Lisle's last speech was first published in 1689, in *The Bloody Assizes* version of her trial. This version is no more than slapdash Whig propaganda designed to demonstrate that she was unfairly treated. Yet a careful analysis of the speech undermines that account of the trial, and is for that reason likely to be authentic. Apart from her concession about the 'discourse with Nelthorp', she emphasises that the only charge against her was for harbouring Hicks, whereas *The Bloody Assizes* report wrongly asserts she was also accused of sheltering Nelthorp. The most probable explanation for these discrepancies is that the authors of *The Bloody Assizes* compiled their trial report from rumour and hearsay, and included her speech without realising its potentially contradictory impact. Had they bothered to check their account against her speech, they would almost certainly have edited what she had said to support the case they were trying to make.

The long-standing myth that Penruddock deliberately allowed the fugitives to reach Moyles Court before raiding the house, to incriminate Alice Lisle and thus avenge the death sentence passed on his father by John Lisle in 1655, almost certainly has its origins in this last speech. Towards the end of the speech, Alice Lisle went out of her way to forgive all who had wronged her and, in particular, 'colonel Penruddock, though he told me, he could have taken those men before they came to my house'. If Penruddock had told her he delayed seizing his prey until they had reached Moyles Court, one could scarcely ask for more convincing confirmation.

That, however, is unlikely. The truth, if one takes Dunne's evidence at face value, was that he and his companions wanted to make the second journey to Moyles Court alone because of their fears that Barter would inform on them, as indeed he did. Had they met him as arranged, north-east of Fovant at eleven o'clock on the

Tuesday, they would have fallen straight into Penruddock's ambush. As it was, they did not leave Warminster until about that time, and tried to find their own way south-east of Fovant. Even though they got hopelessly lost, they successfully gave Penruddock the slip. It is therefore much more likely that Penruddock told Alice Lisle that he 'could have taken these men before they reached Moyles Court had they kept to their arrangement with Barter', which was the substance of what he said during the trial. But the vindictive gloss – that he deliberately delayed his capture – became accepted folklore, and has been kept alive by repetition since.

In his *Antiquities of Winchester* (1798), Milner was quite clear:

> Colonel Penruddock, of Wiltshire, son of that Colonel Penruddock, who had been condemned to death by Mrs Lisle's husband, then Oliver Cromwell's chief justice, was in search of these . . . men, and could have apprehended them sooner than he did, but probably having good information of their intention, and being actuated by resentment for the murder of his father, he waited until they were actually harboured in Mrs Lisle's house.

James Waylen, the nineteenth-century Wiltshire historian, made the same point more pompously:

> An unsatisfied grievance, in the estimation of Royalist gentry, survived in memory of the fact that at the trial and condemnation of the agents in the Penruddock rising, John Lisle had sat as Lord President of Cromwell's High Court of Justice. We are not therefore surprised to find the Penruddock of the next generation joining in the hue and cry after a delinquent bearing the name of Lisle. Unfortunately for himself, he was induced to execute the function in such a manner as seriously to tarnish the lustre of his own house, while he canopied that of his rival in a halo of undoubted martyrdom.

The *Country Life* writer of 1909 concurred:

> It has even been surmised that [the fugitives'] arrest could quite well have taken place before they reached Hampshire, but was

purposely postponed in order to implicate Dame Alice. One would, however, prefer to believe that Colonel Penruddock did not design to be revenged against a dead foe in the person of that foe's widow. Yet so it turned out to be.

These assessments of Penruddock's motivation are no more probable or fair today than they were when they were written.

TWENTY-ONE

Forfeiture of Assets and Rehabilitation

At the foot of the page in the Gaol Book recording Alice Lisle's conviction, it is noted that 'William Carpenter and Rachel his wife' were 'remanded without bail to the next [assize]', and are recorded as having appeared at the Winchester spring assize in March 1686. While there is no note of what happened to them, they were probably released under the general pardon issued on 10 March 1686. The confiscation of Alice Lisle's assets following her execution almost certainly meant the Carpenters became unemployed, and it is therefore possible that the William Carpenter convicted of burglary and theft at the Exeter spring assizes in 1687 was her former bailiff doing what he could to make ends meet.

Alice Lisle's conviction triggered the forfeiture process by which a traitor's assets passed to the Crown, either for its own benefit or for distribution to favoured recipients. The inventory of her assets was formally confirmed on 25 September 1686, and her estate given to Louis Duras, Earl of Feversham, one of the king's long-standing and trusted confidants. Born into the French aristocracy as the Marquis de Blanquefort in 1640, he joined the court of James, who was then Duke of York, becoming naturalised in England in 1665. After marrying Mary, the Earl of Feversham's eldest daughter, he succeeded to the title on the earl's death in April 1677. James made him commander-in-chief of the forces sent to oppose Monmouth, when he displayed spectacular ineptitude by sleeping soundly throughout the battle of Sedgemoor. Despite the scorn this brought him, he was installed as a Knight of the Garter towards the end of August 1685. According to Burnet, he accepted £1,000 to seek a pardon for Alice Lisle, but James refused this request, having already given his word to Jeffreys not to interfere. Burnet considered Duras 'an honest, brave and good-natured man, but weak to a degree not easy to be conceived'.

The Lisle property he received was assessed at 'a total annual value of £179 3s 2d'. He was also given what was described as John Lisle's 'concealed' estate. Shortly after John's escape to Switzerland and his attainder, Charles II gave his known assets, mainly in the Isle of Wight, to his (Charles's) brother James. But it was generally believed that John's estate had not been fully disclosed, and the lawsuits brought to discover its true extent were both laborious and incomplete even by the time Alice was executed. It was probably a welcome relief for the Crown to hand over the task of ferreting out the assets, and Feversham was given 'the aid of the Exchequer in suing for same' to ensure that the costs of securing his bounty did not exceed its value. What happened to Moyles Court during the three years of his ownership, and whether he lived there, is not known.

The report of Alice Lisle's trial concludes with the Act of Parliament of May 1689, reversing her conviction and attainder (Appendix Seven). This Act cited the Crown's failure to obtain a prior conviction against Hicks, and Jeffreys' coercion of the jury, as justifying her rehabilitation. By then, the political climate had completely changed: James II had fled, William III was on the throne, and Jeffreys had died in the Tower a month earlier. The Act became law on 24 May and was a direct response to a petition by two of Alice Lisle's daughters, Tryphena Lloyd and Bridget Usher. As a piece of political window-dressing, the propagandist's hand is clearly evident: the Act was as concerned to condemn the legal excesses of the 'bad old days' – underpinning the Glorious Revolution that had substituted the House of Orange for the House of Stuart – as to correct an apparent injustice.

A second petition by Alice Lisle's other daughters, Anne Harfeld, Mary Browne and Mabella Lisle, complained that, because of the way their mother had been treated, they were 'left destitute of their fortune, and forced to subsist on the charity of their relations; all the real estate being entailed on the son, being five hundred pounds per annum'. Could they be reimbursed from Jeffreys' estate? The plea fell on deaf ears. The petition was directed simply to 'lie on the table', and nothing more was done.

These petitions and the Act that followed them, together with the highly partisan 1689 version of Alice's trial published in *The Bloody*

Assizes (Appendix Four), mark the origin of the myth of Alice Lisle's innocence. Burnet's imaginative and misleading defence of her in 1724 (Appendix Five) – that she sent word to a local magistrate as soon as she discovered that Hicks had fought for Monmouth, telling Hicks to try to escape meanwhile – seems to have attracted far more support than Salmon's convincing demolition of the story in 1738.

In 1846, in his *Lives of the Lord Chancellors*, Campbell adopted Burnet's account without question; and in his *History of England* three years later, Macaulay was prepared to believe Alice Lisle's claim to ignorance of Hicks's involvement in the rebellion. The *Gentleman's Magazine* of 1828 and 1884 took the same view, and Frederick Fane accepted Burnet's version in the *Hampshire Field Club Magazine* in 1890. Illogically, others have treated the absence of a prior conviction against Hicks as clear evidence of her innocence.

But two more recent writers who had little doubt about Alice Lisle's guilt were R. Storry Deans (*Notable Trials*, Cassell, 1906), and H. Montgomery Hyde (*Judge Jeffreys*, Harrap, 1940). Storry Deans, while deeply critical of Jeffreys' conduct of the case, concluded:

If the admitted facts are looked at with impartial eyes . . . the accused had very little defence . . . She knew that fugitive rebels were lurking everywhere: that Hicks was asking to be concealed: that he, at any rate, was a partisan of the side that had rebelled and had been defeated. She never asked, according to her own story, why this man was in such danger as to desire concealment. Why not? Was it because she suspected, only too truly, the real reason? If not, again I ask, why did she not inquire? Was it so that she should be able to say . . . that she did not know? . . . Again, when Penruddock accused her of having rebels concealed in her house, why did she deny in toto that anybody was there? She did not merely say 'There are no rebels here', as she well might have said. She said 'There is nobody here'. It is impossible, in my judgment, to resist the conclusion that the unfortunate woman either knew, or wilfully shut her eyes to the fact, that Hicks was a fugitive from Monmouth's army.

TWENTY-TWO

Moyles Court

On the western edge of the New Forest, Moyles Court lies well back from the road from Ringwood to Fordingbridge. Today it is a flourishing preparatory school, and, though it is less isolated than in Alice Lisle's time, now being surrounded by farms, riding establishments and Southern Water Company land, the nearest hamlet is still Rockford, half a mile away, where the Alice Lisle Inn serves Alice Lisle bitter. It is a country backwater of slow-moving peace and charm.

Over three centuries, the house has undergone extensive renovation, having three times fallen into near-total disrepair. Its ownership and occupation during the eighteenth century, after Alice's son John had retrieved his inheritance, can be reasonably clearly established. A lease to Admiral Lord Windsor came to an end in 1694, after which John, a widower since Catherine's death in childbirth in 1684, lived there with their two sons, Charles and John Croke Lisle. John's second wife, Anne Howe, joined the household on their marriage in 1702, and he died in 1709. Thereafter the succession can be traced through various genealogies and the voluminous abstracts of title prepared for its sale in 1820 to Henry Baring, the third son of the founder of Britain's oldest merchant bank, Sir Francis Baring.

Alice Lisle settled Moyles Court on John when he and Catherine Croke married in 1679, and John disposed of it by will to his son Charles. Charles and his wife Lucy being childless, Charles bequeathed it to his second cousin, Edward Lisle 'the elder', the son of Alice's brother-in-law, Sir William Lisle, directing that it should then go to each of Edward's seven sons in the order of their birth.

Edward, a close friend of the poet Alexander Pope and sheriff of Hampshire in 1702, was a barrister of Lincoln's Inn. He married

Mary, a daughter of Sir Ambrose Phillips, in 1688. In contrast to Charles and Lucy, they indulged a gargantuan appetite for procreation at their home at Crux Easton in north Hampshire. Mary gave birth to her first child, Edward 'the younger', in 1692, and between then and 1717 she produced nineteen children.

Charles Croke Lisle died in 1721, so that Edward the elder owned Moyles Court for the two years before he died in 1723, to be succeeded by Edward the younger, MP for Hampshire from 1734. This Edward fled to France in 1740 when the house and other property was threatened with seizure in a Chancery action, claiming he had failed to pay an annuity of £400. The Commons evidently disapproved of his reliance on parliamentary privilege to avoid his obligations, because he was suspended and lost his seat the following year. Despite this, he still owned the house on his death in June 1753.

Moyles Court then passed to a younger brother, John, who remained in possession until his death in 1759. His successor was another brother, Charles, who survived until 1772, to be followed by his son, then a minor and also named Charles. Thereafter, the position becomes more complicated, minor shares in the house being taken mainly by the younger Charles's sisters, their spouses and their children. All these interests had to be identified, defined and bought out to ensure that Henry Baring acquired a clear title in 1820.

One may assume that those who inherited the property, from Alice's son John down to the younger Charles, also actually lived there at one time or another, because documents describe each of them as 'of' Moyles Court. Charles's married sisters are also thus described, so that, though a lifelong bachelor, he can scarcely have been without company. His death in July 1818, at the age of 64, ended the Lisle succession and occupation of the house.

Henry Baring married Maria, an American heiress and the divorced wife of the Comte de Tilly, in 1802. Though a partner in the family firm from 1803, his playboy lifestyle made him far less successful as a banker than his two elder brothers, Sir Thomas Baring and Alexander, who later became Lord Ashburton. In 1811 Henry acquired his main residence, Somerley, an extensive mansion on the west bank of the Avon, to which in 1820 he added Moyles Court and its adjoining properties for £29,905.

His main weaknesses were philandering and gambling. Marriage proved irksome: he was as unfaithful to Maria as she was to him, and by 1821 things had deteriorated to the point where she had the family portrait, by one of the finest artists of the day, Sir Thomas Lawrence, sawn off at the left to exclude him, and re-titled it *Mrs Henry Baring, Her Two Children and Their Dog*. Because his addiction to gambling was regarded as incompatible with the bank's image (wisdom long since forgotten by the end of the twentieth century, when the gambling instincts of its Far Eastern dealer caused Barings' ignominious collapse in 1995), he was dismissed in 1823. Despite his behaviour, Henry held on to most of Maria's £200,000 fortune on their divorce in 1825, and immediately married Cecilia Windham, of a distinguished naval family from Norfolk.

He saw Moyles Court as more of an investment than an alternative residence. A note about it in the *Gentleman's Magazine* (1828) records that 'Henry Baring, esq. of Somerley, the present possessor, has taken down great part of the building, leaving only sufficient to serve as a habitation for the farmer renting the estate'. This demolition presumably included the 'malthouse', Hicks's and Dunne's refuge before their arrest, since it appears only in outline on a map of 1828 and is omitted from subsequent maps. Henry's loyalties now made Norfolk more attractive, and in 1829 he sold both Somerley and Moyles Court to Welbore Ellis, 2nd Earl of Normanton, since when Somerley has remained that family's country seat to the present day.

Moyles Court gradually fell into disrepair, and was virtually derelict by the mid-1860s. But it was about this time that a former clergyman, Frederick Fane, was offered it rent-free for life by the 3rd Earl of Normanton, on condition that he brought it and the gardens up to Victorian standards. Fane, a widower whose recent remarriage had left him with two substantial fortunes, did not hesitate, and went about his task with great determination.

But his granddaughter was appalled. In her *Dusty Pages*, privately published in 1956, Joyce Carew had nothing but contempt for what she and her mother saw as self-indulgent extravagance. 'Being a selfish man, he gave no thought to the future generation, his children or their descendants, and accepted Lord Normanton's offer . . . The money grandfather lavished on Moyles Court made him, in spite of the two heiresses, a comparatively poor man.'

Born in 1892 to Fane's third daughter, Lilla Fortescue, Joyce Carew describes her visits to Moyles Court, and these accounts and her mother's recollections give a vivid insight into the hierarchical structure of an upper-class Victorian household. Fane's rule over it seems to have been generally benign, if somewhat distant. Joyce recalled that, 'when he was not suffering from gout, he was a good companion to the young'. But of his earlier years as a clergyman, she concluded: 'I do not think he ever wished to take Holy Orders, and as far as I can make out no one was less fitted for a saintly life.'

After his remarriage, she observed: 'My grandfather lived rather a useless life. He fished and during the winter was out shooting most days.' In Ellingham Church 'grandfather would read the lessons on Sundays (the only useful thing he did in the week) and my mother and her sisters attended two and sometimes three services each Sunday'.

Fane's household was hardly exceptional for a Victorian country squire. Deference was expected, and given; and, despite his outlay on Moyles Court, he was able to take his family on European holidays. In 1888, he compiled an article for the *Hampshire Field Club Magazine* about the house's history and the task he originally faced:

The house had been uninhabited for sixty or seventy years, and the architects had given their opinion that nothing could be done but to pull it down. Part had already been destroyed: the cellars were full of water, the windows boarded up and broken, the whole place a prey to the spoiler. When bricks were wanted a room was pulled down; when a fire was wanted a floor was pulled up or the old panelling torn away. Owls resented interference vehemently, and long after the house was again inhabited, screamed and hooted down the chimneys, till they made the night a terror. With patience and care the house is now restored, as nearly as possible, as may be in the style in which it originally stood . . .

Fane died in 1902. In 1903 the house was leased to Reginald Barclay, who, as a Wiltshire militia colonel, had just returned with his regiment, the equivalent of today's Territorials, from two years'

Boer War service running a prisoner-of-war camp on St Helena. For Barclay, Moyles Court was conveniently close to the regimental headquarters at Devizes. Shortly before Barclay's departure, a *Country Life* writer of 1909, though critical of some of Fane's restoration, concluded that the house was 'a thoroughly agreeable and comfortable home . . . environed by thoroughly adequate and characteristic gardens . . . but the joy of the vicinage is towards the east, where the wooded slopes invite the pedestrian into the open glades and sheltered recesses of one of England's most choice sylvan tracts'.

Barclay was followed at the house by John Howard Thomas, of whom little is known. It was then leased in 1920 to Edward Goschen, a stockbroker, following his overseas service in the Boer War and as a diplomat. He was succeeded in 1931 by Charles Henry Waring, a First World War captain in the 18th Hussars who later transferred to the Royal Flying Corps.

Waring, seventeenth in line to the Italian dukedom of Valderano, extensively repaired and renovated the property, converting the chapel into a gunroom and servants' quarters, and renting some 1,500 acres of adjoining land for shooting. His son, Ronald de Valderano, the 18th Duke, lived there from the age of 13 until he joined the King's Royal Rifle Corps in 1937. He explored the cellars and discovered a hidden stairway inside the house leading down to a tunnel, which, though blocked by a fall of earth after some 200 yards, ran southwards from the house towards a gardener's cottage. He also explored part of another passage leading north-east towards a small clump of trees on Mockbeggar Common, where it was believed to end in a concealed exit.

Charles Waring was an adventurous soldier. Despite a serious riding accident shortly before the First World War in which he lost the ability to grip with his legs, he tried to continue as a cavalry officer simply by balancing himself on horseback. This was not acceptable to his regiment, however, and he was compulsorily retired. He thereupon joined the Royal Flying Corps. Though he shot down a number of German planes over France, his RFC superiors invited him to leave after he had crashed three British aircraft. He then joined the Machine Gun Corps, with which he served in Mesopotamia.

His contribution to the Second World War was to form a 'Dad's Army on Horseback' well before the infantry version first appeared on Britain's television screens in 1968. Raised in 1941, the New Forest Cavalry comprised a group of neighbours and friends equipped from the Moyles Court gunroom with sabres, lances and sporting rifles, an elephant gun serving as their anti-tank weapon. Mounted on hunters and New Forest ponies and supported by a Boy Scout bugler, they trained with great enthusiasm. A general's inspection was arranged at a forest clearing near Pickets Post, but the staff officers found not a horse or soldier in sight when they arrived. Moments later, the bugle sounded and the cavalry emerged from the trees at first a trot, then a canter, a gallop, and finally full tilt in a charge. The inspecting officers took cover behind their staff cars, and the only casualty was the man who broke his shoulder firing the elephant gun. Though apparently impressed, the general was mainly interested in why a man in cavalry uniform should be wearing RFC wings above his medal ribbons. 'Because I bloody well earned them!' barked the duke. But the War Office was in no mood to tolerate private military units, and a week later the New Forest Cavalry was officially disbanded.

The house was requisitioned in 1941 as headquarters for a Fighter Command station at Ibsley. The oak-lined avenue from the Fordingbridge road was cut down, as were also Old House Copse and much of Cherry Orchard Wood to make way for the airfield. It was first used by Hurricanes, but then a succession of Spitfire squadrons, and occasionally US Air Force Lightnings and Thunderbolts, flew from the base throughout the war. The house itself suffered badly: the Elizabethan garden walls were severely damaged by 'sticky-bomb' practice, and by the time it was derequisitioned in 1946 most of the ceilings had come down. The Air Ministry paid £20,000 in compensation. After restoration of the property, Charles Waring twice let it to aspiring, but unsuccessful, preparatory school head teachers. It was put up for auction in 1962 amid stories about Alice Lisle's ghost, when Southern Television pictured the house with a spectral figure superimposed, and a board saying 'For Sale – Vacant Possession?' It was bought with 50 acres and three cottages for £10,500 by the Manor House School, Wimbourne, which moved there in 1963. The headmistress, Vesper

Hunter, thus inherited and restored, for the third time in a hundred years, what she described as 'a vandalised shambles'.

Now renamed Moyles Court School, the main house comprises classrooms, staff rooms and the school library downstairs; the large front room, in which a false ceiling conceals the original minstrel's gallery, has an open hearth with a fireback dated 1674. The 'hole by the chimney', where Nelthorp hid, can still be seen in one of the rear staff offices next to an arched recess that probably housed an ancient kitchen range. Some of the panelling in the adjoining room is distinctly hollow, and could contain the hidden staircase down which the duke found his way to the south-leading tunnel. The first floor is mainly dormitories and staff accommodation.

Outside, the chapel has been converted to a two-storey building, the school dining-hall being on the ground floor and a housemaster's flat upstairs. The old walled garden is the sports area, and the small granary still stands on its original 'staggle-stones' (mushroom-shaped supports about 2 feet high, the seventeenth-century method of preventing rising damp) and is now a ceramics studio. Twenty yards west of where the great granary stood, opposite the main school entrance, is 'Dame Alice House', which is girls' boarding accommodation.

Generally, the school buildings blend comfortably with the style of the old house, leaving the main features of its seventeenth-century reconstruction dominant and intact. Home to a lady who deserved better of the law than she got, it stands as a gentle reminder that the purpose of the law is to secure justice for those bound by it, rather than the political convenience of those who govern them.

APPENDIX ONE

Katherine Hyde's Petition[1]

Katherine Hide, widow. For the forfeited estate of John Lisle, attainted for treason, that she may better subsist and may show kindness to Wm. Lisle, his second son, who married her daughter, and on whom the estates of £500 a year in possession, and £300 in reversion, were entailed for want of issue, but John Lisle cut off the entail in revenge, because William adhered to the late king.

This description of William as 'his second son', implying he was John's offspring, conflicts with the text of the original petition clearly describing William as the second son of Sir William, and John Lisle as his eldest. The original reads:

To the Kings Most Excellent Majesty
The humble Petition of Katherine Hide widow:
Sheweth:
That Sir William Lisle entailed in 1630, about five hundred pounds per annum in possession, and about three hundred in reversion . . . Upon John Lisle, his eldest son and the heirs males of his body, which for want of such issue, was to come to William Lisle his second son from whom the said John cut it off, by fine and Recovery, because the said William did . . . constantly adhere to your Majesty and Royal Father; that the entail being so cut off, the said Estate is forfeited to your Majesty for the treason of the said John.

May it therefore please your most sacred Majesty to grant the forfeiture of the said estate to the Petitioner that she may be enabled thereby to testify her kindness to the said William Lisle . . .

And your petitioner shall ever pray for your Majesty's Long and Happy Reign.

APPENDIX TWO

Arundel and John Penruddock's Letters[2]

Arundel Penruddock's letter of 3 May 1655

My dear Hart
The sadd parting was soe far from making me to forgett you that I have scarse thought upon myself since but wholy of you. Those dear embraces that I still feel and shall never lose (being the faithful testimony of an indulgent husband) have charmed my soul to such a reverence of your remembrances that were it possible I would with my owne blood lament your dead limbs to life again and with reverence think it no sin to robb heaven a little longer of a Martyr Oh my dear you must now pardon my passion this being the last (Oh fatal word) that ever you will receive from me and know that until the last minute that I can imagine you shall live I will sacrifise the prayers of a Christian and the groans of an affected wife and when you are not which sure by sympathy I shall know I shall wish my owne dissolution with you and so we may go hand in hand to heaven it is to late to tell you what I have (or rather have not) done for you how turned out of doors because I came to beg mercy, the Lord lay not your blood to their charge, I would fain discourse longer with you but dare not my passion begins to drown my reason and will robb me of my devoirs which is all I have left to serve you Adeue therefore then thousand tymes my Dearest Dear and since I must never see you more take this prayer that may your faith be soe strengthened that your constancie may continue And then I hope heaven will receive you wher greyfe and love will in a short time after I hope translate my Deare
Your children beg your blessing and present their dutys to you.
Your sadd but constant wife ever to love your Ashes when dead
    A Penruddock
    May the 3rd 1655 11 o'clock at night.

John Penruddock's reply of 7 May 1655

My dearest Heart

I even now received thy farewell letter: each word whereof
represents unto me a most lively Emblem of your affection, drawn
with thy own hand in water colours, to the figure of a death's
head. My dear, I embrace it, as coming first from God, and then
from man: for what is there done in the City that the Lord hath
not permitted? I look upon every line of thine, as so many threads
twisted together into that of my life, which being now woven, my
meditations tell me, will make a fit remnant for my winding sheet,
Upon the reading thereof, I may say with the Prophet, I should
have utterly fainted but that I believe verily to see the goodness of
the Lord in the land of the living. As this is mine my dear, so let it
be thy consolation. When I think what a wife and children I go
from, and look no further, I begin to cry, O wretched man that I
am! But when my thoughts soar higher and fix themselves upon
those things which are above, where I shall find God my Creatour
to my Father and his Son my Redeemer to my Brother (for so
have they vouchsafed to term themselves) then I lay aside those
relations, and do of all love, my dear, desire thee not to look
towards my grave where my Body lies, but toward the heaven
where I hope my Soul shall gain a Mansion in my Father's house.
I do stedfastly believe that God hath heard the prayers of my
friends, and thine and mine: how knoweth thou, O woman,
whether thou hast not saved thy husband? Let those
considerations raise thy spirits, I beseech thee; and that for God's
sake and mine. Though I ly among the children of men, which are
set on fire against me; yet under the shadow of the Almighties
wings I will hide my self till this tyranny be overpast. The greatest
conflict I have had in this extremitie was my parting with thee; the
next encounter is to be with Death: and my Saviour hath so pulled
out the sting thereof that I hope to assault it without fear. Though
the Armies of men have been too hard for me, yet I am now lifting
my self under the conduct of my Sovereign and an Army of
Martyrs that the gates of hell cannot prevail against. My dear, I
have now another subject to think on; therefore you must excuse
the imperfection you find here. I have formerly given you

directions concerning my children, to which I shall referre you. May the blessing of God be upon thee and them and may there not be a man of my name ready to be a sacrifice in the cause of God, and his Church so long as the Sun and Moon shall endure. I shall now close up all, with desiring you to give testimony for me to the world, that I die with so much charity as to forgive all my enemies. I will joyn them in my last prayers for my friends. Amongst which, you and my children are for my sake obliged to pay a perpetuall acknowledgement. To Mr Rolles and his Lady, and my cousin Mr Sebastine Isack for their sollicitations in my behalf. If I should forget this City of Exeter for their civilities to my own self in particular and indeed to all of us, I should leave a reproach behind me. I will give them thanks at my death and I hope you and yours will do it when I am dead. My dear heart I once more bid thee adieu and with as much love and sincerity as can be imagined, I suscribe my self Thy dying and loving Husband,

John Penruddock

Exon, May 7th and the last year and day of my date, being the year of my Saviour 1655

This concluding note indicates he expected to be executed the following day.

APPENDIX THREE

Lady Mary Howard's Petition to the King[3]

The humble petition of the Lady Mary Howard
   Humbly sheweth

That whereas it hath pleased your Majesty to express a gracious sense of the sufferings of your petitioner and withal a Princely and favourable inclination for your petitioner's satisfaction, And your petitioner having, as she humbly conceiveth, found out a certaine and easy way for her relief.

It may therefore please your Majesty to appoint your Attorney Sir Geoffrey Palmer to draw up a grant for your Majesty's signature to put Mrs Lisle into possession of the estate (she having seven small children) the greatest part of which is her Jointure, and her husband being only tenant thereto for life.

And your petitioner shall ever pray etc.

APPENDIX FOUR

The 1689 Bloody Assizes *Account of Alice Lisle's Trial*[4]

Had those Persons who suffered about Monmouth's Business, fell only into the Hand of Cannibals, some of 'em, at least, had 'scaped better than they did from Jeffreys. Those more tame and civil Creatures would have spared the Old and Withered, though they had devoured the Young and Tender. But no Age, no Sex made any Difference here; and as those who had just come into the World, Children and Girls of ten or a dozen Years old were refused Pardon; so those who were half out of it, would not be suffered to tumble into the Grave entire . . . An instance of this was my Lady Lisle, of such an Age, that she almost slept on her very Trial, condemned for as small a Matter as has been known, by one of those dormant Laws . . . but hardly ever executed, only for corresponding with Nelthorp, an out-law'd Person, and, as was pretended, giving him Shelter at her House, and Hicks, who brought him thither. For Hicks, he was not then convicted, nor in any Proclamation, and so 'tis a Question whether she could, even in Rigour of Law, deserve Death on his Account. For Nelthorp, he himself says in his last Speech, (That he was wholly a Stranger to that worthy Lady; neither did she, as he verily believes, know who he was, or his Name, till he was taken.) For this she was found Guilty, and lost her Head at Winchester. Her case was thought so hard, that the Honourable House of Parliament have now reversed her Judgment.

APPENDIX FIVE

Burnet's Account of Alice Lisle's Trial⁵

The other execution was of a woman of greater quality: the lady Lisle. Her husband had been a regicide, and was one of Cromwell's lords, and was called the lord Lisle. He went at the time of the restoration beyond the sea, and lived at Lausanne. But three desperate Irishmen, hoping by such a service to make their fortunes, went thither, and killed him as he was going to church; and being well mounted, and ill pursued, got into France. His lady was known to be much affected with the king's death, and not easily reconciled to her husband for the share he had in it. She was a woman of great piety and charity. The night after the action, Hicks, a violent preacher among the dissenters, and Nelthorp, came to her house. She knew Hicks, and treated him civilly, not asking from whence they came. But Hicks told what brought them thither; for they had been with the duke of Monmouth. Upon which she went out of the room immediately, and ordered her chief servant to send an information concerning them to the next justice of peace, and in the mean while to suffer them to make their escape. But, before this could be done, a party came about the house, and took both them and her for harbouring them. Jefferies resolved to make a sacrifice of her; and obtained of the king a promise that he would not pardon her. Which the king owned to the earl of Feversham, when he, upon the offer of 1000l. if he could obtain her pardon, went and begged it. So she was brought to trial. No legal proof was brought, that she knew that they were rebels: the names of the persons found in her house were in no proclamation: so there was no notice given to beware of them. Jefferies affirmed to the jury upon his honour, that the persons had confessed that they had been with the duke of Monmouth. This was the turning a witness against her, after which he ought not to have judged in the matter. And, though it was insisted on, as a point of law, that till the persons found in her house were convicted, she could not be found guilty, yet Jefferies charged the jury in a most violent manner to bring her in guilty. All the audience was strangely affected with so unusual a behaviour in a judge. Only the person most concerned, the lady herself, who was then past seventy, was so little moved at it, that she fell asleep. The jury brought her in not guilty. But the judge in a great fury sent them out again. Yet they brought her in a second time not guilty. Then he seemed as in a transport of rage. And they, overcome with fear, brought her in the third time guilty. The king would shew no other favour, but that he changed the sentence from burning to beheading. She died with great constancy of mind; and expressed a joy, that she thus suffered for an act of charity and piety.

APPENDIX SIX

Robert Harley's Letter to his Father, 1685[6]

At the trial of Mrs Lisle . . . lasting until one o'clock in the morning, she fell asleep through age, 72. Her allegations were she knew not Nelthorp. The Court told her she was tried for harbouring Hicks. She alleged she knew him not to be a rebel. The Jury after some stay returned and told the Court some of them were not satisfied with the evidence, which they were told was as clear as the sun, and then repeated it all to them; upon which they returned her guilty and the Lord Chief justice told her that according to the power he had received at London she should be burned the next afternoon; but upon desire he reprieved her until Wednesday when her sentence was changed to beheading which was executed that day at Winchester. When they pressed her to confess I do not hear that she made any answer.

APPENDIX SEVEN

The Act Annulling Alice Lisle's Attainder[7]

Whereas Alicia Lisle, widow, in the month of August, in the first year of the reign of the late king James the Second, at a session of Oyer and Terminer, and gaol delivery, holden for the county of Southampton, at the city of Winchester in the said county, by an irregular and undue prosecution, was indicted for entertaining, concealing and comforting John Hicks, clerk, a false traitor, knowing him to be such, though the said John Hicks was not, at the trial of the said Alicia Lisle, attainted or convicted of any such crime: And by a verdict injuriously extorted and procured by the menaces and violences, and other illegal practices of George Lord Jefferies, baron of Wem, then Lord Chief Justice of the King's Bench, and chief commissioner of Oyer and Terminer and gaol delivery, within the said county, was convicted, attainted, and executed for High Treason: May it therefore please your most excellent majesties, at the humble petition of Triphena Lloyd and Bridget Usher, daughters of the said Alicia Lisle, That it be declared and enacted by the authority of this present parliament: And be it enacted by the King and Queen's most excellent majesties, by and with the advice and consent of the Lords spiritual and temporal, and Commons in this present parliament assembled, and by the authority of the same, that the said conviction, judgment and attainder of the said Alice Lisle be, and are hereby repealed, reversed, made and declared null and void to all intents, constructions and purposes whatsoever, as if no conviction, judgment or attainder had ever been had or made; and that no corruption of blood or other penalty or forfeiture of honours, dignities, lands, goods, or chattels, be by the said conviction or attainder incurred: any law, usage or custom to the contrary notwithstanding.

Notes

Chapter One. Alice and John Lisle

1. Thomas Salmon, *A Compleat Collection of State Tryals and Proceedings upon Impeachments for High Treason and other Crimes and Misdemeanours from the Reign of King Henry the Fourth to the End of the Reign of Queen Anne*, 4 vols (London, printed anonymously, 1719), vol. 3, p. 489. The trial was included – in identical terms, apart from updated spelling – in volume 11 of Howell's *State Trials* at the beginning of the nineteenth century. The 33 volumes of the *State Trials* were edited by Thomas Bayly Howell (vols 1–21; 1809–15) and his son Thomas Jones Howell (vols 22–33). Except where otherwise stated, Howell's *State Trials*, volume 11, is used in this book.

2. The high rate of infant mortality made early baptism obligatory for those anxious to ensure Christian salvation for their children.

3. The dates given in the *Dictionary of National Biography* (repr. Oxford, Oxford University Press, 1998) for Alice Lisle's birth and marriage (1614 and 1630 respectively) are wrong.

4. The *Dictionary of National Biography* and various genealogies cite John as Sir William's second son and William as his eldest, but contemporary evidence demonstrates that John was the eldest. This is confirmed by the heralds' 'visitations', or censuses, of 1622–34 and 1686, Middle Temple records, and a petition by Katherine Hyde in 1660 (see Appendix One). The first visitation, probably compiled in 1622, shows John aged 13, as the eldest of four sons, and William as the second. The updated 1634 visitation confirms John's seniority, noting his first wife's death in 1633, and is repeated in that for 1686. The Middle Temple records John's admission on 16 May 1626 as Sir William's son 'and heir', and William's eight years later, on 21 April 1634, as his 'second son'. John was called to the Bar in November 1633 and William in June 1641. There could be three reasons for the error: that William was named after his father; that the knighthood he received from Charles II after the death of his father, who had been knighted by James I in 1606, has been mistakenly treated as an inherited baronetcy; and that after the death in

infancy of John Lisle's son William, born to his first wife, Mary Elizabeth, his and Alice's third, and sole surviving son, after the deaths of Beconsaw in 1653 and William in 1654, was also called John, and the two generations have been confused.

5. This reconstruction seems to be corroborated by the description of the house during Alice Lisle's trial in 1685 as 'the new house that is built there'.

6. A royal property originally known as Chelsea House, it bordered the Thames in the area of what is now Beaufort Street. On his accession in 1625, Charles I gave it to George Villiers, 1st Duke of Buckingham. On the Duke's murder in 1628, it passed to his second surviving son, also George, and became known as Buckingham House. Cromwell confiscated the property in July 1651. Although returned to George at the Restoration, it reverted to the Crown on his debt-ridden death in 1687.

7. A grandson of Sir John Croke, judge and Speaker of the House of Commons during Elizabeth's reign, and a first cousin of the only daughter-in-law Alice Lisle ever knew, Catherine Croke.

8. On 12 April, a government official related Mr Justice Wyndham's specious attempt to give Cromwell credit for 'directing this offence to be tried by commission in the ordinary legal way, and not by extraordinary commissions' (Lincoln's Inn Library, Thurloe Papers, vol. 3, p. 372). Cromwell's direction was in fact the only one lawfully open to him.

9. Their exchange is at Appendix Three.

10. 'Records of the Rising in the West', 1875, reprinted from the *Wiltshire Archaeological and Natural History Magazine*. The relevant documents now appear to be lost.

11. A modern parallel is *Congreve* v. *Home Office* in 1975, when an attempt was made to charge higher rates for television licences renewed shortly before the increase was due to take effect, on pain of having the licences revoked. In the Court of Appeal, Lord Denning said: 'the demands were an attempt to levy money for the Crown without the authority of Parliament; and that is quite enough to damn them.' He drew attention to the near-Cromwellian attitude of leading counsel for the Home Office, Roger Parker QC (subsequently Lord Justice Parker, since retired), who 'said at one point . . . that if the court interfered in this case, "it would not be long before the powers of the court would be called in question". We trust that this was not said seriously, but only as a piece of advocate's licence.' Parker's comment was vigorously condemned in *The Times* two days later.

12. *Memoirs of Edmund Ludlow, with a Collection of Original Papers, and the Case of Charles the First* (London, 1771), p. 440.

Chapter Two. The Nonconformist Widow

1. The summary of Katherine Hyde's petition printed in the *Calendar of State Papers (Domestic) 1660–1* is misleading, and underlies the error in the *Dictionary of National Biography* that John Lisle had a son named William 'who adhered to the king and married the daughter of Lady Katherine Hyde'. As the original of the petition makes clear (Appendix One), the William in question was John Lisle's younger brother. John's two sons of that name, born to Mary Elizabeth and Alice, both died as infants.

2. There are suggestions in the *Dictionary of National Biography* and elsewhere that Alice accompanied John to Switzerland. This is most unlikely. Not merely did she have seven young children, but she is nowhere mentioned by the spies reporting on John to London, which they would certainly have done had she been with him.

3. Whitlock's son was also, according to the Temple Church records, baptised in his father's Middle Temple chambers on 1 December 1647, though there is no mention of who performed the ceremony.

4. Hoar graduated at Harvard in 1650, and after his marriage to Bridget went with his bride to America in 1672, where he became President of Harvard shortly afterwards. He was, however, not greatly liked, and he resigned in March 1675, dying of consumption that November. A year later, Bridget married the Boston bookseller Hezekiah Usher. The marriage was not a success, and she returned to England in 1687. Hezekiah redrafted his will in 1689 to exclude Bridget; but she heard about it, and went back to America, where she was able to retrieve a substantial portion of his estate. She remained there until her death in May 1723.

5. Even if the Crown had been willing to sell to a Regicide's widow, it is doubtful whether Alice Lisle could have afforded a property the size of Bagshot Park; and if it had formed part of her estate, one would have expected it to have been mentioned by name. But the licence entry might have been correct. John Barter's account at her trial of his conversation with her in the kitchen at Moyles Court was as follows: 'she said, what countryman art thou? Said I, madam, I am a Wiltshire man. Said she, do'st thou make bricks? No, said I, madam, I can help in husbandry work. Said she, if thou could'st make bricks, I will give thee ten acres of ground in such a place. I told her, no I could not.' Brick-making flourished in the Southampton area during the later seventeenth century, one of the materials used being Lower Bagshot clay dug from various places in the locality. If Alice Lisle let any of her

Hampshire property on clay-digging concessions, it would be natural for the name of the material to be applied to the land.

6. In *Original Records of Early Nonconformity under Persecution and Indulgence* (London and Leipsic [*sic*], T. Fisher Unwin, 1911) Professor Lyon Turner claims that on this occasion Hicks hid in a nearby hayloft, where 'his pursuers touched him with the point of their weapons, though they knew it not'. This appears to be unsupported by evidence.

7. The authorities appear to have temporarily lost track of him as a result: an anonymous and undated note in the *Calendar of State Papers (Domestic)* of 7 August gives Richard Lloyd's address as 'Aldgate at the Sign of the Mitre'.

Chapter Four. The Report of the Alice Lisle's Trial

1. See Appendix Four.

2. J.G. Muddiman, *The Bloody Assizes* (London, Butterworth [Hodge], 1929). While aware of the page gap in vol. 3 (*Notes and Queries*, vol. 155, p. 149) between the end of Alice Lisle and the start of Fernley (516–77), Muddiman appears to have overlooked the fact that the final page of Oates, p. 576, was out of sequence with the 487 on the preceding page. He considered Alice Lisle was included 'as an afterthought' once printing had finished, and implies that, though available, the report was initially rejected. But this is scarcely consistent with either the need to leave the gap between Oates and Fernley in the first place, or, far less, the quality of the report.

3. S. Schofield, *Jeffreys of 'The Bloody Assizes'* (London, Thornton Butterworth, 1937).

4. G.W. Keeton, *Lord Chancellor Jeffreys and the Stuart Cause* (London, Macdonald, 1965).

5. Statutory licensing of the press had been reintroduced on 24 June 1685.

6. Sir Edward Parry changed his view on this. In *The Drama of the Law* (London, Ernest Benn, 1924) he says Jeffreys examined Nelthorp before he left London, and was 'fully primed with the case for the prosecution' when he rode down to Winchester. But in his book *The Bloody Assize* (London, Ernest Benn, 1929), he says: 'Nelthorp gave him no information of any moment', and concludes that Jeffreys was bluffing.

Chapter Five. The Law of Treason – Then and Now

1. It is not quite the oldest criminal statute in force. That appears to be the Statute of Marlborough of 1267 (renamed, by Act of Parliament in

1948, the Distress Act 1267), under which fines can still be imposed for 'levying . . . any revenge or unlawful distress', i.e. resorting to self-help. No prosecution appears to have been brought under this statute for at least a century, and a landlord today would be more likely to face prosecution under the anti-harassment provisions of the Protection from Eviction Act of 1977.

2. The last public execution was in May 1868, when Michael Barrett was hanged outside Newgate prison for murder. Of the traitors, Lovat was the last to be beheaded, and Joyce the last to be hanged. The last hangings in Britain were those of Peter Allen and Gwynne Evans on 13 August 1964, Allen at Walton gaol, Liverpool, and Evans at Strangeways gaol, Manchester, following their joint conviction for murder. Parliament abolished the death penalty for murder in November 1965, and has since voted regularly against its reintroduction.

3. References throughout this chapter are from the combined work, Robert Holbourne, *The Learned Readings of Sir Robert Holbourne* (London, printed for Sam. Heyrick *et al.*, 1681).

4. With a wide disparity between rich and poor, and the high intrinsic and nominal values of the coinage, successful counterfeiting or clipping must have been as rewarding for the poor as it was ruinous for the rich.

5. These last three disadvantages were removed by the Treason Act of 1695, passed mainly in response to public reaction against the Bloody Assize.

6. This procedure was not abolished until 1948. The last peer tried by the House of Lords was Lord de Clifford, acquitted of manslaughter in 1935.

7. Now the Bay Tree and Old George in Salisbury High Street.

Chapter Six. Winchester Assize, August 1685

1. The other reason was the ancient common law rule, preserved by the Larceny Act of 1916 but abolished under the Theft Act of 1968, that goods of no value could not be the subject of theft.

2. Crimes were classified either as felonies or the less serious 'transgressions', or misdemeanours. Felonies were almost always punishable with death and by confiscation of the offender's goods, whereas misdemeanours involved neither penalty.

3. 'Have mercy upon me, O God, according to thy loving kindness: according unto the multitude of thy tender mercies blot out my transgressions.'

4. As used in the seventeenth century, 'culprit' carried the technical legal meaning of an individual against whom the prosecution was ready to prove its case. It had not acquired its modern meaning of someone who is, or is presumed to be, guilty of a crime.

Chapter Seven. The Jury

1. Seventeenth-century jury service was confined to males, and depended on a property qualification. It was not until 1919 that women became universally eligible, while the property requirement, which excluded women for many years afterwards, persisted until 1974. Today, the majority of voters of either sex may serve. Sheriffs continued to summon jurors until 1972, when the task was transferred to 'jury summoning officers' appointed by the Lord Chancellor.

2. Until 1533, those on treason or felony charges were allowed a total of thirty-five peremptory challenges; in that year, Parliament reduced the total to twenty for felony, leaving treason unaffected. This remained the law down to the twentieth century: in 1948, the figures for both types of offence were reduced to seven; and to three in 1977. The right was abolished in 1989. But the accused has always been able to challenge any number of jurors for cause. The prosecution's unlimited right of peremptory challenge was abolished in 1305, since when it has only been able to have jurors 'stood by' or, since 1825, challenged for cause. The right to stand by was substantially restricted in 1989 to cases where jurors were seen as a potential security threat, open to improper approaches, or so plainly biased or illiterate as to be incapable of acting impartially.

3. A freeman was 'one sworn free of the Guild merchant of the City'. He was one of the citizens, always a small minority of the inhabitants, and had the privileges of voting for the mayor and bailiffs, voting in parliamentary elections, standing for election and, in medieval and later times, carrying on a trade without a special licence. Freemen were thus the local aristocracy of power and status (though by no means always of birth) and, being elected by the existing freemen, formed a self-perpetuating oligarchy who represented and ruled the city.

4. Barbara Carpenter Turner believed the challenges to Kerby, Penton, Wavell and Yalden were made by the Crown on the grounds of their known independence and/or opposition to James II's policies, so that 'the jury was rigged' (*Winchester Cathedral Record*, 40, 31; *Hampshire Chronicle*, 4 April 1964; *Hampshire Hogs*, 2, 34). This is unlikely. First, the report specifically asserts that the challenges were made after 'the

Prisoner was bid to look to her challenges'. Second, Jeffreys later stated that Alice Lisle had 'made what challenges [she] could'. Third, the report describes each as a 'challenge', rather than a 'standing-by'. Fourth, it is difficult to envisage how prosecuting counsel could have had anything like the same knowledge of the jurors' outlook and opinions as Alice Lisle, unless they had had the entire panel comprehensively vetted in advance and were ready to voice their objections at the moment of each juror's random selection. There seems no reason why Alice Lisle should not have had as much to fear from those of independent attitudes, and from sensitive politicians possibly more concerned with their survival than their apparent loyalties, as the Crown.

Chapter Eight. Opening of the Prosecution

1. *Diary of Samuel Pepys*, ed. Latham and Matthews, vol. 11 (London, Bell and Hyman, 1976), pp. 228–30.
2. In vol. 2 of *State Trials* (1826), Samuel Phillips argues (p. 197): 'The language used by [Hicks], reflecting on the king and government, though expressive of disloyalty, and very suspicious in his situation, was not an overt act of high treason.' As a matter of law, this is wrong. Hicks's comments, in so far as they referred to and supported Monmouth's cause, constituted overt acts in the most direct sense, and the history of the offence contains many comparable examples. Moreover, Phillips overlooks Hicks's and Hook's joint efforts to persuade the prisoners to change their allegiance, an even more classic example of treason, as Bacon made clear.
3. Clearly, Hook was as guilty as Hicks. But he managed to avoid capture after Sedgemoor, and spent two years in hiding. Pardoned in 1688, he became a strong supporter of the Jacobite cause. He later fought against Marlborough in the Netherlands in the War of the Spanish Succession.

Chapter Eleven. Dunne's Overnight 'Isolation'

1. Longleat, Britain's most magnificent Elizabethan mansion and still the seat of the Bath and Weymouth family today.
2. Probably the separate building in the courtyard behind the main house, described in eighteenth-century conveyances as the 'carthouse containing six arches', and in the 1819 sale particulars as the 'Farm Horse Stable . . . and Stable with open Stalls'. By 1962, when Moyles Court School bought the house, it appears to have been converted to the 'Garage Block . . . of brick with a tiled roof (and) three sets of double doors', and was demolished shortly afterwards.

Chapter Sixteen. Alice Lisle's Defence

1. This presumably alluded to the order to the lords lieutenant of 20 June for the arrest of 'all disaffected persons, especially dissenting ministers'.

Chapter Eighteen. Jeffreys' Summing-up: Part 2

1. Probably a misprint for 'met'.
2. The possibility that Alice Lisle offered to employ Barter as a brick-maker, or to rent land to him for that purpose, in the Southampton area has been mentioned above. Jeffreys' assertion that Barter had said she offered him land in Carolina is hard to follow. Possibly what Barter told the court was misheard or misunderstood; or Alice Lisle may have made an exaggerated allusion to Barter about her daughter Bridget's connections with America through her husband, Leonard Hoar. There is no evidence that Alice Lisle herself ever owned property in America.
3. Following John Bovett's plea of guilty to treason at Dorchester on 3 or 4 September 1685, Robert Thatcher pleaded guilty at Wells towards the end of the month to having harboured him. Joseph Kelway's plea of guilty to treason at Taunton, where the assize began on 17 September, was followed by Anna Strode's acquittal on 11 March 1686 at the Dorchester spring assize of having knowingly harboured him as a rebel.

Chapter Nineteen. Sentencing and Execution

1. It appears at the end of the account of her trial in Tutchin, *A New Martyrology, or the Bloody Assizes: A Compleat History of all those Eminent Martyrs . . . from 1678 to 1689* (London, J. Dunton, 1689) (see Appendix Four), from which the *State Trials* editor most probably copied it verbatim.

Chapter Twenty. Was Justice Done?

1. *Country Life*, December 1909, p. 876.
2. Howell (ed.), *State Trials*, vol. 11, pp. 353–8.

Appendices

1. *Calendar of the State Papers (Domestic) 1660–1*, p. 341, item 73.
2. W.W. Ravenhill, *Records of the Rising in the West A.D. 1655* (Devizes, H.F. and E. Bull, 1875), pp. 124–5.

3. *Calendar of the State Papers (Domestic) 1660–1*, p. 341, item 71.

4. John Tutchin, *A New Martyrology, or the Bloody Assizes: A Compleat History of all those Eminent Martyrs . . . from 1678 to 1689* (London, J. Dunton, 1689).

5. Bishop Gilbert Burnet, *Bishop Burnet's History of his Own Time* (London, Thomas Ward, 1724), vol. 1, pp. 649–50.

6. TNA: HMC, Duke of Portland MSS, vol. 3, 1894, p. 387.

7. Thomas Salmon, *State Trials* (printed anonymously, 1719).

Bibliography

Birkenhead, Earl of, *Fourteen English Judges* (London, Cassell, 1926)

Burnet, Bishop Gilbert, *Bishop Burnet's History of his Own Time* (London, printed for Thomas Ward, 1724–34)

Calamy, Edmund, *The Nonconformist's Memorial* (London, Button and Son and T. Hurst, 1802)

Campbell, John, *Lives of the Lord Chancellors*, 4th edn, 10 vols (London, John Murray, 1856)

Clarendon, Earl of (Edward Hyde), *History of the Rebellion and Civil Wars in England* (Oxford, printed at the Theater [*sic*] *c*. 1702–26)

Dictionary of National Biography (Oxford, Oxford University Press, repr. 1998)

Halsbury, *Laws of England* (London, Butterworth Tolley, 1994)

Hargrave, Francis (ed.), *A Complete Collection of State-Trials and Proceedings for High Treason, and other Crimes and Misdemeanours*, 4th edn (London, printed by T. Wright, 1775)

Hicks, John, 'True and Faithful Narrative of the Unjust and Illegal Sufferings and Oppressions of Many Christians (Injuriously and Injudiciously call'd Fanaticks) . . . since the 10th of May, 1670' (pamphlet, printed 1671)

Holbourne, Robert, *The Learned Readings of Sir Robert Holbourne, Knight, Attorney-General to King Charles I, upon the Statute of Treasons, to which is added Cases of Prerogative, Treason, Felony, etc.* (London, printed for Sam. Heyrick *et al.*, 1681)

Keeton, G.W., *Lord Chancellor Jeffreys and the Stuart Cause* (London, Macdonald, 1965)

Ludlow, Edmund, *Memoirs of Edmund Ludlow, with a Collection of Original Papers, and the Case of Charles the First* (London, printed for T. Becket *et al.*, 1771)

Lyon Turner, G., *Original Records of Early Nonconformity under Persecution and Indulgence*, 3 vols (London and Leipsic [*sic*], T. Fisher Unwin, 1911)

Macaulay, Thomas B., *History of England from the Accession of James the Second*, 10 vols (Leipzig, Bernhard Tauchnitz, 1849)

Memoirs of Edmund Ludlow, with a Collection of Original Papers, and the Case of Charles the First (London, 1771)

Milner, John, *The History, Civil and Ecclesiastical, and Survey of the Antiquities of Winchester*, 2 vols (Jas Robbins, 1798)

Montgomery Hyde, H., *Judge Jeffreys* (London, Harrap, 1940)

Muddiman, J.G., *The Bloody Assizes* (London, Butterworth [Hodge], 1929)

Oglander, John, *A Royalist's Notebook. The Commonplace Book of Sir John Oglander KT of Nunwell* (London, Constable, 1936)

Parry, Edward, *The Drama of the Law* (London, Ernest Benn, 1924)

—— *The Bloody Assize* (London, Ernest Benn, 1929)

Pepys, Samuel, *The Diary of Samuel Pepys*, ed. Latham and Matthews (London, Bell and Hyman, 1976)

Phillips, Samuel (ed.), *State Trials: or a Collection of the most interesting Trials prior to the Revolution of 1688*, 2 vols (W. Walker, 1826)

Ravenhill, W.W., *Record of the Rising in the West, A.D. 1655* (Devizes, H.F. and E. Bull, 1875)

Salmon, Thomas, *A Compleat Collection of State Tryals and Proceedings upon Impeachments for High Treason and other Crimes and Misdemeanours from the Reign of King Henry the Fourth to the End of the Reign of Queen Anne*, 4 vols (London, printed anonymously, 1719)

—— *A New Abridgement and Critical Review of The State Trials and Impeachments for High Treason; From the Reign of King Richard II down to . . . the Tenth Year of the reign of His present Majesty King George II* (London, printed for J. and J. Hazard *et al.*, 1738)

Schofield, Seymour, *Jeffreys of 'The Bloody Assizes'* (London, Thornton Butterworth, 1937)

Smith, Thomas, *Commonwealth of England* (London, John Smethwicke, 1609)

Storry Deans, R., *Notable Trials: Romances of the Law Courts* (London, Cassel, 1906)

Trussell, John, 'Touchstone of Tradition' (manuscript in Hampshire Record Office, W/K1/12, 1687)

Tutchin, John, *A New Martyrology, or the Bloody Assizes: a Compleat History of all those Eminent Martyrs . . . from 1678 to 1689* (London, J. Dunton, 1689)

Walker, Clem., *The Compleat History of Independency Upon the Parliament Begun 1640* (London, printed for Fic. Royston *et al.*, 1661)

Wood, Anthony A., *Athenae Oxonienses* (London, printed for Thomas Bennet, 1691)

Journals

Country Life
Gentleman's Magazine
Hampshire Chronicle
Hampshire Field Club Magazine
Hampshire Hogs
London Gazette
Winchester Cathedral Record

Index